THE YEAR IN IRELAND

THE YEAR IN IRELAND

by

KEVIN DANAHER

THE MERCIER PRESS
4 BRIDGE STREET, CORK

To Anne
whose gracious silence made it possible

© *Kevin Danaher, 1972*

SBN 85342 280 X

Printed in the Republic of Ireland by the
Leinster Leader Ltd., Naas, Co. Kildare

Contents

List of Illustrations

Introduction

If one were to ask which particular branch of folk tradition most widely reveals the panorama of the whole, the answer would undoubtedly be Calendar Custom.

Calendar Custom is deeply influenced by environment, by climate, by the fertility of the soil, by the proximity of such geographical features as the sea, rivers, lakes, mountains and moors. It is intimately connected with the daily and yearly routine of work. It is associated with travel and trade. It bears upon the social traditions of the community and upon the individual lives of the community's members. It embodies devotional and religious practices, divination, healing, mythology and magic. It abounds in explanatory tale and legend, historical allusion and pious parable. It includes all manner of amusements, sports and pastimes.

Furthermore, it reaches back through time into the remote and unknown depths of prehistory. It contains elements which already were of vast antiquity when the first Christian missionaries came into Ireland, as well as matter which recalls the flowering of early Irish Christianity. It has features derived from the piety as well as from the practicality of the Middle Ages. Every phase of our changing history has affected it; every body of the people who came into Ireland has added something to it; Scandinavian and Norman, English and Scots, all have left some mark upon it. Above all, it shares largely in the common tradition of Western Europe, so many of its elements being but Irish versions of practices much more widely known.

The material in the following pages is derived mainly from printed sources, supplemented by memories of a childhood spent in a district where old beliefs and old customs still survived vigorously, and by more than thirty years of research into Irish folk tradition. It is not claimed here that the material is presented exhaustively, nor, although an effort

11

has been made to suggest the main areas in which local variation of tradition occurs, is it to be supposed that this regional diversity is fully revealed. Many minor and local nuances of belief and custom have, of necessity, been omitted; the scientific mapping of these is a specialized and technical exercise which must await the time when the full resources of our national archive of folk tradition are made available for general study. Irish Calendar Custom is a vast and complicated field, how vast and complicated has been shown in the one comprehensive investigation of an Irish folk festival which has hitherto appeared, Máire Mac Neill's *Festival of Lughnasa,* a work which occupies almost 700 pages.

Many other aspects of the matter are not examined here, or have, at most, been very lightly treated. An obvious and important pursuit is the comparing and contrasting of Irish tradition with that of other areas; this is a field of study in itself. Another, and most tempting, exercise is the delving into the origins of custom and belief; here we are on slippery ground, for the fact is that the materials of folk tradition are so abundant and so varied that evidence may be adduced to prove almost any theory.

I wish to record my gratitude to numerous friends and colleagues who have helped with information and comment; among these are Seán Ó Súilleabháin, Tomás de Bhál, Bríd Mahon and Máire Dillon, of the Department of Irish Folklore, University College, Dublin, A. T. Lucas and John C. O'Sullivan of the National Museum, and Alan Gailey and Aiken McClelland of the Ulster Folk Museum. The many people in the Irish countryside who, over the years, have helped with information are so numerous as to make their listing impossible; may I here express my thanks to them, for it is they who, in the final analysis, have made this book.

Kevin Danaher,
May Day, 1972.

Saint Brighid's Day

In Irish folk tradition St Brighid's Day, 1 February, is the first day of Spring, and thus of the farmer's year. It is the festival of Ireland's venerated and much-loved second patron saint, who is also the patroness of cattle and of dairy work. In the *Journal of the Royal Society of Antiquaries of Ireland*, 1945, p. 164, Seán Ó Suilleabháin wrote:

'The main significance of the Feast of St Brigid would seem to be that it was a christianization of one of the focal points of the agricultural year in Ireland, the starting-point of preparations for the spring sowing. Every manifestation of the cult of the saint (or of the deity she replaced) is closely bound up in some way with food-production, and this must be the chief line of approach to a study of this spring festival.'

A relaxation of the rigours of winter weather was expected at this time, for, according to tradition, the saint had promised:

> *Gach 're lá go maith*
> *Ó'm lá-sa amach*
> *agus leath mo lae féinigh*

> Every second day fine
> from my day onward
> and half of my own day

The farmers now hoped for good weather to speed the spring ploughing and digging, to symbolize which many of them turned a sod or two in a tillage field. Along the coast the fishermen expected an abatement of storms and rough seas, so that they might again begin their work. Weather signs were carefully noted; the wind direction on

13

the eve of the festival betokened the prevailing wind during the coming year; the festival day should show signs of improving weather, although an exceptionally fine day was regarded as an omen of poor weather to come.

To see a hedgehog was a good weather sign, for the hedgehog comes out of the hole in which he has spent the winter, looks about to judge the weather, and returns to his burrow if bad weather is going to continue. If he stays out, it means that he knows that mild weather is coming.

Rain in February, however, was not unwelcome, as it softened the soil and brought an early growth of grass. Proverbially a rainy February gave token of a fine Summer.

For sea-coast dwellers the spring tide nearest to the festival was *Rabharta na Féile Bríde,* and was believed to be the greatest spring tide of the year, and the people were quick to take the opportunity of cutting and gathering seaweed to fertilize the crops and of collecting shellfish and other shore produce. In a few places around Galway Bay, a live shellfish, such as a limpet or a periwinkle, was placed at each of the four corners of the house, to bring fishing luck and ensure plentiful shore gathering.

The lengthening day too, was welcome to people whose artificial lighting was limited. 'On St Brighid's day' the saying ran, 'you can put away the candlestick and half the candle.'

This was a day of stocktaking in household and farmyard. The housewife examined her store of meal, salt bacon, potatoes and other food to make sure it was lasting well and to see how strict her economy must be until stores could be renewed. In the same way the farmer examined the store of hay and other fodder and decided how it should be portioned out to the animals.

In places certain kinds of work were prohibited on the feast day. The inhabitants of parishes dedicated to the saint usually kept the day as a holiday and did only such work as was strictly necessary. Instead, they performed devotions at the local shrine of the saint, as at Dabhach Bhríde in Liscannor parish, County Clare or St Brighid's Stream at Faughart, County Louth.

In some places any kind of work which required the turning of wheels, such as carting, milling and spinning, was carefully avoided. This was especially the case in south County Kerry and west County Cork, from which area we hear of dressmakers refusing to operate their sewing machines, and of men walking long distances rather than use

14

bicycles. In a few localities ploughing and smithwork also came under the ban.

The housewife made sure that the house was clean and tidy for the occasion and no matter how poor the household, always provided a festive supper or at least some tasty dish on St Brighid's Eve. Sowans, apple-cake, dumplings and colcannon were favourite foods, while a Frenchman named Coquebert de Montbret who visited Galway in 1791, saw fruit cakes being eaten on that day (*Journal of the Galway Archaeological and Historical Society, 1952*, p. 11.) and Col. Vallencey in his *Essay on the Antiquity of the Irish Language* 1781, p. 21 also tells of fruit cakes:

'On St Bridget's eve every farmer's wife in Ireland makes a cake called *bairín-breac*, the neighbours are invited, the madder of ale and the pipe go round, and the evening concludes with mirth and festivity.'

Butter always formed part of the meal and fresh butter was sure to be churned on the same day. The more prosperous farmers gave presents of butter and buttermilk to poor neighbours. Some killed a sheep, and sent portions of the meat to friends and to the needy. Others had a fowl or a piece of bacon as the main item of the festive supper.

It was generally believed that the saint travelled about the countryside on the Eve of her festival, bestowing her blessing on the people and on their livestock.

There were various ways of indicating that her visit to house and farmyard was welcome. A very common token was the placing of a cake or pieces of bread and butter on the window-sill outside. In some places this offering was left to be taken away by a tramp or other poor person or by the *brídeóg* party (described below); in others it was brought in next morning and shared among the members of the household. Often a sheaf of corn was put beside the cake, as refreshment for the saint's favourite white cow which accompanied her on her rounds. Others laid a bundle of straw or fresh rushes on the threshold, on which the saint might kneel to bless the house, or on which she might wipe her feet before entering. In County Donegal the offering frequently was a dish of porridge, while many households in County Mayo stuck the handle of the churn-dash into the ground and placed the cake for the saint on its flat top. In County Antrim and other parts of the north a table was set in the kitchen with food as for a guest, and when the time for the saint's visit had passed, the first poor person who came the way was invited to eat the food.

15

There are traditions of dishes of water, salt, pieces of meat or portions of butter being left out as offerings for the saint. After she had passed by, these acquired curative properties and were kept to relieve sickness.

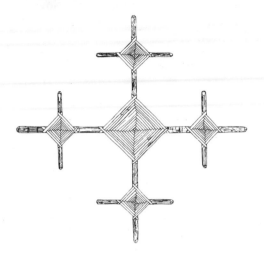

1 Saint Brighid's cross, County Waterford (National Museum, Dublin)

Saint Brighid's Crosses

The most characteristic and most widespread Irish custom connected with St Brighid's Eve was the making of the *cros Bríde* or *bogha Bríde*, (St Brighid's cross) which was hung up in dwelling-house, and often in byre and stable as well, to honour the saint and gain her protection.

The most usual type of cross was the diamond or lozenge of straw. In making the simplest form of this, two pieces of twig or slips of wood are fastened in the shape of a cross, and straw is then carefully woven around them to form a neat lozenge. A more elaborate form is made by securing small lengths of twig or wood across three or all four legs of the cross, thus making smaller crosses at the extremities, and then weaving straw diamonds about these as well as about the central cross. Still more elaborate forms can be made by increasing the number of cross-pieces or by forming a wooden lattice, and weaving a straw lozenge about each intersection. The most elaborate crosses may have as many as twenty-four or even thirty lozenges. Sometimes rushes are used in making this type, but straw is much more usual.

16

These diamond or lozenge crosses were made in all four provinces of Ireland but were most common in Connaught and Munster, and in Counties Donegal, Monaghan and Armagh in Ulster.

The next most popular type, that which has been adopted as its symbol by Radio Telefís Éireann, the Irish broadcasting service, has no wooden foundation, but is made by doubling rushes over each other to form an overlapping cross. The simplest form has only four rushes, but these are most often made by the unskilled hands of small children. More practised makers add more rushes, sometimes up to twenty or more, to each side, thus producing a square of overlapping rushes from half of each side of which a bunch of rushes projects so that the whole forms an irregular cross. Usually the projecting rushes are tied together at the ends, thus making each leg look somewhat pointed.

These crosses are almost always made of rushes, though straw specimens are known from a few localities. This type of cross was well known in many parts of Ulster and Leinster, but only in a few places in Connaught and Munster.

A subtype of this, with three legs instead of four, has been noted in several parts of the north, in Antrim, Armagh, Down and Donegal. Here it is usually made together with the four-legged type but appears to have no special significance, except that in places it is hung in the byre while the four-legged cross is hung in the house.

The four-legged cross has been called a swastika by some writers who have thereupon entered into much speculation regarding magic, mystic symbolism, ancient religions and so forth. To call it a swastika is mistaken since it lacks the essential feature of the swastika (hakenkreuz, gammadion, crux ansata) – the hooked or bent arms, and any speculation based on this name is thus misleading.

A third type, not as common as either of the foregoing, is found in a number of widely separated places in Connaught, Munster and Ulster and was frequent in Sligo, Leitrim and south Donegal. This was made by interlacing a number of strands or groups of strands of straw, reed or rushes in a crisscross pattern and tying each of the four sets of the projecting ends together to form a cross which looks like a four-armed set of interlaced bows. In many homes in south west Donegal, this was made as a third cross, together with a four-legged and a three legged overlapping cross. These latter were hung, respectively, in the house and the byre, while the third type was hung in the stable. Elsewhere, however, it was made and hung up as the regular St Brighid's cross. A rarer type, consisting of a cross within a circle, all formed of triple

17

plaited straw rope is known from parts of County Cork and County Tipperary. Another rare type, a plain latin cross made from two short plaits of straw has been noted in a few places, in Counties Clare, Galway, Longford and Donegal. A few examples of this type with the addition of a straw lozenge in the middle are known.

In a number of widely scattered localities, with concentrations in County Clare, west County Galway, South west County Mayo and County Meath, little crosses of two slips of plain wood, tacked or tied together, were made. These may represent a break-down of tradition, being substituted for older, more complex forms. Occasional specimens made of cloth, paper, cardboard, quills and other materials are also, clearly substitutes for older types. There are, however, some very localized cross types which are well made of traditional materials; these may be survivals of more widespread use, or more recent products of local imagination and skill.

In many localities, but especially in Leinster, where the cross tradition seems to be weakest, there are memories of crosses being made and hung up long ago but no details of which types of crosses.

From Counties Cork, Limerick and Kilkenny there are records of the tracing of a cross on the arm or sleeve or the forehead with the blackened end of a charred stick and from County Meath of marking a cross in the same way on the whitewashed wall of the byre.

One of the earliest references to the cross recalls its power to protect the house and its occupants from fire. This is in the burlesque poem *Hesperi-Neso-Graphia* (1735 ed., 8):

> St Bridget's cross hung over door
> which did the house from fire secure
> as Gillo thought, O powerful charm
> to keep a house from taking harm;
> and tho' the dogs and servants slept,
> by Bridget's care the house was kept.

This belief is still held by many, as is the belief that the cross gives equal protection against lightning. Mr William Monks, Lusk, County Dublin, gives us an example of this:

'The Saint Brighid's Cross was not made in north County Dublin within my memory. This is how I first saw it: when I was a boy, workers from County Cavan and County Monaghan used to come to my father's farm in Spring and Autumn, to do the planting and take

18

the harvest. They lived in a house on the farm. One day there was a fierce thunderstorm, and one of these men got a handful of straw and made a Saint Brighid's Cross to save the house from being struck by lightning. When the storm was over I asked him to teach me how to make the crosses, and he did.'

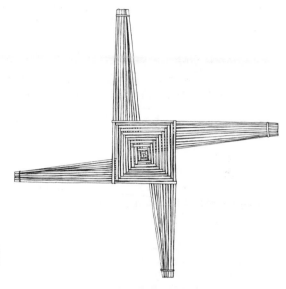

2 Saint   Brighid's   cross, County Leitrim (National Museum, Dublin)

Making the Crosses

Usually the making of the crosses was attended by some ceremony. In the southern half of Ireland the household usually made one cross, of the local type; this was then sprinkled with holy water and hung up above or close to the entrance door with an appropriate prayer, such as 'May the blessing of God, Father, Son and Holy Spirit be on this cross and on the place where it hangs and on everyone who looks at it.' In many parts of this southern area, especially in County Clare, but also in a few places in Limerick, Tipperary, Waterford, Kilkenny, Laois, Offaly and south Galway a second cross was made, similarly blessed and hung up in the byre.

In the northern half of Ireland a much more elaborate ritual, in slightly varying forms from one locality to the next, was used. This was known in every county in Connaught, but especially in Sligo, Leitrim, north Mayo and north Roscommon, and in every county in Ulster (except, apparently, County Down) as well as in the Dundalk district of County Louth.

A very full description of the local form of these ceremonies, written down in Carrickmore, County Tyrone, about the year 1900, is given by John B. Arthurs in *Ulster Folklife* 1957, pp. 42–3:

'One of the family (a girl) representing St Bridget leaves the house, and when outside knocks on the door three times to seek admittance. She carries rushes in her hands. Each time on knocking she says:

"Téighidh sibh ar mhur nglúna, déanaidh sibh umhlaíocht, agus ligigidh Bríd Bheannachtach isteach." ("Go down on your knees, do homage, and let Blessed Bridget enter the house").

'When this has been said for the third time, those inside respond:

"O, tar isteach, tá céad fáilte romhat." ("Oh, come in, you are a hundred times welcome").

'Then she enters and places the rushes under the table. The supper has been already laid out on the table, and the following grace is recited by the father and mother:

"Beannaigh sinn, a Dhia, beannaigh ár mbiadh agus ár ndeoch; is tú a cheannaigh sinn go daor; saor sinn ar gach olc!" ("Bless us, O God, bless our food and our drink; it is Thou who hast redeemed us at great price; deliver us from all evil!")

'When the supper is eaten, the parents recite this thanksgiving:

"Díograis dhuit, a Thiarna, glór, altú agus buíochas dhuit ar son na cod' sin agus gach cod' a thug tú ariamh dúinn! A Shlánaitheoir a thug a bheatha dúinn, go dtuga tú an beatha síorraí ins na Flaithís dúinn! Go rabh seacht fearr i gcionn na bliana a bhéas muid, ins na grásta is mó agus ins na peacaidh is lú! Sláinte anma is cuirp i ndaoine, agus a n-eallach ar sabháil ar thubáiste, ar sheirbhís na bliana, ar fhiabhras nó ar aicídeacha; agus go mór speisialta gan rud ar bith a chur inár mbealach a choinneochaidh an ghlóir shíorraí de dholaidh ar ár n-anaim! Má chí an tAthair Síorraí aonduine againn anseo i láthair eadra dhá chomhairle, go gcuiridh sé i gcomhairle agus i gcasán ár leasa sinn fá choinne ar n-anaim chun na glóire síorraí; le cathaithe an Diabhail agus an tSaoil shaluithe ghránna a choinneáil amach as ár gcroidhibh agus as ár n-intinn, agus ár gcoinneailt ar stáid na grásta fa choinne ar n-anam chun na glóire síorraí. Amen."

20

("Love to Thee, O Lord, glory and thanksgiving for this meal and every meal which Thou hast ever given us! O Redeemer who has given us life, grant us eternal life in Heaven! May we be seven times better off at the end of the year, in the greatest graces and the smallest sins! Health of soul and body in people, and their cattle safe from accident, from the year's hardship (?), from fever and diseases; and particularly (we pray) that (Thou) will put nothing in our path which will deprive our souls of eternal glory! If the Eternal Father sees anyone among us here present in doubt, may He counsel and guide them (us) for our good so that our souls may attain eternal glory; that He may keep the temptations of the Devil and of the ugly besmirched World from our hearts and our minds and keep us in a state of grace so that our souls may attain eternal glory.   Amen.")

'After the thanksgiving the rushes are plaited and made into crosses of varying thickness. The father and mother make a very large cross. The crosses are then sprinkled with holy water and hung on the roof or on the walls, where they remain until the following year.'

In *Ulster Journal of Archaeology, 1945*, p. 64, Oliver Davies quotes a description by one of the Ordnance Surveyors in County Derry in the 1830s:

'A strone or large cake of oatbread is made in the shape of a cross. The rushes are thrown on the floor, and the strone placed on the rushes. All kneel round the rushes and the bread, and at the end of each short prayer a piece is taken off the strone by each person and eaten. When all is eaten the crosses are made, and when blessed by the priest or sprinkled with holy water, are placed over the door, usually by the third day after the Feast in the hope that the family may have a plentiful supply of bread until that time twelve months, and in honour of St Bridget.'

In County Donegal the usual words of the door ceremony are *'Téighidh ar bhur nglúnaibh, agus fosclaidh bhur súla agus leigidh Bríd isteach.'* ('Go on your knees, open your eyes, and let Brighid in') to which is answered *'Isé beatha, isé beatha na mná uaisle'* ('Greeting, greeting to the noble woman').

The person who represented the saint at this door ceremony was often the man of the house, and just as often the eldest daughter. Sometimes a daughter named Brighid was chosen, even if not the eldest.

The material for the crosses, either straw or rushes had already been prepared and laid ready near the door for the ceremony. Where rushes were used, these were fresh and green and should have been pulled, not cut.

In most parts of this northern area there is a distinct connection between the festive supper and the making of the crosses. In places the material for the crosses is placed upon or under the table during the supper. In parts of Donegal and Sligo where a dish of mashed potatoes or colcannon formed part of the meal, this was mashed or mixed in a pot which rested on the material for the crosses.

In other places the crosses were made before supper and laid on the table while this was eaten. Sometimes the dishes holding the food were laid upon the crosses, sometimes the crosses themselves had pieces of bread laid directly on them during supper. Elsewhere the crosses were laid on the floor under the table. In parts of County Leitrim crumbs from the supper were put into the crosses.

In this northern area the bundle of rushes or sheaf of straw was usually portioned out among all the family, and each member made a cross. Usually one of the parents made a larger cross which was put over the door, while the other adults made those to be hung in the byre and stable. The children vied with each other in the making of their crosses, thus learning how to make these neatly. The children's crosses were hung over their beds.

In places the crosses were taken to the church to be blessed. This depended upon the attitude of the parish clergy. While working in County Donegal in January and February 1950 the present writer heard, in one parish, a priest telling his flock that he would attend to bless their crosses at a certain time, while in another parish a priest condemned the making of the crosses as 'superstition'.

In explanation of why the crosses were made and put up, tradition without hesitation answers 'protection'. Protection against fire, storm and lightning is the most usual reason given, but illness and epidemic disease were also held at bay by the cross, while evil spirits could not enter the house where it hung near the door.

In some districts last year's cross was taken down when the new cross was put up. More usually the old crosses were left in position, especially where pinned to the underside of a thatched roof. In places a newly married couple began a new series of crosses which was added to year by year until both partners had died. Perhaps the earliest reference to crosses is by the Rev. Story, a Williamite chaplain in September 1689.

Story reported:

'I went abroad into the Countrey, where I found all the Houses deserted for several miles, most of them that I observed, had Crosses on the inside above the Doors, upon the Thatch, some made of Wood, and others of Straw or Rushes, finely wrought; some Houses had more, and some less: I understood afterwards, that it is the custom among the Native Irish, to set up a new Cross every *Corpus Christi* day; and so many years as they have lived in such a house, as many Crosses you may find; I asked a Reason for it, but the Custom was all they pretended to.'

Since no such custom is known at Corpus Christi, it is clear that Story was mistaken in the date; the source of his information on this point is doubtful too, for he informs us that the district was deserted as all the inhabitants had fled for their lives or had been driven away by the advancing army.

After the making of the crosses the residue of the material was not just thrown away. In parts of Donegal, Tyrone and Antrim it was neatly arranged on the floor near the hearth, sometimes covered with a white cloth, to form a bed for the saint when she visited the house.

In some houses rushlights were made from the residue and lit in honour of the saint.

An Antrim tradition says that a little ring was made from a portion of the rushes and hung on the spinning wheel to bring a blessing on its work during the year.

The straw or rushes left over from the making of the crosses, or from the sheaf or bundle left at the door for the saint or from 'Brighid's bed' was believed to have curative powers. Strands from it were preserved and tied about an aching head or a sore limb during the night. Next morning the wearer might throw the strands on the fire, where by burning quickly they presaged a rapid cure. Others put a wisp under the mattress or pillow to ward off disease. In parts of Donegal the fishermen wove a little ribbon from the residual rushes or straw and carried it when at sea to gain the saint's protection.

In a few places in County Leitrim, children practised a custom which does not seem to be known elsewhere. They got a small piece of a flat wooden board about 30 cms by 15 cms and with the viscous exudation of a partly boiled or roasted potato fixed peeled rushes upon it in figures representing 'the sun, the moon and the stars'; this was then hung up with the cross.

23

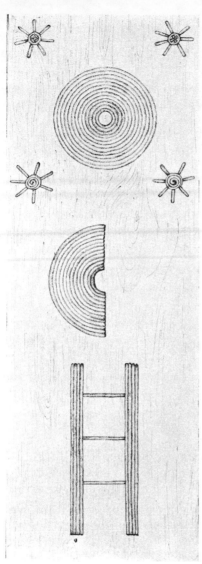

3 "The sun, moon and stars"
(National Museum, Dublin)

The 'Brídeóg'

Over a large part of Ireland, that is to say in places in every county of Munster and Connaught as well as in south and mid Leinster and a few places on the fringes of Ulster, one of the main features of St Brighid's Eve was the going about from house to house of groups of young people carrying a symbol of the saint.

Most commonly this was an effigy supposed to represent St Brighid herself, made with more or less care as local custom demanded. Sometimes this was a nicely-dressed doll borrowed from a little girl; often such a doll was re-dressed or decorated for the occasion. More often the image was specially made; a sheaf of straw might be pushed into shape and suitably dressed or garments might be stuffed with straw or hay to approximate to a human figure. The foundation of the figure might be a broom or a churn-dash, or some sticks or pieces of lath fastened together, and the whole padded and dressed. The churn-dash was widely used, as it could be stood upright on the floor. The head and face might be made from a mask or a carved turnip or a piece of white cloth suitably painted or coloured. Sometimes care was taken to represent the saint's figure with some reverence; other effigies were deliberately grotesque.

The character of the progress from house to house varied from one place to another. Where the custom had weakened, a small group of

24

children carried a doll to a few neighbours' houses and were given a penny or two at each house.

In other places the unmarried girls carried about an effigy which they had made and dressed with care. On coming to each house they were welcomed by the occupants and announced that they were bringing St Brighid's blessing to the household. In some cases they had made a number of St Brighid's crosses and they gave one to the head of each house. Usually it was accepted that the girl who carried the effigy was the most beautiful and the most modest of all. Sometimes no effigy was carried, but a chosen girl, dressed wholly or partly in white, and carrying a finely made St Brighid's cross of the local pattern, impersonated the saint. This procession of girls was known in parts of Counties Cork, Clare, Waterford, Galway, Roscommon, Mayo, Sligo, Offaly, Kildare and Westmeath.

In the *Ulster Journal of Archaeology* (1945, p. 46), T. G. F. Paterson recalls:

'On the Louth-Armagh border I have heard of "Brigid's Shield" and "Brigid's Crown", and was informed of a tradition that in days gone by, the most modest and most beautiful girl of a particular area, wearing a crown of rushes, a shield on her left arm, and a cross in her right hand, was escorted by a group of young girls from house to house on Brigid's Eve or Brigid's Morning, and that special prayers and ceremonies were observed. Unfortunately my informant had no recollection of the prayers or ritual in use, as she had never seen the ceremony performed and had only heard of it from "the old people".'

A more elaborate description of this form of the custom is to be found on pp. 225–6 of the *Louth Archaeological Journal*, iii (1914) in an article by Rev. L. Murray:

'The ceremony which took place on St Brigid's Eve is now remembered by only a few of the older people in Omeath. Nicholas O'Kearney gives a good description of it in one of his manuscripts, and to him I am indebted for the following account:

"It was the universal custom to prepare the *Cros Bhrighite*, the *Sgiath Bhrighite*, and the *Crothán Bhrighite* – i.e., the Cross, Shield and Veil of St Brigid, on the eve of the Saint's festival. They were generally plaited from the strong grass which grows in morasses or about lakes, and they were done with great ingenuity, for the inhabitants of the different townlands vied with one another in producing the neatest and most ingeniously wrought shield and cross. In the evening, the people of each townland assembled into one place to perform the pious ceremony. The most exemplary virgin in the townland was always chosen as An Bhrídeog, to bear the cross, shield and veil, and if her name was Brigid it was an additional recommendation. The maiden thus selected put on the veil, took the cross in her right hand and the shield in her left, and proceeded to each house, followed by the people who were engaged in humble prayer, invoking the Almighty Ruler of the universe to fill, with His Holy Spirit, those of His servants who dwelt in that house, and to enable them to keep His commandments according to the example of the great St Brigid. When the procession reached the house, the Brídeog put the question to those inside:

" 'Are you resolved, with God's assistance, to obey His laws and those of His Church, and to lead blameless lives like the great St Brigid?' The answer was usually in the affirmative, upon which the Brídeog presented the cross made for that house, with the words, 'Take the sword with which the great St Bridgid fought against her enemies, the world, the flesh and the devil, and remember to bear the crosses of this life with true Christian fortitude after the example of the great St Brigid.' On presenting the shield, she said, 'Take ye this shield, the shield of Faith; remember the many victories gained by St Brigid under its protecting influence, and bravely follow her example.' On presenting the veil, she asked, 'Will you follow the rules of virtue, piety and general good conduct laid down for your guidance by St Brigid?' The mistress of the house then called on the daughters and female domestics to answer in the sincerity of their hearts, and she presented the veil, saying, 'Be modest, chaste, and virtuous according to the example which the saint, whose festival we celebrate, has left for your imitation.' Then the cross was held up, and the whole assembly were called on to remember their redemption on that instrument, upon which exhortation, all would fall on their knees and join in fervent prayer to Almighty God that with the assistance of His divine aid, they might spend the coming year in piety and virtue.

"Thus the pious procession proceeded from house to house, and after the ceremony the crosses, shields, and veils were placed over the doors, in order that they might never be out of sight of the inmates, and especially that their attention might be frequently called to the promises made to God on St Brigid's Day. In case the sons or male inmates were suspected of a breach of the laws of God, parents did not fail to call their attention to the cross and shield placed over the door, and the mothers frequently put their daughters and female domestics in memory of the veil and ceremonies of St Brigid's eve. Rarely, we are told, were they appealed to in vain. It was by these and similar means that the seeds of piety, virtue and morality were sown and nurtured in the minds of the people of Ireland, and it is to be regretted that these old customs were often ridiculed, even by some of those whose duty it was to guard the morality and piety of the people.

"In Omeath, this custom was sneered at so long that it gradually fell into disuse, but St Brigid's crosses can still be found in a few of the houses." '

One wonders if this elaborate ceremony can be a survival from some medieval religious procession, or if it springs from a late eighteenth or nineteenth century refinement of local piety.

In most places the progress with the effigy was less reverent and more robust. In County Kildare, a century ago (*County Kildare Archaeological Journal*, V, p. 441) it took this form:

'On St Brigid's Day "the Breedhoge" was carried round by the young people from house to house, at which collections of food and money were made "in honour of Miss Biddy". This custom was probably a survival of a religious ceremony in which a statue of St Brigid was carried at the head of a procession.

' "The Breedhoge" consisted of a churn-dash, round which wisps of hay or locks of straw were tied to resemble a human figure. A ball of hay served as a head, and was covered with a white muslin cap, such as worn by old women. The figure was clad in a woman's dress, and a shawl completed the costume.'

In many parts of the south and west, only youths and young men went about. In recent times they usually dressed fantastically in coloured garments, with ribbons, sashes, fancy hats and face masks, but formerly they usually wore women's skirts, white shirts and conical straw hats which came down over the face, and often one or more of them wore outer covering made entirely of straw. We may note that this garb was also worn by the 'strawboys' or 'soppers' at wedding celebrations (see p. 45 below), and that disguise of shirt, skirt and mask was adopted by the dreaded 'Whiteboys' in the agrarian disturbances of the late eighteenth and early nineteenth centuries.

The group of young men on St Brighid's Eve brought musical instruments with which they entertained the households visited.

A memory of their procedure is recorded by the late T. H. Mason from friends in the Killarney district:

'As a small child I remember waiting in the kitchen for the knock which would announce "The Biddies". They were dressed in weird costumes, caps back to front and ferocious masks. They carried the "Biddy" – a large doll. We children were awe-stricken and tremendously excited when they trooped into the kitchen.' . . . .

'The figure they carry – the "Biddy" – is supposed to be an effigy of St Brigid. They do not sing, but dance to the music of a concertina. Their dress is anything they can get in the way of fancy smock and trousers and the masking of the faces I thought was for disguise. They collect for the "Biddy" and nowadays spend the money on drinking.' (*Journal of the R. Society of Antiquaries of Ireland*, 1945, p. 165).

A child's impression of these weird figures is given by Cáit Ní Dhonnchadha in *An Claidheamh Soluis* (6 August 1910) which may be translated as follows:

'When we heard the noise approaching the house, we would run upstairs and listen from there to their talk and their capers. However,

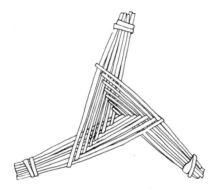

4   Saint Brighid's cross, County Donegal
(National Museum, Dublin)

on this night, I do not know what tempted me, as we all sat by the fire, but I said boldly that I would bet that I would not be frightened, by the *Brídeog*, but would stay below while she was there.

' "If so," said my father "I bet you that you'll be sorry in the end. I'll warrant that you'll not be as bold then as you are now."

'Soon we heard the noise coming. The other children ran upstairs. I sat on a stool in the chimney corner. Soon a terrible knock was struck upon the door. It was opened for them. In they came with a leap, one after the other, the man with the *brídeóg* in the lead. He had a great tall old hat on his head, two hand-lengths of rusty beard hanging from his face. He wore a flannel coat tied about with a large straw rope and a woman's old skirt down to his heels. There were about ten in the group, each of them in clothes funnier than the next.

'These devils were not long inside when they spied me seated in the corner. Up came the *brídeóg* man and thrust it before my eyes. Oh! I screamed and covered my face with my kerchief to shut out the horrid sight. I would have given a lot then to be upstairs with the others, I was so shaken with fear.

'Soon two of them stood out on the floor and recited for us *"Aighneas an Pheacaigh leis an mBás"* (The Sinner's Dispute with Death).

'That done, another sang "An Brianach Óg" ("Young O'Brien"). I had my face covered, determined not to move, but I liked the song so much that I lifted my face from the kerchief. But my friend, the *brídeóg* man, was beside me and he shook it at me, and waggled his beard at me so that I went into cover more quickly than I had come out.

'However, they were given some money and they went away to another house. But for a long time the rest of the family laughed and joked about my wonderful bravery before the *brídeóg*.'

Usually those carrying the effigy had a short verse to say in each house visited. A Kerry version went:

> Something for poor Biddy!
> Her clothes are torn.
> Her shoes are worn.
> Something for poor Biddy!

While a County Clare verse went:

> Here is Bridget, dressed in white.
> Give her a penny for her night.
> She is deaf, she is dumb,
> She cannot talk without a tongue.

On Inisheer, as John Messenger tells us in his *Inis Beag*: 'At the beginning of this century, a destitute woman who lived alone used to go from door to door begging for food and carrying a large "Brighid's Doll" made of straw and dressed immaculately in white with a picture of the saint on its breast. Some of the folk pulled straw from the doll to manufacture their crosses. After the woman recited the following poem, she was presented with food in honour of the saint, for which she blessed each person in the house with the doll:

29

Here comes Brigid dressed in white
Give her something for the night.
She is deaf, she is dumb,
For God's sake, give her some.

'Today, small groups of girls travel about the island emulating their predecessor by begging for coins to buy candy and donate to the church. A Brigid's Doll dressed in confirmation garb is carried by the leader of each group, and is used to confer blessings after the girls have recited in unison the two verses.' In this instance the use of a verse in English on an Irish-speaking island may point to a recent introduction of this form of the custom, perhaps by the 'destitute woman' mentioned above.

Tomás Ó Crohan describes the custom in another island community, the Great Blasket, (*Allagar na hInise*, 158):

'St Brighid's Day, 1922. When I opened the door early in the morning, two pilgrims were on the threshold, a little girl with the figure of a child in her arms and, her companion, a little boy . . . When they came in and when I had pulled myself together I looked carefully at them. They were sister and brother and closely related to me.

'Then I asked them what they would like to have – money, an egg, bread or sugar; and if I had named gold they still would prefer the sweet. Then I gave them some sugar and in going away they left me their blessing. No other one came to me during the day, although they told me that another one was going about.

'Many a year, when I was young, there were six or seven of them going about this island . . . An egg and a penny is what they used to take then.'

A Fermanagh tradition says that the visitors knocked on the door and waited until those inside called out 'who is there' – 'This is Biddy' – 'Welcome, welcome in,' on which they went in, sang a song or two and received the usual small gift. A similar welcome *Dé bheathasa, a Bhrídeog'* is remembered in South County Kerry.

While the tradition flourished it was considered wrong as well as mean to refuse a gift. Formerly, eggs or cakes were given instead of money, and the visitors brought baskets or other containers to hold these. In some houses, the housewife stuck a pin in the effigy's clothing.

Usually, when their round was completed, the *brídeóg* party returned to the house where they had made their preparations and had a feast and a dance there on the proceeds.

30

Of late many groups carried no effigy or other symbol with them, but merely solicited gifts at the houses visited. Sometimes they continued to make their rounds on two or three nights following, a departure from custom which was generally unpopular.

The effigy was usually called the '*brídeóg*' or the 'biddy' and those who carried it '*brídeóga*', 'biddies' or 'biddy-boys'.

Each group of '*brídeóga*' or 'biddies' visited only the houses of a certain circuit or area, and intrusion into the domain of another group was considered unfair and unmannerly. For this reason the group usually revealed its identity, although not necessarily that of its individual members, the guessing of whose names was part of the fun. Richard Hilliard, in a note in *Ulster Folklife* 1962, pp. 100–2, describes the custom in Killarney, County Kerry, where his family owned the Lake Hotel. He remarks:

'When the Biddies called at the Hotel they knocked at the door and the "captain" said: "God bless all here, can we come in?" If an invitation was extended the captain might then be asked: "What Biddies are you?" and he would raise his visor and say, "We are Muckross." This plan prevented "poaching" from other areas'. Having described the jollifications he goes on to tell of the rivalry between different groups.

'Before our time, the great centre for the Biddies was Muckross House, where the Herbert family lived until 1898, indeed all the local gentry seem to have encouraged the Biddies, and each crowd had its own territory. This led to an interesting situation, as far as we were concerned. Father moved to South Hill in 1926, an estate which adjoined Flesk Castle where the late Major Macgillicuddy had gone to live in 1918. Major Macgillicuddy had joined his place to the Lisavageen Biddy area, which was actually divided from his estate by the River Flesk. South Hill was in the Muckross Biddy territory, but when we moved there, and mother asked the Muckross Biddies to call with us, we found that the Major had persuaded the previous proprietors of South Hill to join his Lisavigeen group! Mother however, would only receive the Muckross Biddies and hunted the others; this actually started a feud between Muckross and Lisavigeen which persisted in sports and games for quite a long time.'

Brat Bríde

In the *Journal of the Cork Historical and Archaeological Society*, 1895,

p. 416 in an article by 'Mannanaan Mac Lir' we read of another custom then common in Munster:

'On St Brigid's Eve a silk ribbon is placed on the window sill (outside) during the night, in honour of our saint. This ribbon is said to lengthen during the night, and is ever after preserved as a remedy against headache. For this purpose *ribín Bríghid* ("St Brigid's ribbon") is used as follows: – First, it is rubbed or drawn around the patient's head three times, saying each time the invocation, "in the name of the Father, and of the Son, and of the Holy Ghost, Amen," after which it is knotted around the head.'

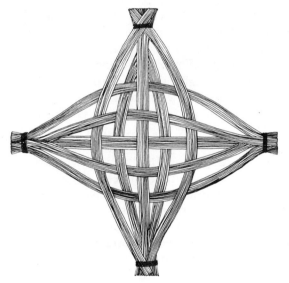

5 Saint Brighid's cross, County Derry (National Museum, Dublin)

In slightly varying forms this custom was widely known in other parts of Ireland, too. In south Leinster, and in north Connaught and west Ulster it was as usual as in Munster, while it is also remembered, if less widely, in places in south Connaught, north and mid Leinster and east Ulster. Its usual name was *Brat Bríde* or *Bratóg Bríde,* St Brighid's mantle.

The general belief was that the Saint, going about the country on the eve of her feast, would touch the *brat* and endow it with healing powers. Once thus touched it kept its virtue for ever, and many held that the older it was, the more potent it became. Some said that its healing power was greatest after it had been kept for seven years.

The *brat* might be a ribbon or a piece of linen or other cloth, or any garment. A sash, scarf or handkerchief thus touched by the saint would keep the wearer safe from harm, and men often put out a belt, a tie or a pair of braces to gain this protection, and to be worn especially when the wearer was engaged in any hazardous pursuit or journey to a distant place; it was often thus worn by fishermen and many stories are told of how this fishing boat or that escaped the perils of sea and storm because one of the crew wore the *Brat Bride*. Migratory labourers from Mayo and Donegal wore it when going to England and Scotland as also did emigrants to America.

Some households set out a basket with several pieces of cloth, all of which were believed to share in the Saint's blessing, and were carefully put away for use when needed.

The ribbon, cloth or garment might be laid on the doorstep or the window sill, or hung up conveniently or thrown on a low roof. In Munster it was often tied to the door latch so that the saint would touch it when entering the house.

The healing power of the *brat* might be employed against any ailment but it was particularly effective in the relief of pains in the head, such as toothache, headache, earache and sore throat.

In Munster, and particularly in east Limerick and south Tipperary and in Clare, the *ribín* or *brat* also gave omens for the future. Its length was carefully measured and marked down, usually on the whitewashed wall of the kitchen. When it was brought in again next morning it was again carefully measured against the marks, and if its length had increased during the night (as it almost always had, since the damp had caused it to stretch) this was a good sign, foretelling long life, plentiful return from crop and cattle, freedom from accident, illness and misfortune.

To some people within this area its increase in length was proportionate to the healing power which the touch of the saint had given it.

As well as relieving illness the *brat* was variously held to cure barrenness, to help women in childbirth and to ward off malign influences such as magic and the evil eye. It saved children from abduction by the fairies, and mothers sewed pieces of a white linen *brat* into the clothes of their young daughters to protect their virginity.

If a farm animal became ill the sign of the cross was made over it with the *brat* which was then laid on the animal's back to ensure the saint's intervention on its behalf. It helped animals to bear their young and ensured a good supply of milk to nourish calves, lambs and foals.

Crios Bríde

In West County Galway the party of young people going about on St Brighid's Eve usually carried the *crios Bríde* (St Brighid's Girdle.) This was a straw rope, some eight or ten feet long, spliced or woven into a loop and with a number – usually four – crosses of plaited straw attached to it.

In some places the boys carried the *crios* while the girls in the same party carried the *brídeóg*, in others the boys carried *crios* and *brídeóg* while in others only the *crios* was carried.

6 *Bogha Bríde*, County Cork (National Museum, Dublin)

At each house visited, the occupants were expected to pass through the *crios*, thus obtaining the protection of the saint and freedom from illness, especially 'pains in the bones', during the coming year.

The bearers of the *crios* said a verse at each house. One version goes:

> *Crios Bríde mo chrios*
> *Crios na gceithre gcros.*
> *Eirigh suas, a bhean an tighe*
> *agus gaibh trí h-uaire amach.*
> *An té rachas tré mo chrios,*
> *Go mba seacht fearr a bheith sé bliain ó iniu.*

34

(Brighid's girdle is my girdle
The girdle with the four crosses
Arise, housewife
And go out three times.
May whoever goes through my girdle
Be seven times better a year from now.)

To which some boys added:

Agus an té ná tugann pingin dúinn
Go mbriseadh sé a chos!
(And whoever does not give us a penny may he break his leg!)

The 'proper' way of going through the *crios* by men was, first the right leg, then right arm and shoulder, next the head, then left shoulder and arm, then left leg: Women put it down over head, shoulders and body and then stepped out of it. Each person was expected to make the sign of the cross and say a short invocation to the saint before passing through the *crios* each of three times.

This custom is still observed in places on the Aran islands and in County Galway west of Loch Corrib. Some memories of it in Mayo and Sligo point to a wider distribution in former times.

In a few places in west County Galway there are memories of passing the cattle through the *crios Bríde*. A large *crios* was woven by the householder when the crosses were being made on St Brighid's Eve. Next morning this was fixed in the door of the byre and the cows were driven out so that each of them passed through the *crios*, thus reaping the benefit of the saint's protection.

Cattle and Crops

In east County Galway a small quantity of seed grain, or the grain from the sheaf from which the crosses were made, was wrapped in a little cloth and hung up beside the cross in the house until sowing time when it was mingled with the general stock of seed grain. Similarly, in the same area, a potato was pinned to the roof by a pointed twig and added to the 'seed' potatoes when the time for planting came.

Some left the portion of grain or potato on the doorstep to gain the saint's blessing, and in due course added these to the seed at sowing time. A County Tyrone tradition tells of a little basket woven from the

35

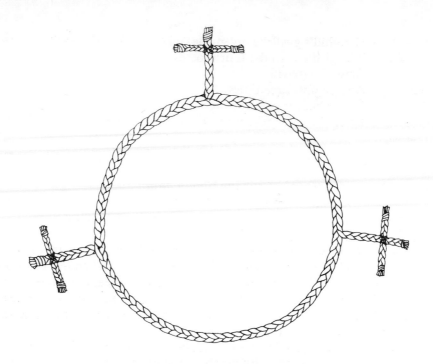

7 *Crios Bríde*, County Galway (National Museum, Dublin)

residue of the cross material and of the sowing from this container of the first grain. In a few places a portion of the residue was chopped and put with the seed grain, or dug into the potato ridges.

The residue from the crosses added to the bedding of horses and cattle warded off illness and danger from them and in south west Donegal the cows were struck with a little switch made from the residue with the same intent. The crosses in the byre might be taken down to bless a sick cow or one milking poorly.

A very widespread custom was the making on St Brighid's eve of spancels and cattle tyings, into which portions of the cross material residue or the threshold sheaf or the Brighid's bed were woven. The use of these in tying or spancelling cows, calves, sheep, lambs, horses and foals had many virtues. The animals were saved from disease and danger and protected from evil magic. Fidgety cows and unruly horses were soothed and calmed by them, and it was very common to use one in leading an animal to a fair; however, care should be taken to bring the rope home and not relinquish it to the new owner who would acquire its luck and blessing to the detriment of the seller.

Other Beliefs and Customs

As well as weather forecasting, some marriage divination was practised. J. B. Arthurs, in *Ulster Folklife*, 1957, p. 43 recalls that:

'In addition to the crosses, imitation ladders and spinning wheels are also woven from the rushes, two or three rushes each being used for the purpose. That night the young men and young women sleep with these under their pillow, the men having the spinning-wheels and the women the ladders. One's future partner would subsequently first be seen climbing a ladder or spinning at a wheel.'

We learn further that these little figures were exchanged as love tokens. The young man made the ladder, the girl the spinning-wheel; they exchanged tokens and put them under their pillows. Then, if they dreamed of each other, they were sure to marry.

In *Ulster Journal of Archaeology* 1945, p. 48, T. G. F. Paterson remarks:

'Saint Brigid's love for birds and their affection for her are well-known, and in County Armagh one will occasionally hear linnets described as "Brigid's Birds". If on Brigid's Day the lark should sing it is accepted as an omen of a good spring.

'The dandelion is sometimes spoken of as "Brigid's Flower". That may be due to the fact that it is almost the first wild-flower to come into bloom following her Festival. Apart from its cheerful aspect it is of some medicinal value, and forms the basis of a very potent but most palatable wine. It is known that the saint entertained in a regal way and was famous for the home-brewed ales that she bestowed upon her visitors without distinction as to rank or condition.'

The oyster catcher, known in Connaught as *Giolla Bríde,* St Brighid's page, is conspicuous on the shore at this time.

Another tradition tells that hoar-frost, gathered from the grass on the morning of St Brighid's day, is an infallible cure for headache. The saint's love of animals was remembered by giving some special, tasty food to the cows and horses. This was also done at Christmas.

Many people brought water from a well dedicated to St Brighid and sprinkled it on the house and its occupants, the farm buildings, livestock and fields, invoking the blessing of the saint.

Candlemas

With the gradual restoration of Catholic ceremonial on the relaxation of the Penal Laws, the custom of blessing candles in the churches on Candlemas, 2 February, again became familiar. As well as donating candles for church use, people brought others to be blessed for use in the home on such occasions as station masses and the administration of sacraments to the sick.

A popular legend to explain why candlemas fell immediately after St Brighid's Day. Because of Our Lady's diffidence in bringing the Infant Jesus to the crowded Temple, St Brighid promised to help her by distracting the attention of the multitude. This she did by appearing with a headdress bearing many lighted candles, and Mary, in gratitude, decreed that St Brighid's festival should be celebrated on the day before that of the Purification and the Candles.

Weather forecasts were made on Candlemas. A fine day was believed to be a token of wintry weather during the rest of February. Thus, in *The Northern Standard* on 6th February 1943 a correspondent from Ballybay, County Monaghan, gave the following note:

'Although many farmers were pleased to see Tuesday morning last so "bright and clear" in order to get out with the plough teams held up by the snow and rainfall of the previous days, yet those who take heed of weather lore didn't like to have such bright sunshine on Candlemas Day.'

Shrove Tuesday

In former times the austerities of Lent were observed with much more rigour and much more devotion than more recently. The faithful were bound to abstain not only from meat but also, even on Sundays, from eggs and from all milk products – that is to say from milk either sweet or sour, butter, cheese, curds and 'white meats', a very severe restriction on people a large part of whose diet consisted of milk products.

This was enjoined on the faithful in Ireland, for instance by the Statutes of Armagh, promulgated at the Synod of Drogheda in 1614 and again in the Statutes of Clonmacnoise, 1649, but undoubtedly is much older, as it was generally the rule in western christendom since the early middle ages. It continued in practice well into the last century, and even when the rigour of the law was modified, many people kept up the custom as a private devotion.

Nothing then, was more natural than the desire to have a 'last fling' just before the beginning of Lent. On the Continent of Europe this became a public, communal revel, the carnival, but generally in Ireland the Shrove Tuesday celebration was a household festival with the family and their friends gathered about the fire-side, when the surplus eggs, milk and butter were used up in making pancakes, and even the most thrifty housewife did not object, as otherwise these perishable foodstuffs might go to waste. Some people kept the Christmas holly for the fire which baked the pancakes.

This was another occasion for divining the future and, probably because of the connection, described below, of Shrovetide with weddings this was mainly marriage divination. In Halls' *Ireland* (I, 315–17) the custom is described thus:

'The family group – and the "boys and girls" of the neighbours – gather round the fireside; and each in turn tries his or her skill in tossing the pancake. The tossing of the first is always allotted to the

39

8 Shrove Tuesday pancake tossing (Hall: *Ireland*)

eldest unmarried daughter of the host, who performs the task not altogether without trepidation, for much of her "luck" during the year is supposed to depend upon her good or ill success on the occasion. She tosses it, and usually so cleverly as to receive it back again without a ruffle on its surface, on its reverse, in the pan. Congratulations upon her fortune go round, and another makes the effort: perhaps this is a sad mischance; the pancake is either not turned or falls among the turf ashes; the unhappy maiden is then doomed – she can have no chance of marrying for a year at least – while the girl who has been lucky is destined to have her "pick of the boys" as soon as she likes. The cake she has tossed, she is at once called upon to share, and cutting it into as many slices as there are guests, she hands one to each: sometimes the mother's wedding-ring has been slipped into the batter out of which this first cake is made, and the person who receives the slice in which it is contained, is not only to be first married, but is to be doubly lucky in the matter of husband or wife. Men also are permitted to have a chance; and it is a great source of amusement to jog their elbows at the important moment, and so compel them to "toss the cake crooked".'

There were other forms, too, of marriage divination but, although some of these were carried out on Shrove Tuesday night they are more closely associated with Hallowe'en, under which date they are described in detail below.

A less amiable custom of the Irish towns is also described by Mr & Mrs Hall (*Ireland*, I, 315): 'The practice of cock-throwing has been long in disuse in every part of Ireland; yet it was at one period a sport almost universal among the lower grades of the various cities and towns. A cock was tied by the leg to a stone or "kippeen"; the thrower, who paid a penny a throw, was to fling a stick, of a fixed size from a fixed distance, at the poor bird, which was to be his property if he killed it. Expert throwers used to carry home many prizes thus obtained, although it was not uncommon to find a cock living through a whole day, in spite of all attempts to destroy it. The day for this sport was Shrove Tuesday, a day which is still dedicated to games and amusements far less cruel and irrational.'

Amhlaoibh Ó Suilleabháin, the schoolmaster of Callan, Co. Kilkenny wrote of this custom in his diary thus on Shrove Tuesday 1831: 'To-day is the day when cocks were pelted. It was a barbarous trick. The poor cock was tied to a post or a stone by a hard hemp cord, and sticks were thrown at it. He who killed it became owner of it. A penny was wagered on every shot. Recently this barbarous custom has receeded. I have not seen it for thirty years. It was an English custom.'

This 'sport' is, happily, long since dead, although we still have in Ireland the word 'cockshot', the equivalent of the English 'cockshy'. As regards Ó Súilleabháin's last observation above, it is perhaps significant that no word of this derivation is to be found in Irish.

Shrove Tuesday is öne of the days when, according to tradition, 'nobody should be without meat', and even in very poor households some meat, if only a little bit of bacon, formed part of the supper. The more prosperous farmers might kill an animal for the occasion, portions of which went as gifts to poorer neighbours. Tradition remembers, too, that in times gone by the head of the slaughtered animal went as tribute to the local blacksmith. John Dunton, a London book-dealer who visited Ireland in the 1690s, remarked in one of his letters (no. 2) upon the eating of meat in profusion at Shrovetide, even among the poorer people:

'A gentleman in Galway to whom I was recommended by one who was friend to us both in Dublin gave me his recommendatorye letters to one O'Flaghertie the most considerable man in this territorye. He was son to one Sir Murragh na Mart O'Flaghertie; the name of na Mart was added uppon the occasion of his killing and devoureing in his own house, among his servants and followers everye Shrove Tuesday at night fifty beefes, and this I am told of the Irish papists in generall that the eve of their Lent they doe lay in a greate deale of flesh, gormandizeing that night enough to serve them until Easter, at which time they rise early in the morning to swallow down more of their beloved flesh; but this you must take notice of in the vulgar and poorer sort of people, not among the gentry.'

In parts of Counties Limerick, Cork, Tipperary and Waterford the head of the household took a small scrap of the meat from the Shrove Tuesday supper, and pinned it to the kitchen roof or inside the chimney, where it remained until Easter Sunday. This was said to bring good luck and prosperity to the household and especially to ensure that there never was a shortage of meat.

We may note another custom mentioned by Dunton (letter no. 4), this time at Naas, Co. Kildare:

'The inhabitants of this place and the neighbourhood have a custom (how begun I could not learn) on Shrove Tuesday to meet on horseback in the fields, and wherever they spy a hare in her form, they make as wide a circle as the company can and the ground will permit, and someone is sent in to start poor puss, who cannot turn herself any way but she is repulsed with loud cries and so frightened that she falls dead in the magical circle, though sometimes she breaks through and escapes, if a greyhound or any other dog be found in the field, it is a thousand to one he loses his life; and thus after they have shouted two or three hares to death they disperse.'

In Skibbereen, County Cork, after the fall of darkness on Shrove Tuesday evening the boys of the town amused themselves by discharging home-made firecrackers. These were made by wrapping gunpowder in paper with a short fuse attached and enclosing the packet in a tight covering of the lead-foil lining of tea chests. Some, even more dangerous, were made from a short length of lead pipe stuffed with powder. These miniature bombs were thrown about the streets, at groups of people, when the sight of the glowing fuse flying through the air was the signal to scatter and run. The bang from these fireworks is said to have been very loud and when thrown at a belated wedding cavalcade, usually caused the horses to bolt, much to the public danger. Towards the end of the last century this custom was finally suppressed by an active police official.

There was a common belief that to lick a lizard endowed the tongue with a cure for burns and scalds; this was especially effective if the lizard was licked on Shrove Tuesday.

Shrovetide Weddings

The traditional time for marrying, in rural Ireland, is Shrovetide. In the nineteenth century and on into the twentieth it was taken for granted that those who wished to marry did so at that time and at no other; there was scarcely a parish church in the country which did not have at least one wedding on Shrove Tuesday, the most favoured day of all. When this custom began we do not know; clearly it seems to be connected with the canonical prohibition of the solemn celebration of the sacrament of matrimony during the penitential season of Lent – a regulation often misunderstood to prohibit any marriage whatever during that period. It is probable that the popular reasoning ran thus: we cannot marry during Lent, thus we must marry before Lent, therefore just before Lent is the proper time to marry. This was held firmly as far back as folk-memory goes, and has, probably, been part of the accepted pattern of belief for several centuries. The ecclesiastical prohibition of the solemn celebration of marriage during Lent was set forth in a decree of the Council of Trent, the Decree on Matrimony, dated 11 November, 1563, ch. x. This decree, however, expressly states that this is no innovation but rather a confirmation of ancient prohibitions long in use in the church. We may take it for granted that such prohibitions were current in Ireland, where a most rigorous observance of Lent was practised in medieval and Early Christian

43

times, and we may postulate, too, a respectable antiquity for folk belief and custom derived from these prohibitions.

Shrovetide, then, was the time to marry. From Little Christmas (Epiphany) onwards the matchmakers had been busy and many unions were planned and eagerly awaited not only by the parties principally concerned but also by the whole district which would share in the merrymaking, feasting and drinking.

On the morning of the wedding the bridal party, in the south west of Ireland, left the house of the bride's parents in horse-traps or side-cars, the bride and her parents in the first vehicle followed by relatives and guests of the bride and groom, the groom joining in at the house or at some point along the way and taking up position at the end of the cavalcade. On the return journey bride and groom travelled together in the first vehicle, with the bridesmaid and groomsman. Many such little processions might be seen on the road on Shrove Tuesday morning.

Other customs prevailed elsewhere in Ireland, many of them much less formal, with the various parties coming separately to the church.

9   A wedding party (Hall: *Ireland*)

An elderly Donegal fiddle-player, Michael O'Doherty, recalls the time, sixty or seventy years ago, when the wedding party walked in a group to the church headed by a violinist playing merry tunes which always included 'Haste to the Wedding' on the way there, and *Tá do mhargadh déanta*' (your bargain is made!) during the walk from the church after the marriage ceremony.

Among the prosperous farmers of east Munster and Leinster it was, and in places still is, customary that when the newly married couple came out of the church, the groom was handed a dish or tray containing some handfuls of copper and small silver coins, which he threw into the air to scatter among the crowd, where children and others scrambled for them. In former times numbers of beggars and tramps assembled for this occasion and sometimes quarrels and brawls occurred between them.

The whole wedding party returned to the house of the bride's parents where feasting, music, singing and dancing continued until late at night. During the return journey the wedding party was sometimes halted by boys holding a rope across the road, on which the bridegroom had to buy the right of passage by giving a small gift of money. On arrival at the house her mother broke a small cake over the bride's head to give her luck and prosperity.

During the festivities the house might be visited by a party of young men of the locality, masked and disguised in much the same fashion as the 'Biddy Boys' on St Brighid's Eve. Usually they wore hats, masks or cloaks made of straw, for which reason they were called 'soppers' in west Munster and 'straw-boys' more widely, especially in Connaught. Usually they were made welcome and having danced with the bride and her attendants and friends, were entertained to food and drink before they left the house again.

Before the coming into common use of horse-drawn passenger vehicles the wedding parties often travelled on horseback, the women on pillions behind the men. On the way to the ceremony the bride was carried behind her father or another male relative, and on the way back, behind her husband. On these occasions the young men often raced their horses furiously across country from house to church or from house to house, the prize being a bottle of liquor. This mad gallop was usually known as 'the race for the bottle', and at Knocknagoshel in County Kerry the sad day is still recalled when three riders collided at the church gate and one was killed in the fall.

A relic of the Penal days, one which continued late into the

45

nineteenth century in many localities, was the performance of the marriage ceremony in the house, not in the church. On such occasions it often happened that several of the more important guests were invited to have their names entered in the record as witnesses to the marriage while the rest of the company was included in the blanket phrase ' . . . *cum multis aliis*'.

Of course these marriage customs might be seen at other times than at Shrovetide, but were most in evidence at this time when most country weddings took place, and are remembered in tradition as part of Shrove.

In his *Parochial Survey* Mason mentions an unofficial kind of calling of banns at Ballymahon, County Longford: 'For a fortnight before Shrove Tuesday, the great day for weddings, it is the practice for persons in disguise to run through the street of Ballymahon, from seven to nine or ten o'clock in the evenings, announcing intended marriages, or giving pretty broad hints for matchmaking, in these words, "Holla, the bride – the bride, A.B. to C.D." &c.; these jokes some times prove true ones.'

Chalk Sunday

As a converse to the marrying and merrymaking it was taken for granted that those who did not marry at this time did not intend to do so that year. This, in the popular mind, was a neglect of social duty. In rural Ireland the unmarried person never had the same status as those who were married. An unmarried man of fifty was still a 'boy' while his married nephew of twenty-five was a man; the young wife of twenty had the full status of a matron while the spinster of forty-five was practically a nobody. The position of the unmarried was emphasized at Shrovetide by the good fortune or the courage of their coevals or juniors who were marrying, and popular disapproval was not wanting. The broken match, the jilted flirt, the unfaithful swain, the crusty old bachelor, the 'boy' of fifty kept from wedlock by a doddering but still tyrannical parent, the vinegary old maid, all these were part of the rural comedy and matter for the rural wits and tricksters. In several parts of Ireland there were customarily accepted ways of showing this popular condemnation of the unmarried state.

A visitor to almost any village or small town in Munster or south-west Leinster in the latter part of the nineteenth century might be surprised at seeing people being marked with chalk when on their way to or from the church on the first Sunday in Lent. This was 'Chalk Sunday' when those who remained unmarried at Shrove had their clothes decorated with stripes and squiggles of chalk. Small boys rushed from doorways and made their mark; young men and girls whipped out concealed bits of white or coloured chalk and did the same. For the most part the victims took the chalking cheerfully if somewhat sheepishly. The younger men and women could afford to laugh it off with some remark about their chances in the following year, but a hardened old bachelor might round on his tormentors with vocal abuse and flourishing of a walking stick. And, naturally, the more disagreeable

CHALK SUNDAY IN THE COUNTY OF KILKENNY, IRELAND

10   Chalk Sunday (*Ill. London News*, 1854)

individuals were singled out for special attention, so that by the time they escaped from the village the backs of their coats were profusely ornamented. Some of the chalkers carried pieces of raddle, the colouring matter employed by shepherds to mark their sheep, which they used on selected victims, and this was particularly unwelcome as it was much more difficult to remove from the clothing than ordinary chalk. About the middle of the last century this custom was in full vigour all over the counties of Limerick, Clare, Tipperary and Kilkenny, as well as in north County Kerry and parts of Counties Cork, Waterford, Galway, Laois, Offaly and Westmeath. In a few places the chalking was done on the Sunday immediately before Shrove Tuesday, but this was exceptional. In the 1920s and 1930s the custom was still observed in a dwindling area, but it has now almost completely disappeared; where it does persist it consists only of children chalking each other in fun.

'Going to the Skelligs'

In much of the south-west of Munster there is a vague tradition that the festival of Easter was celebrated a week later on the island sanctuary of Sceilg Mhichíl than on the mainland. Whether this tradition is a distant echo of the ancient controversy on the date of Easter is a matter of speculation, but it did give the occasion of another form of disapproval of the unmarried. These had lost their chance of marrying this year on the mainland, but they still could be married on the Skellig, and steps must be taken to send them there. In places, especially in Cork city and other parts of County Cork, the purpose of the voyage to the Skellig was penitential, as chronicled by 'Mannanaan Mac Lir' in *Journal of the Cork Historical and Archaeological Society*, 1895, 420:

'All the marriageable young people, men and women, in any parish, who are not gone over to the majority at Shrovetide, are said to be compelled to walk barefoot to the Skellig rocks, off the Kerry coast, on Shrove Tuesday night; and have also to bring back home blocks of bog-deal or bog-oak as penance for their misdeed; the amount of the load to be in proportion to their offence. Thus, a young man or woman whose "first offence" it was, was said to be "let off light", but henceforward the offender was said to be "loaded" in proportion to his or her contumacy.'

All over County Kerry, in parts of west County Limerick, in much of County Cork, especially along the coast, and in west County Waterford the negligent were greeted, in the first days of Lent, with a barrage of chaff and banter. 'You're off to the Rock, I suppose?' 'Don't miss the boat!' 'Is it Mary or Katie you're taking on the excursion?' &c. &c. Here again the victims had to grin and bear it, for any objection brought only an increase of the annoyance. And threats of complaining to the parents of the more youthful tormentors, here as well as in the chalking, had little effect, nor would such complaints be welcomed by the parents, for were not the young people only carrying out a good old custom?

In many places the custom was carried further, and local poets were encouraged to compose verses on the occasion, verses which told of a grand sea excursion to the Skelligs, praised the splendid vessel which would take the party there and gave a long list of the participants, linking together the names of the bachelors and old maids as incongruously as possible. These verses – most of them mere doggerel –

were written out and circulated about the parish so that all might enjoy them, and were sung to popular airs, often in the hearing of those lampooned in them. In Cork city, we are told, they were printed; in a note in *The Journal of the Royal Historical and Archaeological Association of Ireland*, 1889, 144–5, we read:

'These were printed and sold in immense numbers on Shrove Tuesday. Many of them were rather witty productions, the poetasters endeavouring in the most absurd manner to join the most incongruous pairs together. The printers' names were never appended to these lists, and of course an opportunity was sometimes taken of venting personal spite, so that advertisements in the local papers are occasionally to be met with, threatening to indict persons who may be discovered to have taken liberties with the names of the advertiser or his lady friend. The lists of the "Pilgrims to the Skelligs" were called by all manner of names, such as "The Paul Pry Skellig List," "The Corkscrew Skellig List," "The Simple Paddy Skellig List," "The Virgins of the Sun Skellig List," "The Shrove Tuesday or Spiflicator List" &c. The custom reached its height about 1840, but has since gradually died away, so that at present no such lists are published.'

The custom in more recent times has taken the form of large posters, giving details of the 'Grand Excursion' with a list of the couples taking part in it. These notices were hung in prominent positions on the first Sunday of Lent, where they might be read by all on their way to church; often they were torn down by some indignant victim, but spare copies were at hand to be displayed without delay.

In south-east County Cork the Skellig joke appeared in its most extreme form. Here bands of young men went about on Shrove Tuesday evening, and if some inveterate bachelor ventured out and fell into their hands he was bound with ropes and had his head ducked under a pump or in a well, or was even thrown bodily into a pond; this drenching was called 'going to the Skelligs'.

'The Ash Bag'

The tradition in a few places is that ashes were sprinkled on the bachelors and old maids on Ash Wednesday; in the Moate and Mullingar districts we are told that small bags of ashes were surreptitiously pinned or tied to their clothing, and the saying 'You'll have the ash-bag thrown at you' was the equivalent of 'Nobody will propose marriage to you.'

Sprinkling of Salt

In parts of north County Galway and south-east County Mayo salt was sprinkled on the bachelors and spinsters 'to preserve them hale and hearty until next Shrove'. At Dunmore this was done on the day after Ash Wednesday, this being market day. At Ballinrobe it was done on the first Monday in Lent, and this was known as 'Salt Monday'.

Domhnach na Smúit; 'Puss Sunday'.

Those who remained unmarried after Shrove Tuesday were popularly supposed to be disappointed and filled with self-pity. In places as far apart as Donegal, north Mayo and Westmeath the first Sunday in Lent was called 'Domhnach na Smúit, 'Puss Sunday' or similar names. Here Smúit means a scowl, and 'Puss' is, of course the Gaelic *pus*, with the same meaning. The first appearance in public of the bachelors and spinsters after their time of grace had expired was on the first Sunday in Lent, and they could not help their frustration appearing on their faces; hence the name, and, needless to say, their facial expressions were not rendered any sweeter by their neighbours' sallies of wit on their sad state. In Kilkenny it was '*Domhnach na nDeóirín*' – ('Sunday of the little tears').

Some other customs

In places Shrove Tuesday night was taken as a time when practical jokes on hardened bachelors were allowed by custom. These took many forms. Horns were blown about the house; the door was tied and the chimney blocked so that the house filled with smoke; cart-wheels and other pieces of farm equipment were tied to the chimney; cabbage heads were pulled from the victim's garden and thrown at his door. In Tralee the delinquent bachelors were 'serenaded' with shouting and 'music' performed on buckets and tin-cans. In parts of County Waterford a frequent joke was the drawing on the whitewashed house wall of a grotesque caricature of the owner, while in places in County Donegal a 'wife', in the form of a scarecrow-like effigy, was provided for the bachelor and set up opposite his house for all to see. In Hall's *Ireland*, 1842, I, 315 we read that in Waterford City an unruly crowd of 'the lower classes' dragged a large log through the streets with ropes, preceded by a musician, and compelled unmarried men and women to sit on the log, sometimes even tying them to it; this was done on Ash Wednesday.

In places, pranks were played on newly married couples. This was, however, rare, except in cases where the marriage, for some reason, did not meet with popular approval. If, for instance, an elderly farmer with grown-up sons, married again, and this time took a young wife who might bear him other children, thus disrupting and confusing the normal course of inheritance and succession, the wedding night might be interrupted by raucous blowing on home-made trumpets, by cat-calls, smashing bottles, beating on tin cans and shouted nicknames and insults.

In some places Shrove Tuesday practical jokes might be played on anybody, not merely on bachelors and old maids. A favourite jest in Monaghan town and other places in the north east was to send some unwitting victim to the house next door for 'a loan of the Pancake sieve', where the poor innocent was sent on to another house and so on, until the truth dawned.

Ash Wednesday

On this, the first day of Lent many people ate only one meal and drank only water.

At least one person from every household went to the church to have his or her brow marked with the penitential ashes and to bring home a pinch of the ash so that the rest of the family too could have their foreheads marked. In many places there is a tradition that the people brought their own ashes – usually a small quantity of turf ashes – to be blessed in the church. Some burned the palm from last year's Palm Sunday to make ashes for Ash Wednesday. Any unused portion of the ashes was carefully wrapped up and put away.

Lent

As mentioned above, the Lenten fast and abstinence were very strictly observed in Ireland, and on all the days of Lent no animal products of any kind were eaten or used in the preparation of food. This meant abstinence from meat, eggs, butter and milk. It also meant that animal fats were not used in cooking, and we must remember that vegetable fats were hardly known in Ireland, which made this restriction much more severe than in those countries where olive oil or other vegetable oils were in common use. Along the sea coast there was some chance of getting fish oils, but these for the most part were unpalatable, although there is a tradition that people drank the oil extracted from the livers of the larger fish, and here no distinction was made between the oil obtained from codfish or halibut and that of the marine mammals such as whale or porpoise. However, these oils came as a bounty or windfall rather than as a regular supply.

The ban on animal products also affected the people's daily bread, for the typical Irish bread is leavened with sour milk and baking soda. Milk was not used for bread-making during Lent, and yeast, barm or sourdough were substituted as leaven. It appears, however, that many of the poorer people had neither the knowledge nor the baking equipment for the use of these, and so must be content with unleavened bread, such as oatcakes. It appears, indeed, that the lopsided economy of the eighteenth and nineteenth centuries had reduced the poorest section of the population – the landless agricultural labourers – to almost entire dependence on a diet of potatoes. Pamphlets circulated widely in Ireland during the famine period of 1846–48 among these poor people told them how to make bread, and how to bake it wrapped in cabbage leaves and in other simple ways in the absence of baking utensils.

Ecclesiastical authority tempered the austerity of Lent for people who thus lived on the edge of hunger by the wise provision that those whose meals were 'scanty and uncertain' should eat whatever they could get when they could get it, without reference to fast or abstinence.

For the average farming family which enjoyed some degree of frugal comfort the Lenten fast meant a small meal of dry bread, or porridge, and black tea in the morning and again in the evening, and a midday dinner of potatoes seasoned with fish or onions. On the coast, shellfish and edible seaweed appeared as relish with the potato meal. Instead of the usual sweet or sour milk, water, to which a handful of crushed oats was added and left to stand until the fermentation of the grain gave the beverage a sour taste, was drunk.

Children, if they were over seven years old, got no milk, and even the younger ones were given it sparingly. 'The very infant in the cradle was allowed to cry three times before he got milk on the fast days', as tradition puts it.

All who could afford to do so laid in a stock of fish, large or meagre according to their means, for Lent. In the large farmhouse a barrel of salt herrings was at hand. Smaller people might have a dozen or two of salt or red herrings hung up by a string or a withy near the fireplace where they grew harder and harder as time went on. Pieces of dried and salted stockfish, usually ling, hung from a rafter.

The pot and the frying pan used to cook meat were cleaned and put away on Ash Wednesday. The herrings were grilled on a gridiron or a tongs, the ling was boiled in a skillet, and even of these the household partook sparingly, merely as a savour to the potatoes and not as a main part of the meal.

There was no merrymaking during Lent, no music, dancing, card playing, or visiting friends. No mother would visit her daughter newly married at Shrove until Lent was over. Musical instruments were stored away. In many houses the pack of playing cards was burned and a new pack was bought at Easter.

Many people, women (who were equally addicted) as well as men, gave up smoking and some in an excess of zeal broke or burned their tobacco pipes. And although some topers found solace in the old couplet:

> Good luck and long life to the
> Council of Trent,
> It took away meat but it left
> us the drink,

55

large numbers took a pledge against alcoholic drinks 'for the duration'.

The rigid austerities of Lent were relaxed gradually over the years so that by the middle of the nineteenth century the 'black fast' was obligatory only on Ash Wednesday and on Good Friday. Nevertheless very many people, especially the elder, continued to observe the old penitential customs in whole or in part.

A curious sidelight on the Lenten fast is the eating of the barnacle goose (*branta leucopsis*) and, possibly, the brent goose (*branta bernicla*) as fish. This is first mentioned in Ireland by Giraldus Cambrensis, who visited this country in 1183 and again in 1185. Having described the wonderful way in which the geese came not from eggs but from shellfish (a common belief of the time) he goes on to say (*Topography of Ireland*, 23): 'Accordingly in some parts of Ireland bishops and religious men eat them without sin during a fasting time, regarding them as not being flesh, since they were not born of flesh.'

Many medieval writers mention the wonderful geese of Ireland and Scotland which spring from shellfish or from trees. Thus William Caxton in his *Mirrour of the World*, a Latin work which he translated in 1481 (p. 98):

'Ther is toward Irlond on the one syde a maner of byrdes that flee, and they growen on trees and on olde shipp sides by the bylles. And whan they be nygh rype they that falle in the water liue and the other not. They be callyd barnacles'.

Bartholomaeus Chassanaeus in *Catalogus Gloriae Mundi* (Cologne edition, 1617, p. 596) repeats the fabulous origin of the geese and adds 'Quia ex avium genere non aviuntur, his quadragesimali ieiunio sale conditis homines vescuntur'. ('Because they are not hatched in the manner of birds people eat them salted during the lenten fast'), while a 'Description of the Barony of Forth, County Wexford,' written about 1680, tells of 'Barnacles becoming in the month of May so ponderously fatt, that not having activity nor strength to flie, are by the adjacent inhabitants in small boats pursued and taken. They are not produced nor breed in these parts, are never hardly from them three months absent, yet returning are found to be of the ordinary proportion of equal corpulency. It is the received opinion (as in the Irish History and Scottish description of blacke Geese) that they have their originall and naturall production from pieces of Timber long remaining in the ocean, and cannot but improperly be esteemed flesh.'

Max Müller remarks (*The Science of Language*, II, 1891, p. 676): 'I am informed that in Brittany Barnacles are still allowed to be eaten on Fridays, and that the Roman Catholic Bishop of Ferns may give permission to people out of his diocese to eat these birds at table', while Heron-Allen, in his *Barnacles in Nature and in Myth*, 84, writes:

Mr Martin Duncan, the learned librarian of the Zoological Society, tells me that shortly before the Great war, when lecturing in the North of Ireland on marine animals, a parish priest who had attended his lecture – in which he had not mentioned the Myth – wrote asking him whether he had told the whole story of the Barnacle "because his people were in the habit of eating the Barnacle-goose during Lent under the impression that it was more fish than fowl", and stating that a comparatively recent pope had granted a dispensation to the people of Derry permitting them to continue to eat the Barnacle-goose during Lent as an ancient and established custom.

'Sir Edward Sullivan tells me, on the authority of the late Sir John Neligan (sometime Recorder of Cork and a notable ornithologist), that the same licence obtained all along the Kerry coast "not because they had any belief in the mythical story of its origin, but because they knew that it lived more on the sea than on land, and so acquired fishy character".'

The tradition of the eating of these geese during Lent is well known in many parts of the west of Ireland. In Tralee, County Kerry, it is related that the custom was kept up until quite recently, and that a well-known hotel in the town made a point of serving brent goose during Lent, mainly for the benefit of the clergy. As Edward Armstrong remarks in *The Folklore of Birds*, p. 227: 'Vincent of Beauvais (*Spec. anim.* xvii, 40) records that at the General Lateran Council in 1215, Pope Innocent III forbade this practice, but news of this does not seem to have yet reached the west of Ireland.'

Saint Patrick's Day

St Patrick's Day is now one of our most important festivals, a national as well as a church holiday. It is celebrated with ceremonies, parades, sports, exhibitions and entertainments of many kinds, most of them having a distinctly national or 'Irish' flavour. All this is relatively new, for, when compared to the numerous and varied traditional customs and practices associated with other great festivals such as May Day or Christmas those belonging to St Patrick's Day appear few and meagre. There are, indeed, associated with the festival of our national patron only two main customs which appear to derive from older tradition, namely, the wearing of an emblem or symbol, and the. 'drowning of the shamrock'.

The first of these, the wearing of an emblem in honour of the saint and of his day is first noted by an English traveller in Ireland, Thomas Dinely, in his *Journal* which appears to have been written in 1681. He says:

'The 17th day of March yeerly is St Patrick's, an immoveable feast when the Irish of all stations and condicions wore crosses in their hats, some of pins, some of green ribbon, and the vulgar superstitiously wear shamroges, 3-leaved grass, which they likewise eat (they say) to cause a sweet breath. The common people and servants also demand their Patrick's groat of their masters, which they goe expressly to town, though half a dozen miles off, to spend, where sometimes it amounts to a piece of 8 or cobb a piece, and very few of the zealous are found sober at night.'

He does not explain why he regards the wearing of the shamrock as superstitious while inferring that the displaying of the cross is not, but he does seem to indicate some kind of social distinction between the two emblems – people of 'all stations' wear crosses, while only the 'vulgar' sport the shamrock.

58

Dean Swift in his *Journal to Stella* shows us that the wearing of crosses was not confined to Ireland, but that the Irish abroad held to the custom. On 17 March 1713 he wrote from London, 'The Irish folks were disappointed that the Parliament did not meet to-day, because it was St Patrick's day; and the Mall was so full of crosses, that I thought all the world was Irish'. Later in the same century we have evidence of St Patrick's crosses farther away. The *Annual Register* for the year 1766 records:

'On the 17th of this month his Excellency Count Mahony, ambassador from Spain to the court of Vienna, gave a grand entertain-

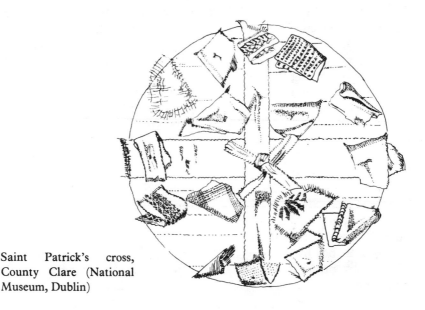

11 Saint Patrick's cross, County Clare (National Museum, Dublin)

ment in honour of St Patrick, to which were invited all persons of condition, who were of Irish descent, being himself a descendant of an illustrious family of that kingdom. Among many others were present Count Lacy, president of the Council of War, the Generals O'Donnel, M'Guire, O'Kelly, Brown, Plunket and M'Elligot; four chiefs of the grand cross; two governors; several knights military; six staff officers; four privy-counsellors, with the principal officers of state, who, to show their respect to the Irish nation, wore crosses in honour of the day, as did the whole court.'

A good description of these crosses, as they were known in the 1890s is given by 'Mannanaan Mac Lir' in *Journal of the Cork Historical and Archaeological Society*, 1895, 553–55:

'For a week or so preceding the National Festival, the grown members of the family are occupied in making "St Patrick's Crosses" for the youngsters, boys and girls; because each sex have a radically different "Cross". The "St Patrick's Cross' for boys, consists of a small sheet of white paper, about three inches square, on which is inscribed a circle which is divided by elliptical lines or radii, and the spaces thus formed are filled in with different hues, thus forming a circle of many colored compartments. Another form of St Patrick's Cross is obtained by drawing a still smaller circle, and then six other circles, which have points in the circumference of this circle, as their centre, and its centre as their circumferential point, are added; after which one large outer circle encompasses the whole, thus forming a simple and not inartistic attempt at imitating those circles or bosses of our beautiful Celtic cross pattern. The many spaces, concave, convex or otherwise, thus formed, are then shaded in; each a different hue, and this constitutes the "St Patrick's Day Cross", of which our little ones are so proud. In our time, when every school boy is supplied with a pair of compasses and a box of water colours, the making of a St Patrick's Cross is only the work of a few idle moments, but it was a different matter in olden times. A quill pen and the index finger were extemporized as compass, and the ingenious methods adopted for coloring in the spaces were amusing and sometimes painful. For yellow the yolk of the hen egg did duty, while laundry blue added another color to the list. Green was obtained (or supposed to be) by chewing rich young grass, while red was usually obtained by pricking with a needle the end of one's finger. The little boy wears his paper cross on his cap, and, military fashion, like a cockade over his ear.

'The little girl's "St Patrick's Day Cross" – which is made by an elder sister, or if sufficiently skilled, by herself – is formed of two pieces of card-board or strong thick paper, about three inches long, which are placed across at right angles, forming a *cross humette*. These are wrapped or covered with silk or ribbon of different colors, and a bunch or rosette of green silk in the centre completes the tasteful little girl's "St Patrick's Cross", which is pinned on the bosom or shoulder.

'I have known two or three old priests in Cloyne diocese break up and distribute among the poor girls of their respective parishes their old and worn vestments, for the purpose of being made into St Patrick's

60

crosses. The cross thus made (from a priest's vestment) to people of a simple faith was an object of veneration; and I have known many such forwarded by their owners to their kindred in America, where they were doubtless received as welcome souvenirs of an ancient custom in the land of their fathers.

'Not a little curious is the etiquette of those children's "St Patrick's Crosses," for whereas it would be considered effeminate of a little boy to wear "a girl's cross", it would be considered most unbecoming on the part of the little miss to don a boy's paper cross. Another form of a "St Patrick Cross" is that which is made of twig of wild sallow, and is only

12 Saint Patrick's cross, County Kildare (National Museum, Dublin)

made by men. . . . Like the St Brigid's Cross . . . it also is pinned to the thatch interiorly, a new one being added at each recurring festival. In a new house, the rule is to fix the first of those St Patrick's Day crosses (i.e. twig crosses) over the door-way, the succeeding ones being pinned on anywhere else in the (interior) roof of the kitchen. I have counted over thirty such twig crosses in the houses of some of my acquaintances where old customs still prevail.'

Some years later, as we learn from the *Journal of the Kildare Archaeological Society*, 1908, 443, only girls and small children still wore the crosses in Dublin and Kildare:

'Young girls and small children wear on the right shoulder "a St Patrick's Cross", consisting of a single or a double cross formed of pieces of narrow silk ribbon stitched to a circular disk of white paper, nicked at the edge, and measuring from 3 to $4\frac{1}{2}$ inches in diameter. At the ends of the arms of the cross a very small bow or rosette is stitched, and one a trifle larger at the junction of the arms; the more and the brighter the colours of the silk, the more handsome is considered the St Patrick's Cross. Those crosses sold in the Dublin slums are made on the same principle, except that instead of gaudy pieces of silk being stitched to the disk, coloured paper, cut into devices, is gummed on as a substitute.'

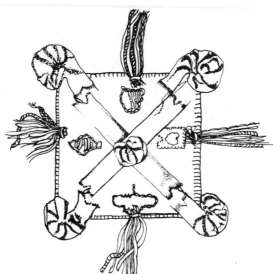

13 Saint Patrick's cross, County Meath (National Museum, Dublin)

Since then, the wearing of crosses on St Patrick's Day has died out completely. Small children now wear a little harp-shaped badge, or a rosette, of green ribbon, while older children and adults wear the shamrock.

In a work called *Synopsis Stirpium Hibernicum*, published in Dublin in 1727, the botanist Caleb Threlkeld identified the shamrock as white clover (*Trifolium repens*), saying:

'This plant is worn by the people in their hats on the 17th day of March yearly, which is called St Patrick's Day, it being a current tradition that, by this three-leaved grass, he emblematically set forth to them the mystery of the Holy Trinity. However that be, when they wet their seamar-oge, they often commit excess in liquor, which is not a right keeping of a day to the Lord; error generally leading to debauchery.'

About seventy-five years ago another botanist, Nathaniel Colgan, set about a definite identification of the shamrock by asking a number of people in different parts of Ireland to send him living rooted specimens of 'the real shamrock' from their districts, which he carefully planted and labelled. In due course the plants matured and blossomed, so that there was no doubt at all as to what they were. Colgan found that four different plants were represented in the collection. The majority of the votes for the real shamrock were divided about evenly between ordinary White Clover (*Trifolium repens*) and Lesser Trefoil (*Trifolium minus*) which has a yellow blossom. A few votes each went to Purple Clover (*Trifolium pratense*) and Black Medick (*Medicago lupulina*). And, interestingly enough, several people who saw the fully grown, blossoming plants in Colgan's collection, refused to admit that anyone of them could possibly be the real shamrock.

One of the reasons, perhaps the principal reason, why St Patrick's Day is traditionally a time for feasting and drinking is that, while it always occurs during Lent, all Lenten restrictions are set aside on this day. We have seen above, p.58, that Dinely in 1681 mentions drinking as part of the celebration, while Caleb Threlkeld refers to 'wetting the shamrock' in 1727.

In most parts of Ireland the men repaired to the local tavern after church to drink the '*pota Pádraig*' or 'St Patrick's pot'. Seldom did the drinking stop at one pot, and both Dinely and Threlkeld may be forgiven their implication that drunkenness was usual on St Patrick's Day. Fitzgerald and M'Gregor, in their *History of Limerick,* 541, say that in that city 'Patrick's-day commences with numerous acts of devotion at a well dedicated to the saint in the neighbourhood of the city and ends with copious libations to his memory.'

The term '*pota Pádraig*' or 'St Patrick's pot' has been in use for centuries. The poetaster Farewell used it in his lampoon 'The Irish Hudibras' in 1689, where his hero proclaims that he will:

> Ordain a Statute to be Drunk,
> And burn Tobacco free as Spunk;
> And (fat shall never be forgot)
> In Usquebah, St Patrick's Pot.

In 1828 Amhlaoibh O Súilleabháin wrote:

'The seventeenth day, Monday. St Patrick's Day. A fine dark calm day; people merry drinking their 'St Patrick's Pot'; a shamrock in every hat, low and tall, and a cross on every girl's dress.' Two years later he wrote 'This is a specially blessed St Patrick's Day, for I do not see a single person, man, woman or boy, drunk, a thousand million thanks to God. This happened owing to the sermons of Father Thomas Doran, with the grace of God, through Jesus Christ.'

'Pota Pádraig' and 'St Patrick's pot' continued in fairly general use until recently to denote a drink on St Patrick's Day; it was also applied to any treat to friends or gifts of money or sweets to children on the festival.

The *Journal of the Kildare Archaeological Society*, 1908, 443, assures us that:

' "The drowning of the shamrock" ' by no means implies that it is

14   Saint Patrick's Pot (*The Shamrock*, 1867)

necessary to get drunk in doing so. At the end of the day the shamrock which has been worn in the coat or the hat is removed and put into the final glass of grog or tumbler of punch; and when the health has been drunk or the toast honoured, the shamrock should be picked out from the bottom of the glass and thrown over the left shoulder.'

In some parts of the south of Ireland, a cross was marked with a burnt stick on the sleeve of each member of the family, with a prayer that the person so marked might be steadfast in the faith of St Patrick.

Everybody should have meat for dinner on St Patrick's Day both in honour of the festival and as a relief from Lenten abstinence. This tradition seems to be very old. Jocelin, who as a monk in the Abbey of Furnes wrote, early in the twelfth century, an account of the life of St Patrick tells us (in his twenty-third chapter) how Patrick, during his religious training in France was tempted to eat meat and for that purpose hid some pieces of pork, but repented so sincerely that God sent an angel to comfort him, and goes on:

'Then St Patrick, rising from the earth, utterly renounced and abjured the eating of flesh-meat, even through the rest of his life; and he humbly besought the *Lord* that he would manifest unto him his Pardon by some evident Sign. Then the *Angel* bade Patrick to bring forth the hidden meats and put them into Water; and he did as the Angel bade; and the flesh-meats being plunged into the Water and taken thereout, immediately became Fishes. This Miracle did St Patrick often relate to his Disciples, that they might restrain the desire of their Appetites. But many of the Irish, wrongfully understanding this miracle, are wont on St Patrick's day, which always falls in the time of Lent, to plunge Flesh-Meats into Water, when plunged in to take out, when taken out to dress, when dressed to eat, and call them Fishes of St Patrick. But hereby every Religious Man will learn to restrain his appetite, and not to eat meat at forbidden seasons, little regarding what ignorant and foolish Men are wont to do.'

If Jocelin was correctly informed about such an Irish custom in his time, it means that about the year 1100 Irish people ate meat on St Patrick's Day, whether they really pretended that it was fish, so as to evade the Lenten law, or ate it with the church's sanction and jokingly referred to it as St Patrick's fish in contrast to the Lenten fish.

St Patrick's day was generally taken as the middle day of Spring. Improved weather was expected from then onwards, all the more confidently because of the saint's promise that every day would be fine

c

after his festival. To the farmers this meant that the time for planting the main potato crop had come, and those who delayed this work long after 17 March were regarded by their neighbours as slovenly and lazy.

Lady Day

25 March, the feast of the Annunciation, was a Holiday of Obligation on which the Lenten fast was relaxed although there was in Ireland no extensive merry-making as on St Patrick's Day. It had some legal significance for, until Britain belatedly accepted Pope Gregory's calendar in 1752, the year began officially on 25 March, which was thus of importance as regards contracts, leases, rents and so on.

Apart, however, from its religious and legal significance, it had little effect on popular tradition. High winds were expected on this day, and if it coincided with Easter Sunday people feared that the following harvest would be poor, with consequent scarcity of food.

Palm Sunday

At least one member of every household brought home from the church a piece of the palm blessed on this day in commemoration of Christ's entry into Jerusalem. Usually every member of the family was at Mass and each brought home a piece of palm. The men and boys broke off a sprig of it when leaving the church and wore it all day in hat or cap band or coat lapel.

In Ireland the 'palm' is usually conifer such as silver fir, spruce, cypress or, very often, yew. Indeed, Palm Sunday was *Domhnach an Iúir* (Yew Sunday) to many Irish speakers.

Formerly, and until recently in some districts, the people brought their own sprigs of 'palm' to be blessed in the church. One old resident of County Fermanagh recalled with gratitude the thoughtfulness of a Protestant neighbour, who, although he had no palm ceremony in his own church, always cut a pile of sprigs from his yew trees and left it on the garden wall so that his Catholic neighbours could take them on the way to their place of worship.

A sprig of the palm was hung up in the house, and farming families usually put a sprig in the byre, too, so that the cattle might share in the blessing and protection. A sprig was set aside for use when occasion arose as a holy water sprinkler.

It appears that in places the palm was worn for several days after Palm Sunday, thus Spencer T. Hall wrote in *Life and Death in Ireland* (1850), 35, at Limerick: 'On the first of these occasions – Palm Sunday – most of the men and boys I met had small bunches of palm in their hats or button holes, which they said had been consecrated by the priest, and which many of them wore or renewed for nearly a fortnight afterwards.'

In parts of Galway and Mayo, we are told, a small quantity of the palm was shredded and mixed through seed grain, a more widespread

68

custom was the marking of a cross on eggs being set for hatching with a charred stem of the palm.

Sometimes children visited friends and neighbours to begin collecting eggs for Easter.

It was especially ominous if Palm Sunday fell upon another festival. If 'the Shamrock and the Palm were worn together', that is to say if Palm Sunday coincided with St Patrick's Day something unusual was expected to occur, although opinions varied as to what this might be. Usually it was taken as a happy omen – the summer would be exceptionally fine, or Ireland's troubles would come to an end. Similar prognostications were confidently made when Palm Sunday fell upon 25 March, the feast of the Annunciation.

Easter

Tradition demanded that the dwelling house and all its appurtenances should be thoroughly cleaned and set in order in preparation for Easter, and this occupied much of the time of the housewife and her helpers during Holy Week. The house was everywhere swept, and cleaned. The walls were whitewashed inside and outside. Woodwork was repainted, furniture scrubbed white, pots and containers scoured, delf and ornaments washed and polished.

Meanwhile the men of the household were equally busy in the farmyard, where the byre, stable and other outbuildings were cleaned and whitewashed and the whole yard and surroundings swept and tidied. Any failure in this regard brought adverse comment from the neighbours and marked down that household as slovenly and unworthy.

To the best of their means, too, people provided themselves with new clothes at this time, and the country tailors and dressmakers were kept busy. Especial pains were taken to dress the children in new garments, and presents of wearables such as hats and caps, ribbons and neckties, stockings and shoes came to the little ones from relatives and friends. All of this finery was shown off by the proud owners at church on Easter Sunday.

Good Friday

This was a day of severe austerity when most people voluntarily exceeded even the rigorous fasting prescribed by the church. Many people ate nothing until midday; many, even then, took nothing more than three mouthfuls of bread and three sips of water.

Usually no work was done on the land on Good Friday; instead, the day was spent in cleaning and tidying by the women in the dwelling house and the men in the farmyard and outbuildings. Most farmers would, however, plant a small quantity of grain or potatoes on this blessed day, thus invoking a blessing on the crops.

The women and girls let their hair hang loose as a token of mourning, while they, as well as the children and many of the men went barefoot all day.

Nobody would move house or begin any important enterprise on this day.

No blood should be shed, thus no animal or bird could be slaughtered, no wood should be worked or burned and no nail should be driven on the day on which the Saviour was crucified, while from noon until three o'clock, the period according to tradition when Christ hung on the cross, silence was observed as far as possible, and prayers were said by the whole household gathered together. The sky was expected to darken at this time.

As many people as possible visited the church to pray, and those who were still wearing shoes took them off when going into the church. It was while engaged in this pious exercise that John de Courcy was taken prisoner by Hugh de Lacy on Good Friday, 1204, in the churchyard of Downpatrick. Visits were also made to graveyards, to pray for the dead, and to holy wells and other local shrines. This was noted at Clonmacnoise by an English parson, the Reverend James Hall, in his *Tour through Ireland* 1813, i, 336;

'Daily prayers are put up for the dead here; and, on Good Friday, thousands are to be seen prostrate over the graves of their friends, praying for the repose of their souls, and for their speedy escape out of purgatory; and people on pilgrimages often go round the well a number of times, on their bare knees.'

Regular fishing with nets or lines was discouraged on Good Friday, and no fishing boat put to sea. Against this, all along the coast people went to the beach and gathered shellfish and edible seaweed which they ate as their main meal; as there is always a full moon in Holy Week there usually is no shortage of this *bia tragha*, 'shore food'.

Cold and wet weather was expected on Good Friday, and welcomed as a sign of nature's mourning for the death of Christ.

Men and boys trimmed their finger and toe nails and had their hair cut on Good Friday. This cutting of hair prevented headaches during the coming year.

Water taken from a holy well on Good Friday was believed to have curative properties and was kept for use in illness. A child born on Good

Friday and baptized on Easter Sunday had the gift of healing, and, if a boy, was confidently expected to enter the ministry and reach high dignity in the church. Similarly, one who died on Good Friday and was buried on Easter Sunday was sure of immediate entry into Heaven.

Eggs laid on Good Friday were marked with a cross and each member of the family ate one of these on Easter Sunday. Eggs set to hatch on this day were sure to produce healthy birds.

Easter Saturday

The blessing of holy water for use in Catholic ritual is part of the church's ceremonies of Easter Saturday. In popular belief this water has power against illness and danger, and one member of every household brings home a small container of it.

Each member of the family took three sips of the Easter water in the name of the Trinity as a preventive of disease, and it was sprinkled on the house and its occupants, on the farmyard outbuildings, livestock and growing crops. The rest of the water was put away for use in illness or danger, and, according to tradition it remains fresh for ever.

A cinder from the Paschal Fire also brought prosperity and blessing, being especially effective in preventing damage by fire. In Limerick, Tralee and other towns people brought turf cinders to the church to be blessed for this purpose.

Herring Processions

In a number of towns the butchers, who had little sale for their meat during Lent, celebrated the coming of Easter and the return of normal business by holding a mock funeral of a herring, symbolizing abstinence.

The custom in Dundalk was described by Henry Morris in *An Claidheamh Soluis* (12 April 1902) thus (translation):

'The people of that town kept the fast of Lent so manfully that no meat was eaten there during Lent. This greatly set back the killers of beef, the butchers, and on each Easter Saturday, when their good season was returning they bought a herring, and hung it upon a straight strong lath nine feet long. Then they got big long rods and walked through the town from Gallows Hill to the Big Bridge, beating the poor herring until hardly a fin was left. On reaching the bridge they hurled the horrid herring into the water with insult, and hung up a

72

quarter of lamb decorated with ribbons and flowers in its place, and went back to the market place, playing tunes and loudly boasting to each other.' Similar processions were held in Drogheda and Cork.

A note in the *Evening Herald*, (4 March 1966) by Liam Ryan describes the Drogheda procession:

'For the elderly people of Drogheda, Lent recalls a quaint custom observed in the town for many years, eventually dying away in the early part of the century.

'The custom was dubbed "Whipping the Herring" and heralded the last day of Lent. Little business came the way of the butchers and the custom was their way of "taking it out" on the herring.

'The ritual usually got under way early on Easter Saturday morning in a laneway off West Street, now known as the Meat Market. Here, the butchers' boys assembled and tied dozens of herrings to a long, light rope which one of the boys would fling over his shoulder. The boy would then run from the laneway, dragging the line of fish behind him.

'The other boys would follow, all armed with sticks or whips, and would constantly flog the fish until not a trace was left on the rope.

'The butcher's boy who for years shouldered the rope of herring was known locally as "Jimmy the Melt". He was a man of great physique and had served in the Peninsular War.'

In Cork a single herring was borne aloft by the butchers and subjected to insult and ridicule as it passed through the streets.

In Dublin, as revealed by Sir Charles Cameron in his *Autobiography* (1920), a related custom was observed on Easter Monday:

'When I was a child, Lent was kept much stricter than it is at present with respect to fasting and abstinence: consequently the trade of the butcher declined considerably during the forty days of Lent. The work of the porters and men engaged in the slaughter-houses was much reduced. I remember seeing on at least two occasions processions of those persons, some dressed in fantastic garments, through the streets on Easter Monday. An ass formed part of the procession, its back covered by a cloth on which a cross was painted. The object of the procession was the collection of donations to compensate the processionists for the loss of employment during Lent.'

An account, given in *Ireland's Own* (26 April 1916), shows us that the public at large could grow weary of the tedious diet of Lent and vent their dislike for it upon the unfortunate herring. A ceremony at Carrickmacross, County Monaghan 'about eighty or a hundred years ago' is described thus:

73

'On Easter Sunday morning, immediately after last Mass, all the young men and maidens, dressed in their best, flocked into the town of Carrickmacross, where they formed into a procession, headed by one of their number carrying a long pole, from the top of which dangled a herring, and marched to the tune of whatever musical instruments they could muster (fiddles were the most common in those days) till they came to the lake just outside the town, when the herring was taken down from the pole and thrown into the water amidst the cheers and laughter of the spectators'.

The account goes on to say:

'The herring, being the cheapest and most plentiful fish, was the principal dish of the poorer classes, and of some of the better-off people, too; consequently the people grew so tired of seeing him day after day on their tables that they conceived the idea of getting rid of him by drowning, after which they would indulge in all kinds of games and pastimes, and amply make up for the quiet time they spent during Lent, as no one would think of enjoying themselves during the Holy Season.'

The Dance of the Sun

People in all parts of Ireland held to the pious belief, common in many areas of Europe, that on its rising on Easter Sunday morning the sun dances with joy at the Saviour's resurrection.

Generally it was held that one should go up to a hill top or other high place to witness this. Patrick Kennedy (*Banks of the Boro* p. 195) mentions this in his memories of County Wexford a hundred and fifty years ago:

'So at last came the bright Easter morn; and Peggy, and Pat, and others were out at sunrise on the top of a hillock, to see the sun dancing, just as he came above the rim of the earth. Those that did not care to face the bright orb with the naked eye, were content to look at its image in a tub of clean water.'

Often there was a special place from which this could best be seen. Thomas Crofton Croker records this from Killarney in his *Legends of the Lakes*, 30:

' "Where does that road lead?" said I, pointing to a road on the left of the one we were pursuing.

' "The road is it?" said the man with the cloak, "why, then, what road should it be, but the road to Sunday's Well, a fine well it is, and a blessed place, for sure they say, though myself never see it, that if one

74

was to go there at peep of day on an Easter Sunday, they'd see the sun dancing a jig on the rim of the sky for joy; and I suppose that's the reason they calls it Sunday's Well".'

Children are normally cautioned not to look directly at the sun with naked eyes and because of this, as Kennedy mentions above, it was usual to view the early morning sun on Easter Sunday reflected in a pan or tub of clean water, and often a parent or other adult person managed to agitate the surface of the water so that the sun appeared to dance and the little ones were not disappointed. Some people set out a tub of water on the evening of Easter Saturday in readiness for this. Others set a vessel of water inside a door or window to catch the sun's rays so that when the surface of the water was disturbed the reflection of the sun 'danced' on the wall or ceiling. In County Kerry it was held that the rising sun danced on Palm Sunday also.

Easter Eggs

The association of eggs with Easter is familiar to us all, especially in recent times in its modern commercialized form of the sale of chocolate Easter eggs. This, of course, springs from the Easter egg beliefs and customs found in almost every corner of Europe and in the areas of European settlement overseas. There are numerous Irish Easter egg customs, which include eating of eggs, presents of eggs, decoration of eggs, and games played with eggs.

There has been much speculation upon the origins of the association of eggs with Easter, with copious invocation of life-forces, magico-religious significance, creation, resurrection and pre-Christian symbolism. The real origin is much more likely to lie in the custom, common to both Eastern and Western Christendom, of fasting from eggs – as well as from all animal products – during Lent. This is summed up in a Greek saying regarding the Lenten fast: 'With an egg I close my mouth (Lent); with an egg I shall open it again (Easter).' Abstention from eggs during Lent meant that all eggs were used up before Lent began (e.g., in the feast of pancakes, as in Ireland) and that there was a large accumulation of eggs by the coming of Easter which provided a surplus for feasting, presents, games and so on. The practice of including eggs in the produce blessed in the church at Eastertide, formerly known in many parts of the Christian world and still common in some Oriental rites, added to the fame of the egg as an accessory of the Easter rejoicing.

Eggs in large quantities must appear on the Easter Sunday breakfast table, and everybody should eat as many of them as possible. Failure to consume at least four or five is looked upon as a very poor effort, while some heroes put away a dozen or more. And someone is sure to tell how, in his grandfather's time, a stout servant boy devoured the most incredible numbers of them, for no housewife would venture to call a halt for reasons of economy to such a spirited observance of the time honoured ritual. Even those who normally did not eat eggs ate at least one in honour of the day, while an inevitable question among children was 'how many eggs did you eat?'

The general feeling was that 'nobody should be without an egg at Easter' and most farmers' wives (for fowl and eggs in Ireland were always under the women's care and disposal) gave presents of eggs to their workpeople and poorer neighbours, and no tramp or beggar coming to the door was denied an egg at Easter.

Mothers often added a little colouring matter, such as washing blue or onion skins, to the water in which the eggs were boiled, so that the children got theirs attractively dyed, or drew various patterns and decorations on the egg shells. The writer recalls seeing a small child's refusal to eat the 'little man' on being given an egg embellished with a drawing of a funny face on Easter Sunday morning.

During Holy Week children often received presents of eggs from friends and neighbours. Sometimes they went to relatives or god-parents, or made the rounds of nearby houses to collect eggs, the usual container for which was a strong woollen stocking.

With the eggs thus gathered, supplemented by other 'goodies', bread and butter, cakes, sweets and so on, the children made their own Easter feast. They retired to a quiet place in an outhouse or the corner of a field where they could build a little 'house' or fireplace on which to cook the eggs. This custom was widely known as the *clúdóg* or *clúideog*, a term applied variously to the custom as a whole or to the collected eggs or to the little structure in which they were cooked. In recent years this children's custom seems to have been confined to the northern half of Ireland but Kennedy describes it, about 1820, in County Wexford (*Banks of the Boro*, 233):

'During the last week of Lent, as nobody dreamed of eating an egg, eggs in abundance graced the Easter breakfast table, and on Easter Monday the little men and women under thirteen years of age assembled in some dry sheltery ditch or quarry-hole, bringing their supplies of griddle-cakes, eggs, butter, dry sticks or turf, and egg-spoons fashioned by themselves of ash or oak boughs, or any suitable chance

15 Painted Easter eggs, County Dublin (from a photograph by the author)

splinters that had come in their way. A roaring fire was soon made, the eggs roasted, and the social meal proceeded.'

And tells of a sad little incident; (id. 152):

'I was at the time with those relatives near Ross; and some of my young cousins and myself were on the point of starting for the town on Easter Monday morning. We were standing at the door just ready for the road, enjoying the fine sunny fresh atmosphere, when I saw James Breen come into the yard. I guessed in a moment that he was the bearer of some sorrowful news, and so it proved. He told me all the particulars as they fell out the day before: how poor little Peggy and her young companions were in such glee, running with their Easter eggs to lock themselves up in a room at Daniel Foley's and hold their feast; and how, just as they were going carelessly behind one of the horses, as he was eating his chopped furze at the stone trough, he threw out his legs, struck the poor little creature behind the ear with his iron shoe; and till God was pleased to release her from her sufferings, she never opened her mouth nor her eyes again.'

77

Kennedy also informs us that a similar custom was current in parts of County Wexford among grown up young people (id. 232):

'Among some dim recollections of ours are scattered the "Tobies" whose ruling superstition was a belief in the virtue of eggs collected at Easter. They were not much respected in general. They dressed themselves as fantastically as they could in scraps of drapery of all descriptions, went in companies of from four to six, and demanded their spare eggs from disturbed housekeepers. As they approached farm houses in the absence of the menkind, their appearance was not agreeable in the eyes of the women. Their habitat was the eastern portion of the county of Wexford. We do not recollect seeing them west of the Slaney. It was once our lot to see in their corps as fine a specimen of a young fellow as could be met with, a profusion of rags hanging round him in the most picturesque disorder, and his manly, sun-burnt features glowing with careless enjoyment. They occasionally sang and danced, but rarely went to the expense of a paid musician. They did not remain together so long as the mummers or the Mayboys. Having collected a sufficient stock of eggs, they made their feast. Under happy circumstances they converted part of their hoard into whisky, got flat cakes and butter for the trouble of asking, and roasted their eggs. Any other chance delicacies that came in the way were not rejected, and at the termination of the festival and the separation of the allies the usages of sober and polite society were not in request.'

In those districts where May bushes were set up, as described later in connection with May Day, the shells of the Easter Eggs, especially those which had been dyed or decorated were kept by the children to be hung as ornaments on the May bush.

In many parts of the north of Ireland 'egg rolling' still is or until recently was, usual. The children rolled hard-boiled eggs on the ground, usually down a slope, in games like marbles, and when an eggshell cracked in collision with another the child who owned the uncracked egg took both. Each egg of a child's store was coloured or marked so it was known, and the game ended in the eating of the eggs. This custom was formerly more widespread; it is still remembered, for instance, in parts of County Limerick.

Mason (*Parochial Survey*, iii, 207–8) notes from Holywood, County Down: 'The trundling of eggs, as it is called, is another amusement which is common at Easter. For this purpose the eggs are boiled hard, and dyed of different colours, and when they are thus prepared, the sport consists in throwing or trundling them along the ground, especially down a declivity, and gathering up the fragments to eat them. Formerly it was usual with the women and children to collect in large bodies for this purpose, though nothing can be, to all appearance, more unmeaning than the amusement; and they yet pursue it in the vicinity of Belfast. Here it is confined to the younger classes. It is a curious circumstance that this sport is practised only by the presbyterians, though it is admitted that it is a very ancient usage and was spread over the Russian Empire and Greek Islands long before the Reformation.'

If Mason is correct in stating that only Presbyterians played this game in this area, this may point to an introduction from Scotland, from which country most of the Presbyterians of the region ultimately derive.

Feasting

The Easter Sunday dinner was a festive meal, second in importance in the round of the year only to that on Christmas day. All who could afford to do so ate meat, roast veal or a young lamb or kid roasted whole being a favourite dish. Better-off farmers killed a beef for the festival and sent presents of portions to friends and to their poorer neighbours. Very often the beef had been slaughtered in the early winter and salted down; special joints of this graced the farmhouse table on the festival days, while lesser portions went to the labourers and poorer people who had no meat of their own. This custom is hardly remembered in Ireland now, but the memory of 'corned beef and cabbage' as the Irishman's festive meal crossed the Atlantic with emigrants and still survives in America.

Spóilín méith na hInide, the little bit of meat pinned up during Lent (p. 42 above) was taken down early on Easter Sunday and burned 'to put a fine rich smell around the house'.

The Cake Dance

Easter Sunday may fall on any date between 22 March and 25 April, that is to say in late Spring when lengthening days and brightening weather made outdoor recreations pleasant, and all the more so as jollifications of all kinds had been discouraged during Lent. One recreation beloved by young and old alike was dancing, a community outdoor affair when weather permitted, and there were few parishes in

79

Ireland in which an outdoor dance was not held on the evening of Easter Sunday.

Often this took the form of, or at least included, a contest for which a large cake was the prize, and although such 'cake dances' were held on other festive occasions also, they are particularly associated with Easter Sunday, probably because the dance held on this day was almost always the first in the year.

In *A Choreographical Description of the County West-Meath*, written by Sir Henry Piers in 1682, such a dance is thus described:

'On the patron-day in most parishes, as also on the feasts of Easter and Whit-suntide, the more ordinary sort of people meet near the ale-house in the afternoon, on some convenient spot of ground, and dance for the cake; here to be sure the piper fails not of diligent attendance; the cake to be danced for is provided at the charge of the ale-wife, and is advanced on a board on the top of a pike about ten foot high; this board is round, and from it riseth a kind of a garland, beset and tied round with meadow flowers, if it be early in the summer, if later, the garland has the addition of apples set round on pegs fastened unto it; the whole number of dancers begin all at once in a large ring, a man and a woman, and dance round about the bush, so is this garland called, and the piper, as long as they are able to hold out; they that hold out longest at the exercise, win the cake and apples, and then the ale-wife's trade goes on.'

There are several descriptions of the 'cake-dance' by nineteenth-century observers, and all of these are from the west of Ireland. Typical of them is this by Sir William Wilde in *Irish Popular Superstitions*, 14–15:

'In Connaught, in former times, when a dance was held on a Sunday evening at a cross-roads or any public place of resort, a large cake, like what is called a barnbrack, with a variety of apocryphal birds, fabulous fishes, and outlandish quadrupeds, such as are only known in heraldic zoology, raised in bold relief on its upper crust, was placed on the top of a churn-dash, and tied over with a clean white cloth; the staff of the churn-dash was then planted outside the door as a sign of the fun and amusement going on within. When they had danced and drank their fill, the likeliest boy took the prettiest colleen, and led her out to the cake, and placed it in her hands as Queen of the Feast; it was then divided among the guests, and the festivities continued.'

Although the custom has now died out it is still remembered in tradition in north Connaught, as, for instance, from Cloone, County Leitrim, in *Béaloideas*, 1939, 139:

'The cake dance was held only on Easter Sunday. On all other Sundays throughout the Summer the "ball" was collected for the travelling piper or musician.

'On Easter Sunday the cross-roads dance was held. A cake was baked – it might be a boxty cake, a griddle cake, or a barley or oaten bannock. A churn-dash was placed in a field, and the cake was placed on its top, and some flowers were placed on top again. There was no cloth placed on the cake as far as I recollect. All the "courting" couples of the neighbourhood assembled, and each boy courted his girl. Then the dance started, and the girls shook their flounces, and twirled their hoops, and the boys pounded the ground with their feet. When the bout of dancing was over, the best boy and girl dancer went out and took down the cake, and it was divided among all the dancers. It was regarded as a great privilege to have the dividing of the cake. The dance was over before sunset. The old saying, still common in the country, "that takes the cake" comes down from these Easter Sunday dances. The dance on Easter Sunday was called a *pruthóg*.'

Other Easter beliefs and Customs

Many holy wells, especially those designated *Tobar Rí an Domhnaigh* or 'Sunday's Well' were visited on Easter Sunday, and water taken from them on this day was held to have more than usual curative virtues.

It was believed, too, that a boy born on Easter Sunday was destined for high office in the Church.

Sometimes the outdoor amusements on the Sunday included the lighting of a bonfire, but this appears to have come from the high spirits of the young people and to have no connection with Easter Saturday's Paschal fire.

Many people, instead of joining in the dancing, made an excursion into the countryside if the day was particularly fine. Amhlaoibh Ó Súilleabháin describes such an outing from Callan in 1827.

'The fifteenth day, Easter Sunday. A beautiful day: midday, five of us left Callan to go to Desart. We went through Graigueooly, through Derrymore, through the Lord's Plantation, skipping like goats, through Derreen, Oorachilleen, to the fishponds, to Desart. The landscape from this delightful summer-palace is exquisitely beautiful. There was a gaseous exhalation from the sun: the mountains to the south were dark-blue. Knocknacarrigy (now, Ballykeefe Hill) near us to the north newly planted, and Knocknaraha to the northwest likewise. There were sheltering woods all round us, ash and oak without foliage growing among evergreen pines; meadows smooth as silk or satin and green as corn-grass. It is a veritable earthly paradise. We bent our steps eastwards to the green beside Ballygelly, to Butler's where we got white baker's bread, fat pork, delicious mutton, whitish pudding, and a drop of whiskey, or barley juice, to drink from a handsome hostess. We went merrily home through Tullamaine, Knockgreagh etc.: as fine an afternoon as I have ever seen.'

While more recently E. E. Evans, in *Mourne Country*, 134, tells of visits to places in the Mourne Mountains of County Down. 'These landmarks, natural or man-made, were gathering places at certain times of the year for the folk of the neighbouring townlands. On Easter Sunday fires would be lit and eggs rolled, and young people would go sliding down between the rocks on flat slabs of stone. Father J. B. Mooney tells me that the Grey Woman on Crotlieve used to be elaborately dressed up like a woman for the easter festivities.'

The 'Grey Woman of Crotlieve' appears to be a pillar stone set up in prehistoric times, and its decoration is not unique.

Easter Monday

Easter Monday was a favourite day for fairs and markets at which there were not only buying and selling of livestock and merchandise, but also games and sports, sideshows, dancing, eating and drinking, gambling and faction fighting. It was also a holiday of obligation on which Catholics were required to go to Mass and to abstain from work, and the Church authorities decided that this sacred character accorded ill with the riotous behaviour at many of the secular gatherings on the same day. The bishop of Kildare and Leighlin, Dr John Doyle – the famous 'J. K. L.', – described before a government inquiry into the State of the Poor in Ireland (*Parliamentary Papers*, 1830, vii, p. 453) how he prevailed upon his fellow bishops to petition the Pope to abrogate the religious obligation on this day and on Whit Monday, so that Catholics might observe it as an ordinary working day, and how the Pope had acceded to their request. From the year 1829 Easter Monday was no longer a holiday of obligation. Dr Doyle's wish met with some opposition, as shown by a remark of his while giving his evidence to the Commission of Inquiry on this matter:

'A very curious occurrence took place on Easter Monday in Carlow. I am carrying on there a very extensive work. I told the men they should work on that day. There is a work at the other end of the town conducted by a Protestant; and he said to his men, as I was informed, "You shall not work; it is an old holiday, and you shall keep it".'

Before long, however, the fairs and markets on this day lost their festive character and became merely trading occasions.

One interesting result of the change was that some of the customs, hitherto observed on Easter Monday, such as the children's egg-feast, described above by Kennedy (p. 76f.) as being held on this day in County Wexford, either died out or were transferred to Easter Sunday. This is clearly shown by the Callan diarist, Amhlaoibh O Súilleabháin. In 1827 he wrote:

'The sixteenth day, Easter Monday or the day of the Easter eggs: a sunny, joyful still morning: midday, the maidens and youths eating their Easter eggs and drinking in the public houses: evening, the public houses still full of people: the day very fine.' While in 1830, after the bishops' decision had taken effect he reported:

'The twelfth day, Easter Monday, that is the Day of the Parcels of Easter Eggs. A fine mild day: light showers and bright intervals with a gentle west wind. There was no parcel of Easter eggs being consumed by youths and maidens in one another's company. There was neither sport nor laughter, drinking nor dancing. Most (of the young people) stayed at home, for Easter Monday is no longer a Holiday of obligation. They removed the double obligation from it; for their Lordships think that a Holiday of obligation is rather harmful in a heretical land like Ireland: as the Protestants put fairs and markets on Catholic Holidays, of set purpose to bring them into disrepute.'

We may remark, however, that he is not correct in his last observation; fairs and markets on church holidays were common in Ireland even before the Reformation.

April Fools' Day

The custom of playing practical jokes on 1 April has long been current in Ireland. Probably the most popular joke was of the 'send the fool farther' kind, described in *Journal of the Cork Historical and Archaeological Society* 1896, 157–8:

'The first of this month is universally known as "All Fools' Day" but why the name or whence the custom of "fooling" people originated I have not been able to ascertain. Up to recent times the custom prevailed of "raising a laugh" at some simple-minded person's expense by giving him a letter, which he was told was of an urgent nature, addressed to some personal friend of the sender's. When delivered, the enclosed note merely bore the legend, "Send the fool farther", which advice was religiously adhered to, for the addressee merely put this missive into another envelope, and having addressed it to another friend some few miles further on, and having told the guileless messenger that it was a most important matter which was confided to his care, set him again on his fool's errand.'

Amhlaoibh O Súilleabháin could not explain it in 1829:

'I have never read or heard what is the meaning of making an April Fool of a person, but what sense could a foolish thing have to-day or any other day?'

However, in 1835 he makes a surmise, rather, one suspects, to show his classical education than to prove anything:

'April Fools' Day. A barbarous custom from pagan times is still established in Ireland, namely, to make an April Fool of a person. At the time when Venus was worshipped the first day of the month was a festival in her honour, and it was customary to play all sorts of low pranks to do her veneration. However, I think that it is time now to lay aside this heathen custom.'

84

The Borrowed Days

According to the old story *An tSean-Bhó Riabhach*, the old Brindled Cow, boasted that even the rigours of March could not kill her, whereupon March borrowed three days from April, and, using these with redoubled fury, killed and skinned the poor old cow. Henceforth the first three days of April traditionally bring very bad weather and are known as *Laethanta na Riabhaiche*, 'The Reehy Days,' 'the Borrowed (or Borrowing) Days', 'the Skinning Days' and other names.

Some people reckoned the days in the Old Style, thus Amhlaoibh O Súilleabháin in 1827:

'This, the twelfth day of April, is the first of the three days of the old brindled cow, namely three days which the weather of Old March took from the beginning of Old April.'

In parts of the north of Ireland the story was more elaborate, with nine borrowed days instead of three:

> *Trí lá lomartha an loinn,*
> *Trí lá sgiuthanta an chlaibhreáin,*
> *Agus trí lá na bó riabhaighte.*
> (Three days for fleecing the black-bird,
> Three days of punishment for the stone-chatter,
> And three days for the grey cow.)

'The first nine days of April are called the "borrowing days". The old legend relates that the black-bird, the stone-chatter, and the grey cow bid defiance to March after his days were over; and that, to punish their insolence, he begged of April nine of his days, three for each of them, for which he repaid nine of his own.'

(*Ulster Journal of Archaeology*, 1861–2, 225).

85

May Day

May Day, the first day of Summer, was a most important landmark in the Irish countryman's year. It was a 'gale day', when his tenancy began or ended, on which a half-year's rent must be paid to the landlord; this is mentioned in a letter of Sir Henry Sydney to the Privy Council in 1576 (*State Papers, Ireland*, 1576), . . . 'and because at May Day, commonly, the Irish captains and lords use to bargain and compound with their tenants . . .'. The letting of grazing and meadowing usually dated from 1 May, and farm servants and workmen were hired at this time. Hiring fairs were held in many places, to which those seeking work, both men and women, came, often carrying symbols of their skill, a spancel which told that its bearer was an expert milker, or a spade, hay fork, reaping hook, flail or other implement. Farmers and others needing servants and workpeople came to these fairs and bargains were struck between employers and workers. Because of the change introduced at the adoption in Ireland of the Gregorian Calendar, these fairs, in common with others were held since 1752 on the eleventh and twelfth day after the original festival day, thus, in many parts of Ireland, especially in Ulster, servants' and workmen's terms began on 12 May.

May Day was important, too, in the work of the farm, as the beginning of the fresh grass season. Cattle which had been sheltered in the byres and stall-fed during the winter and spring were turned out into the pasture fields and from now onwards, on many farms, milked morning and evening in the fields. This was the season for sending the cattle to the *buaile*, the summer pastures in moorland or mountain, in those areas where this practice was observed. Sheep and dry cattle were moved from the home fields into the rougher pastures, and shepherds docked the lambs' tails and castrated the young rams. Those fields intended for meadow were carefully cleared of stones and other obstructions which might hinder the reapers or injure their implements, and were fenced with care to keep wandering animals out. All the spring work – the tilling of the soil to produce crops – should have been finished by May Day. This was also the time when turf-cutting began, and when turbary was rented.

To have hay still left in the haggard at May Day was a sign of good husbandry and a matter of pride to the farmer. The housewife, too, took stock of her store; she should, if she had managed thriftily, still have meal for bread baking and for porridge. Sir Henry Piers, in his *Description of West Meath* (1682), tells us:

'They have a custom every Mayday, which they count their first day of summer, to have to their meal one formal dish, whatever else they have, which some call, stirabout or hasty pudding, that is flour and milk boiled thick; and this is holden as an argument of the good wives good huswifery, that made her corn hold out so well, as to have such a dish to begin summer fare with; for if they can hold out so long with bread, they count they can do well enough for what remains of the year till harvest; for then milk becomes plenty, and butter, new cheese and curds and shamrocks, are the food of the meaner sort all this season; nevertheless in this mess, on this day, they are so formal, that even in the plentifullest and greatest houses where bread is in abundance all the year long, they will not fail of this dish, nor yet they that for a month before wanted bread.'

Signs of the weather, the appearance of the sky and of the May moon, the strength and direction of the wind, the amount of rain, were all carefully noted on May Day as indications of the coming summer's weather. A cold east wind was a bad sign while frost was ominous of hard times to come, and while the people of Inishowen, as John O'Donovan tells us in his Ordnance Survey letters (Donegal, 1835, Ms. p. 12), expected to see snow still on Slieve Snaght, a north Wexford tradition recalls that snow on Croghan Kinsella on May Day was so evil an omen that local farmers expected their landlord to forego the rent for the coming half-year. Rain was expected and welcomed during the coming month. 'A wet and windy May fills the barns with corn and hay' and 'A wet May and a dry June make the farmer whistle a tune', and, with the coming of the nectar-laden summer blossoms, 'a swarm of bees in May is worth a load of hay'.

In different parts of the country it was held that one should not dig, whitewash, bathe or sail on May Day, the various explanations given for these prohibitions indicate on the one hand a reluctance to engage in any activity which might seem to have a magical purpose and on the other a feeling that danger was to be avoided at a time when ill-luck or evil influence might prevail.

Welcoming the Summer

In Ireland, as in most parts of Western Europe, the principal customs and ceremonies of Maytime were those which welcomed the Summer. Whatever the origin of these, they were in recent centuries mainly of a festive character, an opportunity for merrymaking and holiday fun. Nevertheless there lay behind them a slight element of the magical. The children set up their May bush in the same spirit in which we hang out our flags on a national holiday, to celebrate an occasion, but some, at least, of their parents were glad of the feeling of protection against unseen forces which the May bush gave.

Perhaps the commonest custom of all, examples of which might be cited for every county in Ireland, was the picking and bringing home of fresh flowers. That these were nearly always yellow flowers may have some significance, but probably means no more than that most flowers then in bloom are yellow – primroses, cowslips, buttercups, marigolds, furze-blossoms. Usually these were gathered before dusk on May Eve by the children, although in many places the tradition lingers that they should be picked before dawn on May Day. The children usually made 'posies' of the flowers, small bouquets, which they hung up in the house or laid on the doorsteps or window-sills or hung over the door. Sometimes loose flowers were strewn on thresholds and floors of house and byre or on roofs, or in and around the well, or on the paths leading to house, outbuildings or well.

Sometimes those who took the first water from the well left flowers there as a sign of their success.

Some people tied small bunches of flowers to horses' bridles; this is noted in his Diary by Amhlaoibh Ó Súilleabháin in 1829:

'A cold windy cloudy dark day: green branches in blossom on the mailcoach horses, at half past six, coming from Dublin.'
And again in 1830:

'The Month of May, 1830. The first day, Saturday. A Fair Day in Mullinahone: a moderate price for cattle. A showery day: a brisk south wind in the morning: a west wind towards close of day: it changed by degrees or gradually: the mail coach bedecked with a May Bush: the horses adorned with beautiful little flowers: they are a glad sight.'

Others tied posies to the cows' horns or tails, to churn-dashes and milk-pail handles; in these cases the protective element was at least as strong as the festive.

For many people there was a religious motive in gathering May flowers, as these were picked in honour of our Lady or of the Angels and were used to decorate the household altar or a little altar or shrine set up by the children expecially for the festival. Some made a cross of flowers on a base of twigs or slips of wood and hung this up prominently. Where there were old or lonely or helpless people, the neighbours' children, voluntarily or prompted by their parents, usually picked flowers for these.

In south-west County Cork, instead of flowers, or together with flowers, the long leaves of 'flaggers' (*Iris pseudacorus*) were placed on the doorsteps and window sills or used to decorate the dresser, although the plant is usually not yet in flower in the area until late May or early June. In Cape Clear Island bunches of 'flaggers' were put in the fishing boats for luck.

In most parts of Munster, however, it was more usual to pick and bring to the house 'May boughs' rather than flowers, small branches of newly-leafed trees, as the verse says:

> *Cuileann agus coll,*
> *Trom agus cárthan*
> *Agus fuinseóg gheal*
> *Ó bhéal an átha*

(Holly and hazel, elder and rowan, and bright ash from beside the ford.)

In much of County Cork sycamore, locally called "Summer tree" was the favourite May bough.

These May boughs were, like the flowers, used to decorate the kitchen, to lay on door steps and window ledges or on the roofs of house and byre. They were also, in places, set up in the farmyard or in the fields, where they were held to guard against ill-luck and evil influence, particularly where branches of mountain ash were so used.

Different growths were believed to be lucky or unlucky. These varied greatly from place to place, and whitethorn, blackthorn, elder, broom, woodbine, snowdrops, furze, alder and other plants and trees might be or should not be brought into the house, according to local custom.

The setting up of a green bough in the farmyard brings us to our next popular method of welcoming the Summer, the May bush.

Camden, in his *Britannia*, writing of the middle sixteenth Century, records:

'And upon the Calends or first day of May, they fully beleeve that to set a greene bough of a tree before their houses, will cause them to have great abundance of milke all summer long.'

And it is only a short step from this to the decorated bush mentioned by Sir Henry Piers, in his *Description of the County of West-Meath* (1682):

'On May Eve every family sets up before their door a green bush, strowed over with yellow flowers, which the meadows yield plentifully.'

Commonest in Leinster, where it was known in every county and also popular in south and west Ulster and in a few areas of Munster and Connaught, the May bush was a branch or clump of some suitable tree or shrub, among which whitethorn was the most popular, which was cut down, brought home and set up before the house or in some other conspicuous place and decorated with flowers, ribbons, paper streamers and other bright scraps of material. In some places garlands of egg-shells were hung on it; often these were the coloured or decorated shells of Easter eggs which were saved for the May bush by the children. Sometimes candles or rushlights were attached to the bush and lit at dusk on May Eve.

In Monaghan, according to Wilde *(Irish Popular Superstitions, 60)*:

'The May bush used to be erected several days before the festival, and was illuminated every night; and in addition, pyramids of "penny dips", fixed in lumps of yellow clay, used to be erected in the neighbourhood of the bush, which always stood upon some green or common, or at the cross-roads, or in the market-place of the town or village.'

In County Kildare towards the end of the last century *(Jour. Kildare Archaeological Society* v, 446):

'The "May bush" was cut the day previous and stuck in the ground in front of the house; it was decorated with all the egg-shells which had been saved up since Easter Sunday, along with ribbons, wild flowers, and bits of candles. On May Night the latter were lit, and dancing took place around the May bush. This custom is of Pagan origin, though at the present time it is thought by the people that it is carried out in honour of the Blessed Virgin Mary, to whom the month of May is dedicated.'

While in Laois in 1939 (*Béaloideas*, ix 929):

'On the 30th April, in nearly all parts of this county, a hawthorn branch or bush is cut and brought home, and set in position in front of the dwellinghouse. The bush is usually a holly, but sometimes any leafless bough will serve. It is decorated with egg-shells, coloured paper, bunches of flowers, ribbons, etc. The bush is left in position in some districts until the end of the month; in others, only until the decorations are withered and crumbling. The bush is usually thrown out, but other families burn it. The egg-shells are saved for weeks beforehand, and those of the eggs eaten on Easter Morning are specially prized.'

Occasionally a suitably situated growing bush might be decorated as a May bush.

In more recent times the May bush has been almost entirely a matter for the children, who might request adult help where the task was too great for their strength or skill, for instance in cutting or setting up the bush and who, in places, went in a group around the village or the townland carrying the bush and asking for contributions of material to decorate it, or of sweets and other goodies, or money with which to buy these. In north County Dublin, until recently, one might be accosted by children chanting 'Long life and a pretty wife, and a candle for the May bush', expecting not a candle but a small gift of money.

In former times it was in many areas very much an adult affair, as witness Sir William Wilde's account of the doings in Dublin in the late eighteenth century (*Irish Popular Superstitions*, 47–8, 59–60):

'The preparation for the May Day sports and ceremonial in Dublin, commenced about the middle of April, and even earlier, and a rivalry, which often led to the most fearful riots was incited, particularly between the 'Liberty boys' upon the south, and the 'Ormond boys' upon the north side of the river; and even among themselves, as to which street or district would exhibit the best dressed and handsomest May bush, or could boast the largest and hottest bonfire . . .

'. . . . For weeks before, a parcel of idle scamps, male and female devoted themselves to the task of "collecting for the May"; and parties decorated with ribbons, and carrying green boughs and sometimes escorted by itinerant musicians, went from house to house soliciting contributions of ribbons, handkerchiefs, and pieces of gaudy silk – materials then manufactured, and consequently more common, in the Liberty than now – to adorn the May bush . . .

'Upon May Eve a crowd of persons, often numbering several hundreds resorted to the spot previously arranged, with saws, hatchets

91

ropes, cars, horses, and all the necessary tackle for cutting and carrying home the May bush, and were generally escorted by fifers and fiddlers. Serious rencontres very often ensued upon these occasions, particularly in the neighbourhood of Dublin, where the authorities had frequently to interfere to prevent some lawn or demesne being despoiled of its wide-spreading thorn. The trophy was, however, generally carried off in triumph, amidst the shouts and rejoicings of the people, and erected in its allotted station, and upon its branches were fixed a number of small candles, which at night-fall were lighted, and afforded a brilliant illumination for the dancers, who tripped it round this emblem of the vernal light, as is still practiced in Germany on Christmas Eve . . .

'. . . . Early upon May morning the bush was decorated with flowers, ribbons, and pieces of silk of the most gaudy colours; and at the conclusion of the festivities the bush was consigned to the flames of the expiring bonfire. In former days the Liberty bush was cut in Cullen's Wood. Efforts were often made, particularly in the City of Dublin, to steal away the May bush, to avert which a guard of stout fellows was set to keep watch and ward nightly, from time of its erection until after the festival.'

It was believed that whoever succeeded in stealing the May bush also stole away the year's luck from the rightful owners. From south County Monaghan we read:

'My grandfather had to "rise out" with all the neighbours to defend a local "may bush" about 1840' (*Béaloideas* vii, 175) while the most famous incident of the kind is that described in 'Ireland Sixty Years ago' (*Dublin University Magazine* XXII, 1843, 671) between two rival factions in Dublin:

'A memorable contest of this kind, in which the weavers cut down "the bush" of the butchers, is thus celebrated in song:

"De May Bush"

De nite afore de fust of Magay,
Ri rigi di, ri ri dum dee,
We all did agree without any delay,
To cut a May-bush, so we pegged it away
Ri ri rigi di dum dee!

'The leader of the boys was Bill Durham, a familiar corruption of Dermot, his right name, a distinguished man at that time in the Liberty riots. When the tree was cut down, it was borne back in triumph, with

Bill astride on it, exhibiting a classical picture still more graphic than the gem of Bacchus astride on his ton:

> Bill Durham, he sat astride on his bush,
> Ri rigidi ri ri dum dee,
> And dere he kept singin, as sweet as a trush –
> His faulchin in one hand, his pipe in his mush –
> Ri ri rigidi di dum dee!

' "The Bush" having been planted in Smithfield, contributions were raised to do it honour; and among other contributors were the fishwomen of Pill-lane, who, from contiguity of situation and similarity of dealing, were closely allied to the butchers of Ormond market. A custom prevailed here, of selling the fish brought for sale, to the women who retailed it, by auction. The auctioneer, generally one of themselves, holding a plaice or a haddock by the tail, instead of a hammer, knocked down the lot to the highest bidder. This was an important time to the trade – yet the high-minded poissardes, like their Parisian sisters "sacrificed everything to their patriotic feelings", and abandoned the market, even at this crisis, to attend "de bush":

> From de lane came each lass in her holyday gown
> Ri rigidi ri ri dum dee,
> Do de haddock was up, and de lot was knocked down,
> Dey doused all dere sieves, till dey riz de half-crown,
> Ri rigi di dum dee!

'After indulging in the festivities of the occasion round "de bush" some returned, and some lay about, *vino somnoque sepulti*; and so, not watching with due vigilance, the Liberty boys stole on their security, cut down, and carried off "de bush". The effect on Bill Durham, when he heard the adversary passing on their way back with the trophy, is thus described:

> Bill Durham, being up de nite afore,
> Ri rigidi ri ri dum dee,
> Was now in his flea-park, taking a snore,
> When he heard de mob pass by his door.
> Ri rigidi dum dee!

Den over his shoulders his flesh-bag he threw,
Ri rigidi ri ri dum dee,
And out of the chimbley his faulchion he drew,
And mad as a hatter down May-lane he flew.
Ri rigidi dum dee!

Wid his hat in his hand by de way of a shield.
Ri rigidi ri ri dum dee,
He kep all along crying out – never yield! –
But he never cried stop till he came to Smidfield –
Ri rigidi dum dee!

Dere finding no bush, but de watch boys all flown,
Ri rigidi ri ri dum dee,
Your sowls, ses Bill Durham, I'm left all alone –
Be de hokey de glory of Smidfield is gone! –
Ri rigidi dum dee

'Bill vows revenge in a very characteristic and professional manner, by driving one of the bulls of Ormond market among his adversaries:

We'll wallap a mosey down Meadstreet in tune.
Ri rigidi ri ri dum dee,
And not leave a weaver alive on de Combe
But rip up his tripe-bag, and burn his loom!
Ri rigidi dum dee!'

The impact of Victorian respectability on these revels and on the roystering, drinking and fighting which accompanied them was a main factor in the disappearance of the May bush and May pole celebrations by gatherings of adults. Other forces were against them, too. The authorities held that they were a nuisance on the public roads and a number of laws forbade their erection there, for instance XXXII George III (1792) Ch. 30, 'An Act for improving and keeping in repair the Post Roads of this Kingdom' which includes this provision (par. XXV): 'If any person . . . shall erect any sign-post or maypole or maybush on any part of the said roads . . . every person so offending shall forfeit the sum of twenty shillings.'

Another statute adverts to the all too common practice of stealing bushes for the festival, XV and XVI Geo III (1775–6), Ch. 26 'An act for encouraging the Cultivation, and for the better Preservation of trees, shrubs, Plants and Roots' has (par. IV): 'And be it further enacted . . . . that every person who shall put up any Maybush opposite or near to his or her house, or suffer any Maybush to be so put up, or to remain for the space of three hours opposite or near to his or her house . . . . not being a person lawfully possessed of trees or woods, or not having lawfully obtained the same . . . shall forfeit and pay such sum . . . not exceeding forty shillings.'

Closely associated with the May bushes were bonfires. This was especially the case in Dublin, where great fires were lit, around which the revellers caroused. Elaborate preparations were made for these too. Thus Wilde:

'Turf, coals, old bones, particularly slugs of cows' horns from the tan-yards, and horses' heads from the knackers, logs of wood etc. were also collected, to which some of the merchants generally added a few pitch and tar-barrels. Money was solicited to "moisten the clay" of the revellers; for, whether from liking, or from fear, or considering it unlucky, few ventured to refuse to contribute "something toste de May bush". The ignitable materials were formed in depots, in back-yards, and cellars of old houses, long before the approaching festival; and several sorties were made by opposing factions to gain possession of these hoards, and lives have been lost in the skirmishes which ensued. In Dublin the bonfires were always lighted upon the evening of May Day, and generally in the vicinity of the May bush. The great fire was, as we already mentioned, at the lower end of the Coombe; but there were also fires in the centre and at the top of that classic locality. The weavers had their fire in Weaver's Square; the hatters and pipemakers in the upper end of James's Street; and the neighbourhood of St John's Well, near Kilmainham, beside Bully's Acre, generally exhibited a towering blaze. Upon the north side of the city, the best fire blazed in Smithfield. With the exception of one ancient rite, that of throwing into it the May bush, there were but few Pagan ceremonies observed at the metropolitan fires. A vast crowd collected, whiskey was distributed galore both to those who had, and had not, gathered the morning's dew. The entire population of the district collected round the bush and the fire; the elder portion, men and women, bringing with them chairs or stools, to sit out the wake of the winter and spring, according to the olden usage. The best singers in the crowd lilted up, "The Night before Larry was stretched", or "Hie for de Sweet Libertie"; but the then popular air of "The Baiting of Lord Altham's Bull", and "De May bush"; and another local song of triumphful commemoration of a victory over the Ormond-market men a verse of which we remember:

> Begone, ye cowardly scoundrels,
> Do ye remember de day,
> Dat yes came down to Newmarket,
> And stole de sweet May bush away?

were the "most popular and deservedly admired", from their allusions to the season and the locality. Fiddlers and pipers plied their fingers and elbows; and dancing, shouting, revelry and debauchery of every description succeeded, till, at an advanced hour of the night, the scene partook more of the nature of the ancient Saturnalia, than anything we can at present liken it to, except that which a London mob now exhibitis the night preceding an execution in the Old Bailey or at Horsemonger Lane Gaol.'

There are traditions from many areas to show that the lighting of bonfires on May Eve was common and widespread, but this custom has almost entirely died out. In Limerick city May Eve is still 'Bonfire night' and until recently children in Belfast lit small fires in the side streets in honour of their 'May queens'.

The rural custom survived longest, perhaps, in the south east, where in County Waterford and in the southern fringes of Counties Kilkenny and Tipperary there still are memories of the cattle being driven through small fires or between pairs of fires, of wisps or coals from the bonfire being used to singe the cows' hair or to bless the fields of growing crops.

The tradition of setting up May poles as against May bushes is also known in Ireland, although here, again, there can be a confusion of tradition, as when a May bush was tied to the top of a long stake set in the ground and called, indiscriminately 'bush' or 'pole' as was the case in parts of the north midlands. However, there are from several places, most of them, significantly, towns in Leinster and east Ulster, descriptions or traditions of the setting up of tall decorated poles, like that still standing in Holywood, County Down, and of dancing and other celebrations around these.

In Sir Henry Piers's *West-Meath* we read, in continuation of his mention of the May bush (p. 90 above):

'and in countries where timber is plentiful, they erect tall slender trees, which stand high, and they continue almost the whole year, so as a stranger would go nigh to imagine that they were all signs of alesellers, and that all houses were ale-houses.'

Which might indicate that the custom was formerly widespread in country districts. We may note that in counties Westmeath, Longford, Laois, Offaly and Kildare, and in the southern part of County Leitrim, together forming a continuous area of the north midlands, and including the locality of which Sir Henry Piers wrote in 1682, there was the custom of calling the outdoor dances which began to be held at this time of the year 'May pole dances' and of the setting up of a small pole called a May pole at the cross-roads where the dance was held. Even yet, within this area one may see an ordinary dance, held in a dance-hall, advertised at this time of the year as 'The May pole Dance'.

There are, however, specific descriptions of May poles from certain towns. Thus, in *Ulster Journal of Archaeology* iii, 1855, 164, we read:

'May poles – Until the beginning of the present century it was customary in the town of Carrickfergus for the young men to bring in a tall straight tree from the country and plant it as a May pole on May day. Still earlier a large number of the young men used to assemble on that day wearing white linen shirts over their other dress, decorated with a profusion of lively ribbons tied in knots. Having elected a king and queen, they danced round the May pole and then visited the houses of the chief inhabitants for contributions.'

While from Maghera, County Derry, a local clergyman reported (Mason: *Parochial Survey*, 1816, 593):

'On the 1st day of May, from time immemorial, until the year 1798, a large pole was planted in the market place at Maghera; and a procession of May boys, headed by a mock king and queen paraded the neighbourhood, dressed in shirts over their clothes, and ornamented with ribbons of various colours. This practice was revived last year, and the May boys collected about seventeen pounds at the different places where they called: this defrayed the expense of a public dinner next day. Circumstances, however, occurred soon after, which induced one of the neighbouring magistrates to come into the town, and cut down the pole which had been planted in the market-place.'

At least one other May pole figured in the tragic events of 1798. From Kildare we read (*Jour. Kildare Arch. Soc.* v, 446):

'In some towns the May pole was a permanent fixture: one formerly stood at the junction of the streets in Castledermot; a pump now occupies the site. Earlier still this may have been the site of the market-cross, as funerals passing through the town always make one

D 97

turn round the present pump. Some rebels are said to have been hanged from the May pole in '98.

'The May pole was unknown in the country districts, and was probably introduced into the towns by the English.'

Other towns with May pole traditions are Downpatrick, Kilkenny, Mountmellick, Portarlington and Portlaoise. Most, if not all, of these seem to bear out the remark in the last excerpt quoted above, that the May pole is a medieval or later introduction into the towns from England. More recent attempts are known by people with English associations to introduce the 'polite' English custom of the May pole to the 'wild Irish'.

Thus at Rathkeale in County Limerick, a local landlord's wife, an Englishwoman, had a May pole set up in 1812 and endeavoured to get the local people to dance around it, but when the novelty wore off the experiment failed.

There is, however, no doubt about the immense popularity of the great Dublin May poles at Harolds Cross and Finglas, thus described by Sir William Wilde in *Irish Popular Superstitions*, 62–3:

'The two Dublin May poles were erected outside the city. One of these stood in the centre of Harold's Cross Green, and existed within the memory of some of the present generation. After its decay, an old withered poplar supplied its place for many years; and so recently as the year 1836, the publicans of the village erected a May pole, decorated it, and gave a number of prizes, in order to collect an assemblage of the people, by restoring the ancient festivities. The chief May pole of Dublin, however, was erected at the pretty suburban village of Finglas, to the north of the city, near the Glasnevin Botanic Gardens, a spot which combines the most delicious sylvan scenery with the charm of the associations connected with the names of Swift, Addison, Tickel, Delany, and in our own day of our distinguished fellow-citizen Doctor Walsh. Here it stood until within the last few years; – a very tall, smooth pole, like the mast of a vessel, and upon every Easter Monday it was painted white and encircled with a red and blue spiral stripe like a barber's pole. In latter years, at least, it was not decorated with floral hoops and garlands like the usual English Maypole, but was well soaped from top to bottom in order to render it the more difficult to climb, and to its top were attached, in succession, the different prizes, consisting generally of a pair of leather breeches, a hat, or an old pinchbeck watch. Whoever climbed the pole, and touched the prize, became its possessor. "All Dublin" turned out to Finglas upon May Day to witness the sports and revels of the people, and the streets of the little village and the adjoining roads were thronged with carriages, hackney-cars, jingles, and noddies, filled with the better class of citizens. There were also a gaudily-dressed king and queen of the May, chosen from among the villagers, but they were the least attractive portion of the assembly. The revels consisted of climbing the pole; running after a pig with a shaved and well-soaped tail, which was let loose in the middle of the throng; grinning through horse-collars for tobacco; leaping and running in sacks; foot races for men and women; dancing reels, jigs, and hornpipes; ass races, in which each person rode or drove his neighbour's beast, the last being declared the winner; blindfolded men trying to catch a bell-ringer; and also wrestling, hopping, and leaping. An adjoining field was selected for the celebration of the majority of these sports. Stewards were appointed to keep the course, and see fair play, and twenty or thirty pounds' worth of prizes, consisting of shawls, hats, frieze-coats, handkerchiefs, and women's gowns and bonnets, were often distributed among the winners. Tents were erected, and bands of music paraded through the assembly; and even shows and booths were to be seen scattered throughout the village. In the evening the crowds collected round the May pole, where the boys and girls danced in a ring until a late hour, before the king and queen, who, attended by a man dressed as a Highlander, sat on a raised platform.'

In the 1820s both these May pole customs fell into disuse, and in spite of attempts to revive them, had died out by the middle of the nineteenth century. In Tralee, about 1785, an eccentric lady named Miss Cameron, gave prizes for May Day games (and supervised these from an elevated platform) as described in 'Tralee Seventy Years Ago', *The Kerry Magazine* 1856, 12:

'The scene opened with a dance on a large scale, to the music of several pipers and fiddlers. Foot races, by men, for hats, from the platform to Caherane followed, in what must be considered a most ludicrous mode. Bags or sacks were fastened around the necks of the competitors, and in that way they were to proceed. Of course they could only jump or hop, and were on the ground as often as they missed a step, but were always put in their legs again by the spectators. The tobacco and snuff were dealt out to the best *grinners*, male and female. The amusement was kept up during the day with great order, which was enforced by Miss Cameron from her elevated position. On all other

May days the townspeople repaired to Ballyseedy to amuse themselves by dancing and drinking, a custom which is still partially kept up.'

Other forms of May day revelry are known from other areas. Wood Martin in *Traces of the Elder Faiths*, 1904, ii, 265, records:

'From the diary of Joshua Wight, a Quaker, we learn that so late as the middle of the eighteenth century, propitiatory rustic processions took place in the south of Ireland. The observer records, that about noon in the month of May, 1752, there passed through the streets of Limerick many thousand peasants marshalled in companies, representing various branches of agriculture. First of all came the ordinary labourers, the men in their shirts, in ranks; the women also with green corn and straw; the plough driven along and the harrow; the mowers with their scythes, the reapers, the gleaners, a great number of women, and a great number with their flails, walking in a great procession to congratulate the probability of a good ensuing harvest ... These country people made a second appearance the next day, at which time the country (people) of Clare and Limerick joined together, and were very particular in their representation of personating the several orders of husbandry in all the branches of it'.

And Thomas Crofton Croker (*Fairy Legends of the South of Ireland*, 1st Series, 1825, 306) tells us of what he calls mummers, which, he considers, are related – he does not say how – to English morris-dancers:

'They consist of a number, varying according to circumstances, of the girls and young men of the village or neighbourhood, usually selected for their good looks, or their proficiency, – the females in the dance, the youths in hurling and other athletic exercises. They march in procession, two abreast, and in three divisions; the young men in the van and the rear dressed in white or other gay-coloured jackets or vests, and decorated with ribbons on their hats and sleeves; the young women are dressed also in light-coloured garments, and two of them bear each a holly-bush, in which are hung several new hurling-balls, the May day present of the girls to the youths of the village. The bush is decorated with a profusion of long ribbons, or paper cut in imitation, which adds greatly to the gay and joyous, yet strictly rural appearance of the whole. The procession is always preceded by music; sometimes of the bagpipes, but more commonly of a military fife, with the addition of a drum or tambourine. A clown is, of course, in attendance: he wears a frightful mask, and bears a long pole, with shreds of cloth nailed to the end of it, like a mop, which ever and anon he dips in a pool of water, or puddle, and besprinkles such of a crowd as press upon his compasions, much to the delight of the younger spectators, who greet his exploits with loud and repeated shouts and laughter. The Mummers during the day parade the neighbouring villages, or go from one gentleman's seat to another, dancing before the mansion-house and receiving money. The evening, as might be expected, terminates with drinking.'

Patrick Kennedy, in *The Banks of the Boro,* describes a similar procession:

'After a reasonable pause we had the delight of seeing twelve young men come forth, accompanied by the same number of young women, the boys dressed much more showily than the girls. They were in their shirt-sleeves, waistcoats, knee breeches, white stockings, and turned pumps; sashes of bright colours round their waists, and ribbons of every hue encircling hats, shirt-sleeves, knees and bodies, the shoulders getting even more than their due. The girls, their hair decked with ribbons, were in their Sunday garb; but for once the admiration of the crowd was given to the men and their ornaments. To heighten the beauty of the spectacle, out sprung the fool and his wife, the first with some head-dress of skin, a frightful mask, and a goat's beard descending from it. Though we knew that the big bluff, good-natured countenance of Paudh himself was behind the vizard, we could scarcely refrain from taking flight, not being able any more than other children to look on an ugly mask without extreme terror. His wife (little Tom Blanche, the tailor) was in an orange-tawny gown, flaming handkerchief, and mob-cap, and had a tanned, ugly female mask, fitting pretty close to her face. Paudh's first salute to his friends was a yell, a charge in various directions, and a general thrashing of the crowd with his pea-furnished bladder suspended from a long stick. Mrs Clown had a broom, and used to some purpose when she found her friends disposed to crowd her.'

The players formed a procession and marched to a neighbouring 'big house' where they performed a rustic comedy, chiefly concerned with the attempts of a youth to steal the affections of the fool's wife, and ended with a figure dance. This went on for several days, the players visiting all the larger houses and farms in the district and being hospitably entertained at each. An instance of this in County Antrim is noted in the *Belfast Mercury* on 15 May 1786; here the custom was observed on 'old May Day':

'Friday last, being the 1st May (O.S.), a number of young men, to the amount of 50 and upwards, assembled at Antrim, as May Boys, elegantly dressed, where they had a superb garland prepared for the occasion, with which they paraded at some of the respectable houses in and about the neighbourhood, then marched to the Right Hon. John O'Neill's, and after the usual formalities, presented the garland to Master Charles O'Neill, who with the utmost politeness received the same, and instantly made them a generous reward for their attention; and his father, ever foremost in liberality, ordered them to be treated with wine, etc. etc.'

In a few places in Counties Louth, Meath and Monaghan the carrying about of an effigy by the May revellers is remembered in tradition. The best description of this is that given by John Donaldson in his *Account of the Barony of Upper Fews in the County of Armagh*, written in 1838 and published in Dundalk in 1923:

'On May eve some young persons of both sexes are still in the habit of gathering Mayflowers (*Caltha palustris*) in the meadows which they carry home and strew outside their doors same evening. Of the origin of this custom their traditions furnish them with no account, but the writer is of opinion they are the remains of the Roman Florialia; for on May day, in the adjoining parts of the County of Louth the figure of a female is made-up, fixed upon a short pole and dressed in a fantastic manner, with flowers, ribbons, etc.

'This figure they call "The May Baby" but it is probable that at its first exhibition that it was made to represent Flora, the Goddess of flowers, and also of fecundity. Around this figure a man and woman (generally his wife) of the humble class, dressed also fantastically with straw etc. dance to the sound of a fiddle and entertain the people with indecent shows and postures, the figure at the same time being kept moving by the rustic maiden that supports it. These exhibitions cause great merriment among the assembled populace; women who have no children to their husbands also attend (some of them from a considerable distance) to see this figure and exhibition, which they imagine will promote fruitfulness in them and cause them to have children. Money is always collected at the end of this pantomime, and the exhibitors and musicians, attended by a concourse of people, proceed to gentlemen's houses with the figure where they also get money. When all is collected and the actors and musicians received some remuneration, the remainder is laid out in drink and the evening passes by jovially.'

This is also mentioned by Sir William Wilde, together with something like a hobby horse, (*Popular Irish Superstitions*, 67):

'From Monaghan we have a graphic account of a somewhat similar

proceeding; there the girls dressed up a churn-dash as a "May babby",
like the Breedeogue at Candlemas – and the men, a pitchfork, with a
mask, horse's tail, a turnip head, and ragged old clothes, as a "May
boy"; but these customs have, we believe, long since become quite
obsolete.'

In several of the above accounts, and in others, there is mention of a
May Queen and also, sometimes, of a May King. The only such custom
to have survived into recent times seems to be that described by Mrs
Cooper Foster (*Ulster Folklore*, 1951, p. 41):

'It is odd to find the custom of the May Queen observed in Belfast
and not, so far as I know, in any rural area of Ulster. In nearly every
working-class district of the city, little girls dress up in all kinds of
fantastic finery and, from shortly after Easter to well on in May, they
parade about the streets followed by their courts, singing, dancing and
entertaining generally, and begging with shameless persistence from
every passer-by. On May Eve they light bonfires in the side streets and
dance around them. Last year I asked one of the queens what they did
with the proceeds of their begging, and I was told that they had a
magnificent party, "cake and buns and ice-cream and oranges".

'Although one feels a sense of guilt in encouraging the practice of
begging in the streets by children, it is difficult to refuse these bright
and colourful little ladies. And, I suppose, the alms one gives them
could be looked upon as a subsidy for an old custom which, if it died
out, would leave Belfast vastly poorer.'

Sir William Wilde, however, in *Popular Irish Superstitions*, 64,
states that in country parts he had never heard of a girl being May
Queen, that part in the revels being taken by a young man dressed as a
woman.

May Balls

A picturesque custom which seems to have been well-known in parts of
the south and south-east is that of giving gifts of decorated balls on
May Day. Thomas Crofton Croker makes it clear that these were
decorated hurling balls, for, in his description of May Day revels in
Cork, quoted above, p. 100, he says: 'two of them bear each a holly
bush, in which are hung several new hurling-balls, the May Day
present of the girls to the youths of the village'. This is confirmed by
Amhlaoibh Ó Súilleabháin:

'Half the district came to take the May Ball. Fair Maiden gave it with her white hand to Hero, who gave it to Sturdy Youth. It is taken out on the green under hoops of flowers and greenery. It is placed high upon a bush and the young people begin to dance around it on the green sward to the music of the harp . . . "I challenge you!" says Sturdy Fellow. "I agree!" says Handsome Youth. The golden ball is taken from the May bush . . . It is struck with a tough ash hurley from the hand of Sturdy Fellow, the leader of the Munster centre, putting it over the heads of the Leinster heroes.'

General Vallencey, in his *Enquiry into the First Inhabitants of Ireland* (1781), 65, gives this custom his own peculiar interpretation; transforming a merry country frolic into a mystic rite:

'In some parts, as the counties of Waterford and Kilkenny, the brides, married since the May-day, are compelled to furnish the young people with a ball covered with gold lace and another covered with silver lace, finely adorned with silver tassils; the price of these some-times amounts to two guineas; these balls, the symbols of the Sun and Moon, are suspended in a hoop ornamented with flowers, which hoop represents the circular path of Belus or the Sun; and in this manner, they walk in procession from house to house.'

In his *Essay into the Antiquity of the Irish Language* it becomes 'a large ball covered with gold or silver tissue (in resemblance of the Deity)' (p. 276), and it is amusing to observe how Vallencey's fantasy rather than the prosaic hurling-ball of Croker and Ó Súilleabháin has been accepted by some romantic nineteenth century writers. It seems clear that in Counties Waterford and Kilkenny, the May balls were given by newly married couples to the young men of the neighbour-hood, and that they came to be expected as a right and on occasion demanded. It also appears that money or drink were often claimed instead of the hurling balls and that there were frequent quarrels, bloodshed and even deaths as result. Amhlaoibh Ó Súilleabháin remarks in his diary (30 April 1828):

'I hear that young lads had along with them to-day two golden May balls which they had got from two couples married last Shrovetide. They are wont to have a May bush on top of a short stick or long cudgel, the golden ball in the middle of it, and themselves and young women dancing around it.'

And he adds, 'there has been no May ball in Callan since the year 1782, when Butler was killed by John Saul'. And in the following year (1 May 1829) he wrote:

'Two May balls were taken up (that is a May bush covered in with

104

silk, ribbons, flowers, etc. with the ball in the middle of it hanging down and covered likewise with adornements), the one from the Grants of Coolalong, and the other from the Walshes of the Fair Green. The young men played for one of them (in a hurling match) afterwards. The golden apple that Paris raised aloft among the goddesses did not do as much mischief as some of these May balls do. Up to this day, no May ball has been taken for the past fifty years, since a man was killed on the crossroads of Callan taking a May ball from a newly married minister, Dr Lambart.'

The newspapers of the period have much to say of these disturbances, for instance an indignant letter in *Finn's Leinster Journal* on 4 May, 1768:

'To the Printer of the Leinster Journal.

'Sir – Though the following piece of advice may appear something like – After Death the Doctor – it may, however (like a remedy taken for the ague when the fit is over) contribute in some measure to prevent the next periodical fit of the mob of this town.

'For many years past the peace of this city has been disturbed every May Eve, by a vast multitude of audacious fellows, who assemble together to collect May-balls among the new married folks. They sally out with Herculean clubs in their hands, and as those unmeaning May-balls are seldom or never given without a piece of drink-money to boot, such bloody battles ensure in different quarters of the town, such confusion and uproar, as would induce a passing stranger to believe that a furious band of wild Indians had broken in upon us; that Magistracy was asleep, or that it had lost all power and influence over the subject. The mischief that follows from this barbarous and unheeded custom is more feelingly understood than can be expressed. Not to mention the fractures, contusions, etc. which are well known to happen on such occasions, and by which many of those miscreants are disabled for a considerable time from working for themselves, and for the support of those who entirely depend upon their sound legs and arms, many Gentlemen's gardens are wantonly robbed of all their beauties, the cultivation of which cost the owner a vast deal of trouble and expense; the hedges and fences, in the outlets of our City, are stript of full grown hawthorns, whose late blooming pride and fragrancy is now miserably dying away on dunghills before cabin doors, by way of Maybushes, no longer alas! to afford a nuptial bed to the new married linnet and his mate, but fastened in the ground for the vilest purposes. To hang fifthy clouts upon.

'And shall Magistracy stand by, looking on such mischievous abuses like an unconcerned spectator? No – that same justice and humanity, which has already redressed so many grievances in this City, will certainly prescribe the following remedy, to be used before the mob's fit returns again.

'Recipe – "Twenty-four drams or hours imprisonment; as many blisters as can be placed upon the scapulars; their names recorded with infamy on the Grand-jury's list;" for all those club-bearers, and for all those hedge-robbers, if any of them can be discovered and can be convicted at the next Quarter Sessions; if not, let such public and previous warnings be given for the time to come, by the inferior officers of the City as may deter those wicked bullies and those wild boars who have trampled upon, and ravished all the sweets of our little Edens, as well as all givers of Mayballs, from ever doing the like again. I am Sir, not a sufferer, but a hearty well wisher of the City of Kilkenny, and your constant reader,

"Florus" '

That the writer's indignation was not without cause is shown by contemporary accounts, for instance, in the *Freeman's Journal* 7–9 May, 1778 where we read of a death:

'On Thursday last Patrick Reade, of Johnswell had his skull fractured in a quarrel which arose betwixt some men who assembled to collect Mayballs, in the neighbourhood of Bennet's Bridge. He was taken to hospital, where he was trepanned on Sunday, and shortly after died.'

In 1779 the civic authorities interposed to stop the revelry (*Finn's Leinster Journal* 1 May 1779):

'The peaceable inhabitants of this city (Kilkenny) are much obliged to the Worshipful John Watters, Deputy Mayor, for having exerted himself yesterday evening with peculiar vigilance, resolution and activity, in checking the career of a numerous mob, in their first setting out in quest of Mayballs. His worship seized the bearer of the Mayball and lodged him in jail. Shortly after this mob was dispersed curiosity led a number of the soldiers quartered upon this city to mix with a crowd of idle fellows, and to attempt another parade. But the prudence and humanity of some of their officers, who foresaw the mischief that was likely to ensure, stopped their progress, and ordered them to their quarters. Thus were the citizens happily delivered from the old usual horrors of May-Eve and it is to be hoped that this example will insure, for the future, the peace and tranquility of the public.'

106

However, three years later the disorders were in full swing again. *Finn's Leinster Journal* reports (4 May, 1782)

'On Tuesday a number of people in different parties, assembled at Callan in order to collect may-balls, they disagreeing, a quarrel ensued in which Nicholas Butler, of that town, cooper, unfortunately received a blow of a stone on the forehead and instantly expired.'

This is the death mentioned by Ó Súilleabháin, above. Nor was it the only one, for the newspaper continues:

'On the same day at John's Well Richard Blanchfield received several wounds, on a similar occasion, under which he now languishes, without any hope of recovery.'

At this stage the church authorities took notice of the practice. Dr Troy, the Bishop of Ossory, in a letter dated 12 Dec. 1784, to the 'Rev. Pastors and other Roman Catholic Clergymen of the Diocess of Ossory' orders them:

'6. In order to prevent the tumults and other fatal consequences of requiring and giving garlands, globes, and other decorations generally known by the appellation of *May Balls* because given by young married people and carried about on the 1st of May, I hereby most strictly command each and every one of you not to administer sacraments to any person or persons of your respective parishes who shall hereafter at any time demand said *May Balls* or call for money, liquor, or anything else in place of them, till such transgressors declare their repentance and promise amendment before the congregation assembled as above.

'The same is to be observed with regard to any young marrried couple, or either of them who shall hereafter at any time give or procure said *May Balls,* or money, liquor, or any other things in their stead to any person or persons whatsoever. Moreover, the first child of any couple so offending, is to be baptised in the parish chapel and nowhere else; as to the woman, she is not to be churched till thirty days shall elapse after her delivery. When called upon in future to administer the sacrament of Matrimony, you are to inform the parties and others present of the above, and require their solemn promise of punctually observing the same.'

(Spicelegium Ossoriense III, 380–1.)

This condemnation seems to have put an end to the widespread practice of the custom in that region, and the later examples mentioned by Amhlaoibh Ó Súilleabháin, appear to have been isolated and unsuccessful attempts at reviving it.

May Dew

The learned Dr Gerard Boate, in his *Natural History of Ireland* (1652, chap. XXII, sect. 2) tells of the virtues of May dew:

'Of May-dew, and the manner of gathering, and preserving it.

'The English women, and gentlewomen in Ireland, as in England, did use in the beginning of the summer to gather good store of dew, to keep it by them all the year after for several good uses both of physick and otherwise, wherein by experience they have learnt it to be very available. Their manner of collecting and keeping it was this. In the month of May especially, and also in part of the month of June, they would go forth betimes in the morning, and before sun-rising, into a green field, and there either with their hands strike off the dew from the tops of the herbs into a dish, or else throwing clean linnen cloaths upon the ground, take off the dew from the herbs into them, and afterwards wring it out into dishes; and thus they continue their work until they have got a sufficient quantity of dew·according to their intentions. That which is gotten from the grass will serve, but they chuse rather to have it from the green corn, especially wheat, if they can have the convenience to do so, as being persuaded that this dew hath more vertues, and is better for all purposes, than that which hath been collected from the grass or other herbs. The dew thus gathered they put into a glass bottle, and so set it in a place where it may have the warm sunshine all day long, keeping it there all the summer; after some days rest some dregs and dirt will settle to the bottom; the which when they perceive, they pour off all the clear dew into another vessel, and fling away those setlings. This they do often, because the dew doth not purge it self perfectly in a few days, but by degrees, so as new dregs (severed from the purer parts by the working of the dew, helped on by sun-beams) do settle again; of the which as often as those good women see any notable quantity, they still pour off the clear dew from them: doing thus all summer long, until it be clear to the bottom.

'The dew thus thoroughly purified looketh whitish, and keepeth good for a year or two after.'

With this belief in the powers of May dew among the erudite and the fashionable it is not surprising to find the same notion strongly held by the ordinary people of the Irish countryside. It was often gathered in the way described by Boate and kept as a medicine or an aid to beauty. It was still more powerful if it was taken and used before sunrise on May Day.

There is a well-known riddle referring to this, in several versions both in Irish and in English; one version runs:

> I washed my face in water
>   that had neither rained nor run,
> And I dried it on a towel
>   that was never woven nor spun

– the answer, of course, being that 'I washed my face in the dew and let it dry in the air'; to conserve its power it should not be wiped off.

The young woman who washed her face thus gained a fair complexion, while if she were daring enough to undress and roll naked in the dew she was given great beauty of person. The dew was believed to bring immunity from freckles, sunburn, chapping and wrinkles during the coming year. It also cured, or prevented, headaches, skin ailments and sore eyes. Applied to the eyes it ensured that its user rose every morning clear-eyed, alert and refreshed, even after a very short sleep.

The man who washed his hands in the dew of May Day gained skill in opening knots and locks, in mending nets and disentangling ropes. The woman who did likewise could unravel tangled threads with ease.

To walk barefoot in the dew cured soreness, prevented corns and bunions and ensured healthy feet during the year.

More sinister use of May Dew, in the practice of evil magic is described below.

Charms and Counter-charms

So powerful were the preternatural forces abroad in the night between sunset on May Eve and sunrise on May Day that almost anything might be expected to happen. Dairy produce was especially vulnerable to the working of evil magic, and careful precautions were taken to guard against this. In Camden's *Britannia* (1610) we have a tradition which the author says he had from a priest named Good who 'about the yeere of our Lord 1566, taught the Schoole at Limerick':

'They take her for a wicked woman and a witch what ever shee bee, that commeth to fetch fire from them on May-day (neither will they give any fire then, but unto a sicke body, and that with a curse): For because, they thinke the same woman will the next summer steale awaie all their butter. If they finde an hare amongst their heards of cattaile on the said May daie; they kill her, for, they suppose shee is

109

some old trot, that would filch away their butter. They are of opinion, that their butter if it bee stollen will soone after bee restored againe, incase they take away some of the thatch that hangeth over the doore of the house and cast it into the fire.'

The same tradition is still remembered all over Ireland; no fire must be given out of the house on May Morning and no honest person would ask for it.

Almost anything taken from the house or, indeed, any part of the farm at dawn on May Day could be used to steal the butter, giving the evil-doer a greatly increased quantity while the victims' churn produced nothing but froth.

Dew gathered with a cream-skimmer or soaked up in a cloth or collected by dragging a rope or a spancel over the grass, or water taken from a well or stream on the farm, while repeating a powerful charm such as:

> Come, butter, come!
> Come, butter, come!
> Every lump as big as my bum!!

or water taken from a point where the boundaries of three farms or three townlands met, *uisce na dtrí teorann* or 'the water of three mearings', were more than usually potent.

Any stranger seen upon one's property on May morning was immediately suspect of evil intent, and might be lucky to get away with only verbal abuse. Lady Wilde (*Ancient Cures, Charmes and Usages*, 1890, 100) tells us of one such case:

'A young student was nearly killed one time by the people, for they saw him walking up and down on May morning on the grass, while he read aloud from a book in some strange language; and they concluded that he was trying to bewitch the herbs of grace, which are for healing. Fortunately, however, a priest came by, and having examined the book, found it was a copy of Virgil; so he informed the excited crowd that the young man was simply going through his college duties in the grand old language that St Patrick had brought to Ireland, and which was sacred for ever to the use of the Church. On this they were pacified, and the young student was allowed to depart in safety.'

Strange animals, either domestic or wild, were equally unwelcome. One of the commonest of Irish tales is that of the hare seen sucking a cow's milk on May Morning. The farmer gives chase, the hare is

110

injured and bleeds, and the trail of blood leads to a house where an old woman lies bleeding – she had assumed the form of a hare so as to steal milk to work magic. Hedgehogs were also suspect and often were cruelly killed.

A hair from a cow's tail or clay from its cloven hoof or cowdung from the byre floor or wisps of straw from the roof of the dwelling house or the byre were equally dangerous in the hands of charm-setters. Another powerful charm was to repeat the words:

> The tops of the grass and the roots of the corn
> Give me the neighbour's milk night and morn.

while plucking grass and pulling young corn in the neighbour's field.

Even the smoke rising from the chimney on May morning might be used to steal the butter. The charm setter walked backwards into her own house, all the time watching the neighbour's smoke and repeating *Im an deataigh sin ar mo chuid bainne-se* – 'The butter of that smoke upon my milk'. In parts of Connaught it was said that would-be butter-stealers climbed upon the roof of the house and caught the first smoke in a bag or a can to ensure the efficacy of the charm.

To enter the farm unseen and open every gate and door was thought to be equally effective.

A spancel – the short piece of rope used to tie a cow's legs while milking – or the halter by which the cow is tied to the stall, could, in the wrong hands, be injurious. The tale is told of a farmer's boy who came to his master in some perplexity; an old woman has asked him to dip a spancel in the milk and give it to her. The farmer dips it in the cesspool and tells the boy to give it to the hag; later when she hangs it over her churn and repeats the charm, what drips from it is filth, not cream. Another story tells of the cows refusal to drink until their owner had removed from the water a spancel concealed there by a charm setter.

Another charm was to enter the byre and lay a spancel or a thread across the cows' backs, or to hide at the byre door and tap each animal with a rowan or hazel switch.

Another form of magic attempted about this time was the stealing of the produce of the neighbour's fields by burying in them meat or eggs or bread, by which means the neighbour's crop failed while that of the charm-setter gave a double return. By similar means it was believed that the neighbour's calves died or aborted while the evil-doer's cows had healthy twin calves. In parts of Laois and Kilkenny it is said that old women might be seen sweeping the dust or mud of the high road towards their own houses while repeating the words 'All that passes here be mine! All that passes here be mine!' in the hope of gaining power over all the possessions of the wayfarers on that road. It will be remembered that at the Kilkenny witchcraft trial of 1326 it was stated that Dame Alice Kyteler was alleged to have swept the streets with a broom, repeating:

> To the house of William my son,
> Hie all the wealth of Kilkenny town.

To every charm there was a counter-charm. No fire was allowed to leave the house. A neighbour, or even a man of the household, who lit his pipe at the fire was required to smoke it out before he left the house. Should it be vitally necessary to give fire to somebody, – say, a sick neighbour whose fire had gone out, more fuel was at once added to the fire with a prayer or aspiration such as *Dia idir sinn agus an t-olc* – 'God between us and all harm'. Some held that a twig of mountain ash (*Sorbus aucuparia*) should be added to the fire from which the coal was taken. Others said that the May day fire lit with dried twigs of mountain ash was thereby freed from all evil influence.

People tried not to be the first to light the domestic fire on this morning, watching the neighbours' chimneys to make sure that the smoke of their own fire was not the first to rise and to claim the attentions of the charm-setters.

People willingly went hungry or ate only cold food rather than light the fire. In parts of Connaught the phrase *Colladh Bealtaine* – 'May Day sleep' – was applied to late rising, as, it was said, those who could do so slept late on May Morning rather than get up and light the fire.

Special care was taken not to throw out cinders or ashes from the hearth on May morning. Indeed, nothing whatever should be taken from the house on this day. Food scraps should be burned, not thrown on the refuse heap. Floor sweepings too, must be thrown into the fire. Dirty water must be kept inside, at least until after midday when the evil influences waned. Nothing was loaned or given as a gift or as alms – no decent beggar would ask for anything on May Day. Some went so far as to refuse to pay for anything bought on this day, so strong was the tradition that anything given away could be used to the giver's detriment.

112

In general the rule was 'no spending, no lending, no borrowing'. To ask for the loan of anything aroused suspicion; to ask for anything white – the colour of milk – was doubly suspicious, and even when the request was clearly innocent it was regarded as a breach not only of custom but of good manners. To return borrowed articles before May Day was good manners, to fail to do so brought doubts as to the borrower's intentions.

Care should be taken, too, not to pick up anything found on the roadway, or indeed anywhere, on May Day. A garment, an implement or other article of value should be laid on the fence or on a bush so that the owner might find it again. To keep such an article was most unlucky, as it might be used by a charm-setter to gain power over the finder or his property, or to transfer some disease or ailment to him.

Water, as we are told, was often used in setting charms, thus every precaution must be taken to guard it. Where the farmer owned his own water supply, in a pump or a well, he made sure that it was protected at the vital hour of dawn on May Morning. One elderly farmer of the writer's acquaintance told how, as a boy, he kept watch with his father, both armed with shotguns, over the well and the stream which flowed through the farm, from sunset on May Eve until sunrise on May Day, and how his father told him, not only to warn away anybody seen approaching the water, but instantly to shoot any wild creature coming to drink; this was in the Kildorrery area of north County Cork, but the custom of guarding the well was common throughout the area of large farms in Leinster and Munster, and, indeed, wherever a farmer owned his own source of water. Pumps were commonly chained and locked as a precaution.

The first water taken from the well after dawn on May Day was potent for good or evil. It was known variously as 'the top of the well', 'the luck of the well', *Barra-bua an tobair, sgaith an tobair* and other names. In evil hands it could do great harm; in those of its rightful owners it brought luck, protection and healing. Often it was taken from the surface of the well by the use of a milk-skimmer.

Where the family owned its own supply, the risk and the benefit of the first water belonged to the family; others, such as the farm labourers and poorer neighbours who were permitted to use the supply were expected not to take water on May Morning until the day was well advanced. Things were different in those areas where one source of water was shared by a group of small farmers or by a whole village. There was rivalry, usually friendly but sometimes leading to quarrels and bad feeling, as to who should have the first of the well. Sometimes the young girls raced each other to draw the first can of water, and some arose long before dawn or even sat up all night so as to be first.

All this activity had the advantage of making sure that no evil-doer got the first water and with it the opportunity to work harm on all the families using the well.

Other precautions might be taken, such as sprinkling holy water or salt on the well on May Eve, or dropping into it a twig of mountain ash or a piece of iron while repeating a prayer or aspiration.

Similar precautions were taken with running water, especially at cattle's drinking places. Particular care was taken that no dregs of milk, nor anything, even cowdung, associated with the cattle, was permitted to fall into running water on May Morning. After milking, the hands must not be washed in a running stream nor must the water in which they are washed be allowed to run into a stream.

Since the protection of dairy produce was the main reason for all these precautions it was only to be expected that special vigilance was exercised in the dairy and in the byre. The milk itself was watched and the utmost care was taken that none of it was taken away. People who bought milk, or were given milk as gift or alms, were not surprised if their May Day supply was not forthcoming until after midday, and here, again, to seek it too early in the day was bad manners. Usually, too, when milk was being dispensed on this day a pinch of salt or a drop of holy water or of 'the top of the well' was added to it, and some small payment, a coin or an egg, was expected in return for it. No milk utensil of any kind was allowed to leave the farm on this day, and nobody in his senses would seek a loan of it. When, about the beginning of this century, scientific testing of milk began to come into vogue, many of the older people were doubtful about it or even refused to give samples on May Day. Indeed, the establishment, about that time, of the co-operative creameries, to which was sent all the milk from the surrounding farms and where butter was made communally for the market, was the main cause of the disappearance of all this milk magic, which lingered much longer in those areas where butter continued to be made in the household.

At milking time a cross traced on the cow's flank by a finger dipped in the first of the milk or a stick dipped in fresh cowdung was thought to give protection, as did a red thread or rag tied to the cow's tail, or touching the cow with a mountain ash twig or hanging such a twig in the byre. Pious people made sure to sprinkle holy water on the cows

114

and about the byre on May Morning, while the St Brighid's Cross or spancel and the 'palm' from Palm Sunday, already hanging in the byre, gave added reassurance.

Many people kept the byre doors carefully locked on May Morning and did not let the cows out to pasture until all danger of the day's bewitchment had passed. Some people avoided churning on May Day, while others took precautions to ensure that all went well. A pinch of salt or a drop of holy water or of 'the top of the well' or a nail or other small piece of iron might be put in the churn. A chain bound around the outside of the churn, or a sprig of mountain ash or a ring of hair from the cows' tails tied to the handle or the dash of the churn, or a horse shoe or other piece of iron, a churn scrubber or a coal from the fire placed underneath it were also considered effective, and some people employed several of these safeguards.

During the churning anybody, young or old, man or woman, who entered the kitchen or the dairy must take a turn at churning. Some held that this was merely a pleasant device to lighten the labour of churning, but others maintained that it was to protect the butter against even inadvertent harm. As the churning proceeded an eager eye was kept alert for the first sign of the coming butter, and if this did not appear in a reasonable time, the worst was suspected and immediate steps taken to counteract the wicked spell.

A very potent remedy was the heating of an iron implement in the fire, a pair of tongs, a spade or a plough coulter, which, when red hot, was plunged into the churn or applied to its side, while repeating a counter charm, such as:

'Come, butter, come!
St Peter stands at the gate,
Waiting for a buttered cake,
so come, butter, come!'

Immediately, it was believed, the charm-setter who had stolen the butter was afflicted with the agony of a red hot iron thrust into her vitals and had to undo the charm, or even to run to the house of her victims confess her misdeeds and restore the stolen butter.

As might be expected, matters of this kind often came to the notice of the civil or the ecclesiastical authorities. An example of this is the following case, recorded in the memoirs of the Ordnance Survey in 1835 (R.I.A., folio 6 p. I); it is from Maghera parish, County Derry, and is quoted here from the *Ulster Journal of Archaeology* (8, 1945, 65):

'Blinking Cattle. Two persons, the one a Presbyterian and the other a Covenanter, and near relations – the accused was a woman, a Covenanter, the accuser a Presbyterian – both parties were brought before the covenanting minister, the Rev. W. Smith, in the meeting-house at Knockloughran for the purpose of examining them. The woman was found guilty and expelled the congregation. The woman (had been) pursued from the cows of the Presbyterian into her own house almost breathless; and on further examination a large chest was opened, in which were deposited crocks of milk in a boiling state, as if occaisoned by a very hot fire. Across the mouth of each crock was the form of a cross in wood; attached to each point of the cross was a long hair, supposed to have been taken from the tails of the cows. Her husband, on the shame of his wife being accused and found guilty of so horrible a crime, died the same night.

'It is said the cure was effected and the butter and milk restored by taking a quantity of straw from the eave of the house of the person found guilty, and burning it under the nostrils of the cow or cows blinked. The priests perform the cure by taking all the milk the cow gives and blessing it, and also blessing salt put into it. This (has) to be given to the cow without letting a particle fall to the ground. This cure was given to the cow of a Presbyterian in Td. Tirmoneeny, but without effect.'

The general protection of the farm was not neglected. In *Transactions of the Kilkenny Archaeological Society*, 1849–51, 375–5, Nicholas O'Kearney tells of an elaborate ceremony, which, apparently, had already died out in his time:

'Another custom was scrupulously observed after sunset on the eve of Bealtine. Farmers accompanied by their servants and domestics, were accustomed to walk around the boundaries of their farms in a sort of procession, carrying implements of husbandry, seeds of corn, *sgaith an tobair*, and other requisites, especially the sacred herb, *bean mhín* (vervain), if any person were fortunate enough to possess a sprig of it. The procession always halted at the most convenient stations facing the four cardinal points, beginning at the east, and went through several ceremonies, particularly that of digging a sod, breaking it fine, and then sowing seed, after which they sprinkled the glebe with *sgaith an tobair*. They then drove all their cows into one place, and examined their tails, lest a witch or evilly-disposed person might there conceal a sprig of the rowan tree, or some other bewitched token. If any suspicious bramble were found attached to a cow's tail, it was immediately taken and burned, and a sprig of vervain, if convenient, or a branch of the rowan substituted instead; for the rowan was potent for good as well as evil, if it were cut before sunrise on Bealtine morning. The cows were afterwards sprinkled with *sgaith an tobair,* preserved since last May-Day, which ended the ceremony.'

A simpler ceremony is described by Helen Roe (*Béaloideas* ix, 29) from Laois:

'On the eve of May Day in many districts the father of the house lights a candle and blesses the threshold, the hearth, and the four corners of the house, with Easter Water. He also blesses his wife and the children in the order of their age. The farmer then visits the stable and blesses the animals. One field is blessed for the whole farm. It is wise to put a branch of the quicken-tree in the field. Some people only bless the fields and the stock.'

This sprinkling of holy water on the growing crops and pasture fields was very general, and one wonders if the absence of mention of holy water in O'Kearney's account above did not spring from the nineteenth-century antiquarian fashion of exaggerating the supposedly pagan elements in popular tradition and minimizing the Christian elements.

A story from County Limerick tells of a farmer shaking holy water on his crop with the appropriate prayer. Accidentally he sprinkled a hare which was crouching in terror in the headland, and instantly the hare was restored to its proper from, that of an old hag who was trying to steal his 'increase' by magic.

About this time the farmer looked out for any sign of magical assault on the crops or live stock. Should any object such as meat, bread, eggs, meat offals, or small dead animals be found concealed anywhere on his property, it had to be removed with care to some public road, and there burned, while holy water was sprinkled and prayers said at the place where it was found; it was usual, too, to leave some object of piety, – a small religious medal, a piece of blessed candle, a rosary beads or scapular – at the spot where the evil thing had been hidden.

There appears to have been a fairly widespread custom of bleeding cattle, for health reasons at this time of the year. *In Popular Superstitions,* 56, Sir William Wilde tells us that

'it was not unusual, some fifteen or twenty years ago, to bleed a whole herd of cattle upon a May morning, and then to dry and burn the blood. We have more than once, when a boy, seen the entire of the great Fort of Rathcroghan, then the centre of one of the most extensive and fertile grazing districts of Connaught, literally reddened with the blood thus drawn upon a May morning. Bleeding the cattle at this period of the year was evidently done with a sanitary intention, as some of the older medical works recommended in the human subject; but choosing that particular day, and subsequently burning the blood, were evidently the vestiges of some Heathen rite. In some districts, and particularly during hard times, some of the blood thus drawn used to be mixed with meal, boiled into a posset, and eaten by the herds and the poor people. But many of these ceremonies, having been either laughed at or positively interdicted by the more educated Roman Catholic clergy, are fast falling into disuse.'

While the *Ulster Journal of Archaeology* (1855, 165) says that:

'On May Eve the peasantry used to drive all their cattle into old raths and forts thought to be much frequented by the fairies, bleed them, taste their blood, and pour the remainder on the earth.'

Other cures and remedies too, were given or applied to the cattle at this important time of the beginning of the Summer pasture season.

An unusually liberal outlook on all of this is remembered by an old lady, Mrs Mary Fogarty, in County Limerick, towards the end of the last century (*The Farm by Lough Gur*, 158–62):

'The powers of evil, always on the alert to entangle and destroy souls, being most dangerous and most powerful on May-Eve, on that day the maids were apt to be uneasy and rather sullen, watching us suspiciously lest we might, through our unbelief, frustrate their precautions against danger. They strewed primroses on the threshold of the front and back doors – no fairy can get over this defence – and in the cow-byres they hung branches of rowan while the head dairy-woman sprinkled holy water in mangers and stalls. The milkmaids, at the end of the evening milking, stood to make the sign of the cross with froth from the pails, signing themselves and making a cross in the air towards the cows.

'While the dairymaids were safeguarding the cowsheds, Ellie stayed in the kitchen to see that no fire or ashes were carried out of the house, nor any food given at the door. As a rule no beggars showed themselves, knowing well that neither milk, bread, nor a light for a pipe would be given them by servants anywhere, not even a kindly greeting, for who could tell that they were true beggars and not witches or *Little People* in disguise, come to steal a coal of fire and to weave an evil spell round the house and family. The final precaution against evil spells and danger was to put out the fire on the hearth to the last red ember. . .

'"Why do you let the maids be so silly?" I asked mother when they were out of hearing. "The nuns say we must never miss a chance of curing people of pagan superstition!"

'"You can try," mother said rather coldly; she didn't like me to quote the nuns at her in my "superior manner". "I think only time can cure superstition," she went on. "I don't want to make Ellie and Bridgie unhappy or frightened, as they would be if I were to make up the fire to-night, or if you were to sweep up the primroses."

'"Doesn't God mind?" I asked her.

'Mother smiled at my peevish face. "I feel sure He has a sense of humour" she said.'

Health

'March will search, April will try, and May will tell whether you'll live or die' – so runs the popular saying. May was thought to be a critical time for sick people, and any illness or injury on May Eve or May Day was especially dangerous and difficult to cure.

Nurse Hedderman (*Glimpses of my Life in Aran*, 1917, 105–6) recalls that this belief was, at least with some people, so strong as to hinder her work for the sick:

'The "May Eve" superstition is another popular cause of illness. I visited a small boy with a tuberculous knee. All signs of diseased bone were present. I advised hospital treatment, but the mother would not hear of it. The first pain was felt on "May Eve", consequently cure was hopeless. The fairies are believed to change their residence on that day, and frequently to snatch children met on their way. They must accordingly have taken her boy and substituted this other, and how could she think of getting back her own? She did not protect him sufficiently, and must accept the inevitable; and now she seemed patiently resigned to it, despite the fact that I had the child afterwards transferred to hospital, where he gradually recovered.'

On the other hand, May Eve and May Day were among the very best days of the year for gathering medicinal herbs, and those who were skilled in the craft of healing were sure to be abroad then, searching for these beneficent plants. The first 'All-May' butter, that is to say the first butter made from the milk of May Day, was held to be the best of all bases for salves and ointments. And it was firmly believed that any herb picked at random before sunrise on May Day was an infallible cure for warts.

Everybody was expected to take blood-purifying medicines at the beginning of May. Many older people will recall having, as children, to swallow such noisome concoctions as sulphur-and-treacle. A favourite dosage was three meals of fresh young nettles boiled until tender, or three cupfuls of the liquid from this boiling taken on three consecutive days, beginning on May Day. The liquid from boiled whitethorn blossoms, similarly taken was, according to some authorities, equally beneficial.

The belief that nettle-stings were good for rheumatism and the fact that nettles were applied to rheumatic limbs may have some bearing on a custom which flourished until recently in the southern parts of County Cork. Crofton Croker (*Fairy Legends of the South of Ireland*, I, 308) wrote of this:

'Another custom prevalent on May-Eve is the painful and mischievous one of stinging with nettles. In the south of Ireland it is the common practice for school-boys, on that day, to consider themselves privileged to run wildly about with a bunch of nettles, striking at the face and hands of their companions, or such other persons as they think they may venture to assault with impunity.'

And in Hall's *Ireland, its Scenery and Character*, I, 25, we read:

'Another old custom prevails also to some extent. May-Eve, the last day of April, is called "Nettlemas night": boys parade the streets with large bunches of nettles, stinging their playmates, and occasionally bestowing a sly touch upon strangers who come in their way. Young and merry maidens, too, not unfrequently avail themselves of the privilege to "sting" their lovers; and, the laughter in the street is often echoed in the drawing-room.'

This may have been no more than another aspect of the revelry prevailing at this season, but a similar tradition from the middle of County Limerick recalls that boys went to the river bank on May Eve to pick 'marshmallows' with which they struck the passers-by; these latter, we are told, usually did not resent it because it was thought to give some vague form of protection against illness and fairy influence. Illness or injury was equally dangerous for animals at Maytime. Nurse Hedderman continues her account of the belief on Aran thus:

'The "May-Eve" superstition is specially dreaded in the case of cattle. They have great faith in putting a cross on the cow, and go out early on that morning to plaster the poor animal with her own excrement – a large Roman cross on the right side. This is believed to protect it from all subsequent harm for that year. This is also the case with horses. I knew one that any ordinary person could see was suffering from mastitis, and was evidently in pain. The inflamed tissue need bathing. I suggested this, but was met with the ready reason that the attack dated from "May Day". Under these circumstances they had to seek elsewhere for a cure.'

As in the case of humans, the ingredients of herbal and other remedies for animals were best gathered at this season.

The Fairies at Maytime

Supernatural beings were more than usually active about May Day, and the appearance of a travelling band of fairies, of a mermaid, a *púca* or a headless coach might, indeed, cause unease or alarm but certainly would occasion no surprise, as such manifestations were only to be expected at this time.

The Great Earl of Desmond, a notable wizard in his day, is seen on May Morning in full armour rising from the waters of Loch Gur, in County Limerick, to gallop his silver-shod horse about the lake. O'Donoghue of the Glens – in similar array – rides over the lakes of Killarney. In County Wicklow the 'Motty Stone', a great boulder, leaves its hill-top and comes down to drink at the Meeting of the Waters, while rocks off the coast, such as the Fastnet, shake loose their bonds and sail at will about the sea.

With all this otherworld activity afoot, precautions for one's safety must be taken. Best of all it were to remain in the security of one's own house, or at least to venture afield only briefly and under dire necessity and, above all, not to sleep out of doors. A piece of iron in the pocket gave some protection; a black-handled knife was the best form of iron. Other useful safeguards were a spent cinder from the hearth, or a sprig of mountain ash; the latter, if twisted into a ring and held to the eye would enable its user to see the fairies clearly. In a few places a tradition of active propitiation survives, by leaving small offerings of food or drink on the doorstep, or at the fort, lone bush, or other fairy dwelling place.

Persons straying near forts or other homes of the 'good people' might meet them venturing out to engage in dancing, hurling and other revels or to travel away to visit or do battle with another fairy group. Many

16   The May Morning vision, Killarney (Hall: *Ireland*)

tales are told of these encounters between mortals and fairies, of invitation to the mortal to join in fairy activities and subsequent reward to those who acquitted themselves well, or of intrusion by a mortal into fairy business and the punishment which followed this.

A favourite pastime of the fairies was to cause mortals to lose their way by bringing down mist or by confusing landmarks. To turn one's coat inside out was held to be a useful counter to this, as it disguised the person and so confused the fairies themselves, thus enabling the victim to escape. A more drastic remedy was to wash hands and face in one's own urine, which caused the 'good people' to recoil in horror and permit the victims to escape.

There was a widely-held belief that this was the time of the year when abduction by the fairies was most to be feared. Infants of both sexes and marriageable young women were most in danger of being spirited away. Usually, to confuse matters, the abductors left a changeling behind, which although at first was just like the person stolen, gradually pined away and died, leaving the real mortal in the power of the fairies for ever.

All over Ireland there are tales of fairy abduction, and of how this was recognized and the victim rescued. That this was more than mere legend is shown by many instances of children or even grown people harmed or killed in well meaning but ill advised attempts to drive away the changeling and so cause the real human to return, because the 'cure' might proceed from pleas to threats and on to increased forms of violence. Sir William Wilde, reporting on causes of deaths in the *Census of Ireland Report,* 1851 (Part V, vol. I, p.455) says of wasting disorders:

'It is this affection which has given rise to the popular ideas respecting the "changeling" and in this country to the many superstitious notions entertained by the peasantry respecting their supposed "fairy-stricken" children; – so that year by year, up to the present day, we read accounts of deaths produced by cruel endeavours to cure children and young persons of such maladies generally attempted by quacks and those termed "fairy men" and "fairy women".'

One striking instance of this, which shows that even the law might on occasion take it into account, is mentioned by T. C. Croker in *Fairy Legends of the South of Ireland,* new series, 1828, vii. This case was reported in the *Morning Post* as follows:

Tralee Assizes, July, 1826. – Child Murder.

'Ann Roche, an old woman of very advanced age, was indicted for the murder of Michael Leahy, a young child, by drowning him in the Flesk. This case, which at first assumed a very serious aspect, from the meaning imputed to words spoken by the prisoner, "that the sin of the child's death was on the grandmother, and not on the prisoner," turned out to be a homicide committed under the delusion of the grossest superstition. The child, though four years old, could neither stand, walk, or speak – it was thought to be fairy-struck – and the grandmother ordered the prisoner and one of the witnesses, Mary Clifford, to bathe the child every morning in that pool of the river Flesk where boundaries of three farms met; they had so bathed it for three mornings running, and on the last morning the prisoner kept the child longer under the water than usual, when her companion (the witness, Mary Clifford) said to the prisoner, "How can you hope ever to see God after this?" to which the prisoner replied, "that the sin was on the grandmother and not on her". Upon cross-examination, the witness said it was not done with intent to kill the child, but to cure it – to put the fairy out of it.

'The policeman who apprehended her stated, that on charging her with drowning the child, she said it was no matter if it had died four years ago.

'Baron Pennefather said, that though it was a case of suspicion, and required to be thoroughly examined into, yet the jury would not be safe in convicting the prisoner of murder, however strong their suspicions might be. Verdict – Not guilty.'

Another form of fairy mischief was the *poc sidhe,* 'fairy stroke' or 'blast', caused by a passing band of fairies striking at random at any who came within their reach, as well as at those who had offended them. T. C. Croker refers to this also (*Fairy Legends,* I, 307):

'May-Eve is considered a time of peculiar danger. The "good people" are supposed then to possess the power and the inclination to do all sorts of mischief without the slightest restraint. The "evil eye" is then also deemed to have more than its usual vigilance and malignity; and the nurse who would walk in the open air with a child in her arms would by reprobated as a monster. Youth and loveliness are thought to be especially exposed to peril. It is therefore a natural consequence, that not one woman in a thousand appears abroad: but it must not be understood that the want of beauty affords any protection. The grizzled locks of age do not always save the cheek from a blast; neither is the brawny hand of the roughest ploughman exempt from a similar visitation. The blast is a large round tumour, which is thought to rise suddenly upon the part affected from the baneful breath cast on it by one of the "good people" in a moment of vindictive or capricious malice.'

The 'fairy stroke' took many forms. Any sudden fall or injury or any unexplained laming, deafness, loss of speech, fainting spell, distortion or swelling could be attributed to it, particularly if an unusual puff of wind had been observed about the time of onset. The small whirlwind, which is not unusual in Ireland in certain weather conditions, was known as *sidhe gaoithe* (wind fairies) and greatly dreaded as a cause of 'fairy stroke'.

Cattle and humans were equally susceptible, and the remedies to be applied to both man and beast were as numerous as the forms taken by the 'stroke'. In some northern areas where prehistoric flint tools and weapons occur frequently, these were believed to be the fairy darts which caused the 'stroke'; happily they also provided the cure by being applied to the afflicted part, or put into the vessel from which the victim drank.

Other May Day Beliefs and Customs

A child born on May Day had the gift of being able to see the fairies, but almost certainly would die young; an animal born on May Day was sure to be a weakling.

Marriage in May was considered most unlucky. On the other hand May-Eve was one of the nights when marriage divination might be successful. The girl who looked at the reflection of the 'young May Moon' in her mirror or in a well might see her future husband looking over her shoulder.

T. C. Croker (*Fairy Legends* II 1828, 215) tells us of the 'drutheen' (recte *druchtín*):

' "The Drutheen", which is supposed to possess the power of revealing the name of a sweetheart, is a small white slug or naked snail, and it is the common practice of boys and maids on May morning to place one on a piece of slate lightly sprinkled with flour or fine dust, covering it over with a large leaf, when it never fails to describe the initial of "the loved name".'

Lady Wilde, *Ancient Cures, Charms and Usages,* 1890, enlarges on this (p.106–7):

'Advice to Maidens

'On May morning, before sunrise, go out to the garden, and the first snail you see take up, and put it on a plate sprinkled lightly with flour, place a cabbage-leaf over, and so leave it till after sunrise, when you will find the initial letters of your lover's name traced on the flour.

'Should the snail be quite within his house when you take him up, your lover will be rich; but should the snail be almost out of his shell, then your future husband will be poor, and probably will have no house or home to take you to when you wed him. Therefore take good heed of the warning given to you by the snail, or avoid trying your future fate if you are afraid of the result.'

She also (*id.*101) mentions another method of divination:

'Among others it is thought right and proper to have the threshold swept clean on May-Eve. Ashes are then lightly sprinkled over it, and in the morning the print of a foot is looked for. If it turn inward a marriage is certain, but if outward then a death will happen in the family before the year is out.'

Both of these customs are still remembered in tradition in most parts of Ireland.

The call of the cuckoo is ominous on May Day. On the hearer's right hand it betokens luck, on the left, ill fortune. To hear it sounding from the churchyard trees meant a death in the family, to hear it before breakfast meant a hungry year. Worst token of all was to hear it through the open door or window when the hearer was inside the dwellinghouse.

All corn should have been sown before the cuckoo's first call.

In west Connaught the first Spring-tide of May was known as *Rabhartha Mór na n-Éan* and was believed to be the highest of the year; it got its name 'the great Spring tide of the birds' because all the sea birds observed the tide on that day to ensure that their nests were built above high water level.

In several parts of Ireland the first Sunday in May had special local significance. In parts of Cork and Kerry it was *Domhnach na hEadraí* 'Cow-time Sunday' and it was on this day that the cows were let out to pasture; possibly this arose from the fear of magic on May Day. But it appears that in parts of the north the date was anticipated, (*Ulster Folklife*, 1960, 24):

'The Cattle were put out of all the byres in the early morning till late evening on the last Sunday in April. It was called Donagh Inadru Sunday. They were not let out again for a few days. On May-Eve everyone pulled May Flowers and put them at every door. On May morning someone belonging to the house used to go for a can of spring water. One used to try to get before the other. No person ever kindled a fire or put out ashes or swept the floor on May morning. (Co. Fermanagh)'

Reverend Mr Hall (*Tour through Ireland* 1813, i, 185) tells us:

'On the first Sunday of May, which, at Cork, and in most parts of Ireland, is generally kept as May-day; happening to be there on that day, I found that all the low people, Protestants as well as Catholics, had gone out in the morning to get syllabubs, or milk cooked in a certain way; and that many of them were drunk before breakfast. In the evening, in the vicinity of the city, every inn, nay, almost every house, was full of people, dancing, drinking, singing, &c. &c.'

The practice of going on excursions on the first Sunday in May was still flourishing in County Cork well into this century.

In north County Dublin it was 'Sumachan Sunday', and was the day on which young men and women seeking work gathered outside the churches after Mass, to hire out with the local farmers.

'Ne'er cast a clout until May be out' says the proverb, interpreted by many as a warning not to change into summer clothes until June.

Others have the version 'Ne'er cast a clout 'til *the* May be out', that is to say until the whitethorn is in blossom. Certainly, most country children were permitted to run barefoot from the May Day onward, and mothers usually bought or made summer dresses for small daughters about this time.

Pilgrimages at Maytime might have special significance in relation to cattle, for instance that to the holy well of Cathair Crobh Deirg in south east Kerry, thus described in *Journal of Cork Archaeological and Historical Society* II, 1869, 318:

'Here a large "patron" is held on each recurring May Day. Persons residing at a distance journey to "the City Well" on April 30 (May Eve) that they may have the water to give to their cattle on May Day, but for all within a comeatable distance the "patron" is held on May Day itself. Having taken the morning train to Rathmore on the Killarney line, the pilgrims to "the City Well" there alight and trudge some four or five miles in a southern direction to their destination, where, having performed their devotions, and taken some of the water from the holy well in bottles or a jar for home consumption, they commence the return journey.

'The manner of using the water from this holy well is peculiar. The operator, who is generally the person who performs the pilgrimage, first commences with the oldest cow in the bawn, after which he next takes the youngest, be it cow or heifer, or even weanling calf; after which all the others are treated indiscriminately. Armed with a teaspoon, he first drops three drops of the water into this (oldest) cow's right nostril, then three similar drops into her right ear, after which three similar drops are dropped into her mouth; the invocation in each instance being the usual one, "In the name of the Father, and of the Son, and of the Holy Ghost. Amen." Cattle treated in this way are said to be impervious to all disease, even lung distemper of the most virulent type. The writer knows many persons in Mid-Limerick and North Cork who every year make a pilgrimage to "the City Well" and bring back, as recorded above, the water in jars for their cattle.'

It was generally believed that water taken from a holy well on May Eve or May Day remained fresh and clear during the whole of the ensuing year.

Ascension Thursday

A little ceremony from County Kildare is noted in *The Journal of the Kildare Archaeological Society*, 1906–08, 445:

'The sixth Thursday after Easter Sunday is the Feast of the Ascension of our Lord; it is observed as a holy-day, and blessed water procured from the priest is brought home from chapel, and poured out in the four corners of a farmer's holding, or a labourer's garden, to ensure good crops.'

Since the weather was usually fine, this was a day much favoured for outdoor games and pastimes. At Callan, County Kilkenny, Amhlaoibh O Súilleabháin noted in 1835:

'The twenty-eighth. Ascension Thursday, a holiday of obligation. A fine, cheerful, blueskied, bright, sunny morning with some light woolly cloud and great calm. Hurling and cock-fighting and a long dance called "High Gates" and a cricket match on the Fair Green.'

Whitsuntide

In the Irish tradition Whit Sunday is a very unlucky day, a day on which all precautions must be taken against accident and ill fortune. Nobody should engage in any dangerous occupation nor should anyone set out on a journey.

Water is to be avoided, for the risk of being drowned is very great. Therefore nobody should bathe or swim, or put out in a ship or boat or travel across a ford or walk along the edge of sea, river or lake. Some said, indeed, that all the dead who were drowned in that water rose up on this day to coax or force living people to join them.

Any creature, human or animal, born at Whitsuntide was fated to cause death or to die a violent death. A foal so born would throw a rider or trample or kick him to death, a bull or a cow would gore somebody. Even smaller creatures were fated to cause evil; a dog or cat or fowl might bite or claw an infant. A human so born would either murder somebody or himself be hanged or killed in some startling fashion, or, worse than all, possess an evil eye of unusual virulence.

Such a person or animal was known as a *cingciseach* (*Cingcís* = Pentecost), and while still young must be protected from its fate by taking steps to nullify the evil. The simple way to do this was to make the infant creature kill something. Thus, say, a live fly was put in a baby's hand and the little fingers squeezed upon it to crush and kill it; then the child, having caused a death, was freed from the spell. In the same way a young animal was made to kill an insect or other small creature and so was saved from its fate.

People, especially children, who are ill, are more likely to die at this time than at others. In parts of the midlands a counter-charm to this evil influence was the laying of a green sod on the head of the sufferer; by this mimicry of burial it was hoped that untimely death was warded off.

Until its abrogation in 1829, Whit Monday was for Catholics a holiday of obligation and thus had become a favourite day for patterns, fairs and devotions at holy wells; since that date, however, most such activities on this day have become obsolete.

Corpus Christi

Very little tradition is associated with this festival in rural Ireland. Whatever may have been customary in pre-Reformation times the church processions and other ceremonies now observed by Catholics are mainly of nineteenth century introduction. Amhlaoibh O Súilleabháin calls the day *Diardaoin Álainn na mBinsí Breátha* and explains the name by telling that it was an old country custom to spread fresh rushes and wild iris on benches outside the house doors, where the old people sat telling stories to the young on this day.

In some, at least, of the medieval towns it was customary to hold pageants or religious plays at Corpus Christi. An entry in the Dublin Chain Book (*Calendar of the Ancient Records of Dublin*, I, 239–40) reads, in a slightly modernised version, as follows:

'Corpus Christi day, a pageant.

'The pageant of Corpus Christi day, made by an old law and confirmed by an assembly before Thomas Collier, Mayor of the City of Dublin, and Jurats, Bailiffs and Commons, the 4th Friday after Midsummer, the 13th year of the reign of King Henry the Seventh (1498):

'Glovers: Adam and Eve, with an Angel following, bearing a sword.

'Shoemakers: Cain and Abel, with an altar and the offering.

'Mariners, Vintners, Ship Carpenters and Salmon Fishers: Noah with his ship, appareled accordingly.

'Weavers: Abraham and Isaac, with their altar and a lamb and their offering.

'Smiths, Shearers, Bakers, Slaters, Cooks and Masons: Pharaoh with his army.

'Skinners, House Carpenters, Tanners and Broiders: The body of the camel, and Our Lady and her Child, well appareled, with Joseph to lead the Camel and Moses with the children of Israel, and the Porters

131

to carry the camel. Stainers and Painters to paint the head of the camel.

'Goldsmiths: The Three Kings of Cologne, riding worshipfully with their offerings, with a star before them.

'Coopers: The Shepherds, with an Angel singing Gloria in excelsis Deo.

'The Corpus Christi Guild: Christ in His Passion, with the Three Maries and Angels bearing tapers of wax in their hands.

'Tailors: Pilate with his company and his lady and his Knights, well appareled.

'Barbers: Annas and Caiphas, well arrayed accordingly.

'Cutlers: Arthur and his Knights.

'Fishermen: The Twelve Apostles.

'Merchants: The Prophets.

'Butchers: The executioners with their garments well and cleanly painted.

'The Mayor of the Bullring and Bachelors of the same: The Nine Worthies riding worshipfully, with their followers according.

'The Haggardmen and the Husbandmen to carry the Dragon, and to repair the Dragon for St George's Day and Corpus Christi Day.'

Any of the guilds which did not play its assigned part to the satisfaction of the Mayor was liable to a fine of forty shillings. Incidentally, the last item in the above list refers also to a tableau of St George and the Dragon performed in Dublin on that saint's day, 23 April.

In the Records of the Corporation of Kilkenny there are several references to the Corpus Christi plays performed in that town. For instance, on 20 April 1610 the Corporation resolved:

'That the mayor and aldermen, with advice of the sheriffs and such of the second council as they shall cull, shall order the celebration of Corpus Christi Day in decent and solemn manner as usual, and shall employ carpenters to make rails for keeping out horses and the mob, and for placing strangers at the place where the interlude shall be played.'

On 23 July 1610 the Corporation ordered a sum of 20s 'for keeping the apparel of the morries and players of the Resurrection', and on 13 Jan. 1631 '£3.13.4d. per annum granted to William Cousey for teaching to write and read and instructing the children of the natives for the play on corpus Christi Day'. The stage for the play was set up in the open air, for there is a record of 13 April 1632 which reads:

'The north side of the market cross granted to two persons for shops during the fair time of Corpus Christi, in regard their shops are stopt up by the stations and play of Corpus Christi day.'

The plays continued to be performed in Kilkenny until the Cromwellians gained control of the Corporation in the 1650s.

The Corpus Christi fair at Kilkenny brought traders and others from far and wide. In the *Calendar of Justiciary Rolls 1305–07, 221*, we read of the case of the servingman of William Douce, a Dublin merchant, who was proceeding there with a pack train of wearing apparel in 1306 when he fell in with a lady known as Christine la Sadelhackere in the town of Naas. What transpired is not specified, but in the morning a box containing linen, shoes and hose to the value of twenty pence was missing, and the whole matter was thrashed out in open court, much to the annoyance of all concerned.

Stanihurst's Chronicle tells of another interesting Dublin ceremony at Corpus Christi.

In 1514 when the Earls of Kildare and Ormond had met at St Patrick's Cathedral, Dublin, to settle their disputes, the citizens of Dublin became incensed against Ormond and his followers and invaded the church and shot arrows at random, by which a man named Blandfield was killed. Naturally this dreadful sacrilege aroused the ecclesiastical authorities, and a legate came from Rome to investigate the matter. The Chronicle goes on to tell us:

'The legat upon his arrival indicated the city for this execrable offense: but at length by the procurement as well of the archbishop as of all the clergie, he was weighed to give the citizens absolution with this caveat, that in detestation of so horrible a fact, and ad perpetuam rei memoriam, the Maior of Dublin should go bare-footed through the citie in open procession before the sacrament, on Corpus Christi daie, which penitent satisfaction was after in everie such procession dulie accomplished.'

This penitential exercise continued until the Reformation. In the nineteenth century when Catholics again became Mayors of Dublin, there was some suggestion that the custom should be revived but these were, in some opinions unfortunately, disregarded.

Midsummer

This description of the celebration of Midsummer in the western part of County Limerick was written in 1943 by an old schoolmaster who had lived in the locality since the beginning of the century:

'This feast as far as my experience goes has always been known in West Limerick as St John's Eve or sometimes Bonfire Night. Older people called it *Oiche an teine chnáimh* and I have heard the elders call it *Teine Féil' Eóin*.

'At the present time the observance is almost entirely confined to children who still on 23 June, St John's Eve, gather sticks etc. and light small bonfires to carry on the time-honoured custom. But old people of thirty years ago and more remembered how the fire used to be lit exactly at sunset and had to be watched and tended till long after mid-night. Prayers used to be said to obtain God's blessing on the crops then at the peak-point of summer bloom. In Athea a circular bonfire was made near the blessed well where the patron saint of the parish, St Bartholemew, was honoured (as also the Blessed Virgin and St John).

'Round the fire gathered young and old. There was much fun and music: a dance was started and games were played while some young men competed in casting weights or in feats of strength, speed or agility. I gathered that it was mostly women who shared in the prayers for the gardens and for good weather. Neglect in this respect might lead to a bad harvest or cause "the white trout not to come up the river" (as they usually did with the mid-summer floods). This neglect too might bring a "scab" on the corn or disease on the potatoes.

'Unless the weather proved too cold, summer swimming in the river began on St John's Day and the observance of the festival was supposed to eliminate all danger of drowning. The Well and bonfire site were close to the parish grave-yard, and prayers for the dead were always included in the religious ceremonies of bonfire-night in the townland of Templeathea.

'Old people now living do not remember these things but were told of them by their elders. I know Athea for the past forty years and the only fires of this kind I saw here were those made by young people in a dozen different places – fires made of turf and furze bushes with other fire-wood. I often heard songs sung there and concertina music, or more rarely the local fiddler would be coaxed out to the fire. The interest of the elders in the festival had clearly died out.

'However in my early youth near Knockaderry, County Limerick, I remember similar circular fires and a curious custom repeated each St John's Eve. The young people used to gather from the marshy ground near the river Deel the large leaf and strong stem the *"hocusfian"* as it was called and each youth armed with one of these went around lightly striking each person that he or she met. This was supposed to protect those who were struck from illness and evil influences during the coming year. Afterwards, the *hocus* stems were thrown into the fire. Here, too, people threw into the fire specimens of the most troublesome weeds in the district – this was supposed to protect the fields from these weeds.

'Old people told me that it was customary to jump over the fire from side to side. Some wise elders claimed to be able to tell, from the manner of jumping and the flickering of the fire, whether the jumpers were guilty or not of certain misdemeanours, such as theft or mis-behaviour with women.

'I was told by the old people that Father Maurice Dinneen, P.P. about 1730, on a certain St John's Eve at the fire exorcized the demon from a young girl. Before he was expelled the devil had to answer some very strange questions set by the priest.

'In Athea parish the Parish Priest, in the early nineteenth century, attended the bonfire and led the prayers.

'Some people used to take the ashes from the fire then extinct on St John's morning to scatter them on their fields etc. At the close of the festival too about after midnight any man who had built a new house or had nearly completed it took from the bonfire a shovel of seed or a *sgiath* of red hot sods to his new home so that the very first fire there should be started by the *Teine Féil' Eóin*. Others took similar seed to their homes to bring them good luck in crops and stock and to ensure their having children to succeed to their "possessions".

'I was returning from Newcastle West on the evening of St John's

135

Day, June 24th, of this year when I saw a group of youngsters round a fire at Knockanare cross-roads.

'I saw an old man come out of a house near-by. He said to the children "ye are late now to bring John's blessing on the year". What he meant was that the fire, to have beneficent power should have been lighted on the eve of the festival.

'About the year 1905 a very old man told me that his grandfather had told him that in his young day – in the late eighteenth century – the young men of Athea used to walk through the fields with lighted torches and then cast these into the fire. This was supposed to bring a blessing on the fields and protect the crops from harm. Another old man told me that one man known as *Giolla an teine* was selected to supervise and direct the ceremonies at the fire.

'It was widely believed that a house built on a path frequented by the fairies and other such uncanny travellers would suffer from midnight noises or supernatural manifestations. Perhaps too, ill-luck in the farm or personal illness etc. might afflict the family. One remedy for these evils was to bring on St John's Eve portion of the blessed fire and to build with them on the path in several places small fires which would be left burning until morning.

'There were certain things connected with *piseóga* that people considered they were well rid of by throwing them into the bonfire. As far as I am aware nothing like that is done in our day although *piseóga* and the harm they do are a strong belief still in Athea. As an illustration permit me to recount a peculiar incident of former days here. On the 23rd of June 1904 I was seated in a farm-house in Athea among a few old friends. The man of the house, John O'Connor (1816–1916), then an old hale, hearty man, had just come in, passing the local bonfire on the road-side near the house. He had taken a few drinks in town and was in good form for conversation and spoke about St John's Eve. He recalled how an old fellow of the place had on a former occasion thrown something into the midsummer fire. I asked him what was the nature of the thing he burned as I noticed that two other old men present seemed highly amused.

'He explained the whole business in fluent Irish as he did not wish some of those present to understand him. It seems that over one hundred years before a girl of the parish gave birth to a child – a baby girl. The father of this child was said to be a priest – an unheard of thing.

'Popular superstition attributed strange powers to this girl's inner

136

garment – the *léine céile shagairt*. Thus while the girl lived this inner garment was ever getting lost or torn. If left on a hedge it was either stolen or had a large piece torn out of it.

'If there happened to be a couple in the parish married for quite a long time without any child forthcoming it was advisable then to procure by stealth a patch of that girl's chemise and stitch it on to the *léine mná* of the childless wife. Children then were supposed to arrive as a matter of course.

'At any rate old Johnny's story told how a certain old fellow of the place after his marriage for quite a time had no children. Recourse was had to a patch of that *léine mná* abstracted by stealth and one by one the children arrived. When the couple had six children the old lad thought he had quite enough and hearing of the *teine Féil' Eóin* in the vicinity took this inner garment complete with patch and got rid of it in the great bonfire.

'Now his wife who did not understand the true significance of this patch was furiously angry over the taking of her garment, and a neighbour's wife was called in to explain matters so that peace reigned again. But as old Johnny explained, the spell of this *piseóg* remained and at the end the couple had over a dozen children in all. This explained to me the evident amusement of the other old men present.

'To come back to the point I wished to make clear I found after many enquiries that there was in old times a custom of burning in the *Teine Féil' Eóin* things used in *piseóga* e.g. a spancel, eggs, meat, part of a dead animal or piece of cloth left on a neighbour's property with certain ceremonies to cause loss etc. to that neighbour.

'It also was customary that small objects of piety, such as rosary beads, little statues or scapulars, when they became broken or worn out, were destroyed without disrespect by being burned in the Midsummer Fire.'

The Midsummer Fire

The midsummer ceremonies were almost all connected with the Midsummer fire, and in the greater part of Ireland were observed on 23 June, the eve of the feast of St John the Baptist.

It is clear that a distinction can be made between two fire traditions. On the one hand a large communal fire lit by the inhabitants of the whole townland or village, or of several townlands or even of the whole parish. Such communal fires were lit, in the past, in places in every county in Ireland.

On the other hand there were small fires lit by the members of each household, or on each farm, at which ceremonies, to be described below, were performed for the benefit of that particular household or farm. These, too, were lit in most parts of Ireland, but were, at least in recent tradition, not as widely known as the large communal fires. There is one small area in the south-west, in the Kenmare – Castletownbeare – Bantry – Skibbereen districts, where only the small family fires were lit.

In general it may be said that the large communal fires were mainly celebrated noisily by music, dancing, singing and similar merrymaking, with other ceremonies as a preliminary or a sequel, while the family fire was a quiet affair in which the protective ceremonies were the main concern of those present, and the only merrymaking was the playing of the younger children about the small fire.

Often the communal fires were very large, sometimes so large that a ladder had to be procured to add the last bundles of fuel to the top of the pile. For days beforehand the children and the young people had collected fuel of all kinds, turf, wood, sticks, bushes and brambles – indeed anything which would burn. An old tar or oil barrel or the tarred fragments of an old boat or *currach* were especially welcome. At some recent fires old motor or bicycle tyres added to the blaze, and to the general merriment when the unpleasant smell of burning rubber was blown towards a dwelling house and brought loud complaints from its occupants.

Often the gatherers went from house to house asking for fuel, and, as it was held to be unlucky as well as mean to refuse, they were given not only inflammable rubbish of which the household was glad to be rid, but also turf and firewood. A refusal might result in fuel being stolen, and some householders hid or guarded their fuel store. At some fires the names of generous donors were called out and the crowd responded with cheers, while the names of the niggardly, likewise announced were met with booing and catcalls. In parts of County Clare the young people carried charred sticks or dead embers from the fire to the houses of the generous and placed them on the kitchen hearth, while they threw ashes from the fire on the threshold of the house where they had been refused.

In many places old bones were added to the pile of fuel or thrown into the fire after it was lit, for the most part merely as additional fuel but possibly with some ceremonial intent in former times. Usually the term in common use, 'bonfire', is explained by statement such as 'oh, they burned bones in the fires long ago', while in one case, mentioned by Mrs Jeanne Cooper Foster in *Ulster Folklore*, 26, a much more partisan explanation was given:

'I was much interested in an experience which some acquaintances of mine had last midsummer Eve (1950) at Portnablagh, Donegal. They were watching the fires on the hill-tops and they asked a group of children why the bonfires were lighted. They received the disconcerting reply that they were burning the Protestants' bones!'

There was much rivalry as to which group might have the largest fire; the place noted for a mighty blaze had a reputation to keep up, while others tried to equal or outshine their efforts. Some over-enthusiastic fuel-collectors did not hesitate to raid the fuel heap being gathered for another fire, and disputes or even fights might ensue. Sometimes the competition was so fierce that a rival band might set fire to a fuel pile a day or two before the festival.

Usually there was a set place in each district for the fire, at a crossroads or street corner, on a commonage, on a limekiln, on a height or in some other 'public' place. Sometimes the fire was made on top of a large rock outcrop. In a few places, such as Tinnakilla, County Limerick, or Tawnatruffan, County Sligo, the fire was built on top of a dolmen, and the capstones of some dolmens have been cracked by this thoughtless act, which clearly was motivated only by the wish to have a high platform for the fire.

Usually the fire was made on or beside an open space where the people could assemble and disport themselves. Sometimes seats were brought or extemporized to accommodate the elderly and those wearied by the frolicking and dancing.

The fire was lit about nightfall, and in many places a knowledgable old man was requested to light it and to say the traditional prayer for the occasion, one version of which runs:

In onóir do Dhia agus do Naomh Eoin, agus chun toraidh agus chun tairbhe ar ár gcur agus ar ár saothar, in ainm an Athar agus an Mhic agus an Spirid Naoimh, Amen –

'In the honour of God and of St John, to the fruitfulness and profit of our planting and our work, in the name of the Father and of the Son and of the Holy Spirit, Amen.'

Around the fire were assembled all the people of the locality, from the smallest children to the oldest men and women. In many places the older people began the proceedings by reciting prayers; these were the conventional Catholic prayers, the *Pater*, *Ave* and *Gloria*, repeated three or nine times, or a decade or five decades of the rosary. In places the assembled people knelt down to pray – the present writer joined in such prayers at Waterville, County Kerry, on St John's Eve in 1951. In places in Connaught and Ulster the people walked sunwise around the fire while praying, usually counting the prayers on rosary beads, sometimes keeping tally by holding in the hand a small pebble for each prayer to be said and throwing one into the fire as each prayer is concluded.

Prayers done, the merrymaking began. By now the fire was well ablaze and as flames and sparks shot up, the crowd raised loud cheers, often augmented by blowing on horns or beating on tin-cans. Musicians struck up and the young men led out their partners to dance. Every now and then the dancing was interspersed by songs, individual dances, recitations, storytelling and instrumental solos, as notable performers were called upon to exhibit their party pieces.

At intervals more fuel was thrown on the fire, and cheers were again raised when flames and sparks shot up. Often the young men and boys waved burning bushes in the air or thrust in a pitchfork to impale and hold up a blazing piece of wood. Sometimes more rowdy fellows pelted each other with burning embers, although the more sedate were quick to suppress behaviour of this kind.

A favourite pastime of the younger boys was to snatch burning sticks from the fire and throw these as high into the air as they could. In an article in *The Irish Times* (9 May 1970) Hilary Pyle recalls the feelings of John Millington Synge and his friend Jack B. Yeats at this sight in Belmullet, County Mayo in 1905. They had been saddened by the depressed state of the people of the area.

' "Yet," Synge summed up, "the impression one gets of the whole life is not a gloomy one. Last night was St John's Eve, and bonfires – a relic of Druidical rites – were lighted all over the country, the largest of all being placed in the town square of Belmullet, where a crowd of small boys shrieked and cheered and threw up firebrands for hours together."

'Yeats remembered a little girl in the crowd, in an ecstasy of pleasure and dread, clutching Synge by the hand, and standing close in his shadow until the fiery games were done.'

In places, particularly in west Munster, holy water was sprinkled on or about the fire before or immediately after it was lit, usually by one of

140

17 Midsummer Eve in Belmullet (Jack B. Yeats)

the older people but in parts of County Cork the youngest child was asked to do this. Often, as on other festivals, there was a general sprinkling of holy water on the house and its occupants, the farm buildings, livestock and growing crops, by prayers invoking God's blessing on everybody and everything.

In a few, widely separated places there is a tradition of the making and setting up of an effigy to represent a human figure, made of old garments or a sack, wrapped about sticks and stuffed with straw or dried grass. In north Kerry this figure was 'seated' on a fence near the fire. In places in County Cork it was raised on a pole near the fire. Later the figure had fire set to it or was thrown into the bonfire. No explanation is forthcoming as to whom or what this effigy represented, but in the Draperstown district of County Derry it was said to portray a turncoat or traitor to the Irish cause and had abuse and stones pelted at it before it was burned in the fire.

There was a common practice of burning away scrub, furze, heather and other growths to clear land or improve grazing, and this was sometimes forbidden by landlord or local authority because of danger to trees or to nesting game birds. Ordinarily the setting of fire in such cases was quickly detected, the fire extinguished and the fire-setters penalized. On Midsummer Eve, however, fires blazing on all sides gave cover to this kind of fire-setting, so that not only could the blaze take hold but it could be blamed upon sparks or embers blowing from a bonfire, or to high spirits or rowdyism on the part of anonymous revellers. There were cases, too, where old animosities led to a farmer's hedge or grove being set alight under the cover of the Midsummer fire.

At some bonfires part of the revelry was eating and drinking; those attending brought food and drink and either themselves consumed them or added them to a common store to be shared out all around.

In Connaught the main and usually the only dish was 'goody' – white 'shop' bread soaked in hot milk (sometimes stolen from the neighbours' cows) and flavoured with sugar and spice. This was made in a large iron pot either set upon the bonfire or heated on a smaller fire nearby. The participants brought their own spoons and bowls or plates.

In Sligo town children went around during the day asking for 'a penny for the bonfire', and the money collected was spent on sweets and other dainties which they ate that evening at the fire. At many fires the older men passed about among themselves bottles of whiskey or *poitín*, not neglecting to invite the old ladies to share in the treat, and sometimes the young men collected money to buy a barrel of beer or porter which was shared out and drunk at the fire.

Sometimes over-zealous policemen tried to stop the bonfires. The *Freeman's Journal* reported on 29 June 1888:

'A large number of people were summoned by the police at the Westport Petty Sessions (Mayo) for lighting bonfires on St John's Eve. The Rev Father Begley pointed out that those bonfires never gave the least inconvenience, that they were a source of innocent amusement to the people throughout the country, and that a district so peaceable as Westport should not be exasperated by this unjustifiable interference on the part of the police officers. There never was such a shameless attempt to disturb the peace of any town. Mr Triscott, District Inspector, said there was no part of Ireland or the kingdom so peaceable as Westport. At the same time he pressed the charge against the accused. The Bench, consisting of three local magistrates and one R.M., having heard one case, were unanimous in dismissing all the cases, observing that it was "monstrous" to have such cases brought into court.'

Robert Gibbings recalls, in *Sweet Cork Of Thee*, 151-2, the answer made by his father, who was the Church of Ireland rector of Carrigrohane, County Cork, to a killjoy who smelled paganism or popery in the fire:

'On that particular St John's Eve of which I was telling we had a grand fire. It was so splendid that no horse would pass the crossroads. Well, what matter? 'Twas only a few miles extra to go round the other way. There was a crowd of people of all ages, and while some of them attended to the fire, throwing on extra fuel, others danced to an accordeon. It was great fun to throw a lighted brand high into the air and watch the sparks that marked its flight. If it fell in a field, it could only do good. In many parts of Ireland at that time it was the custom deliberately to throw the brands into the fields, believing as in ancient times that it would increase the crops, though not realizing that it was indeed an offering to the fire god.

'And in the middle of it all, when the higher flames had subsided and we were jumping through the fire, a solemn, miserable-looking man came up to my father. "Have you forgotten Ezekiel and Jeremiah?" he asked "Aren't you ashamed to be putting your children through the fire of Moloch?"

' "Ah, for goodness sake, let the innocent children enjoy themselves" said my father.'

Jumping over the Fire

The custom of jumping over the Midsummer fire was known all over Ireland. Sir William Wilde, (*Irish Popular Superstitions*, 49) gives some of the benefits which the jumpers expected:

'If a man was about to perform a long journey, he leaped backwards and forwards three times through the fire, to give him success in his undertaking. If about to wed he did it to purify himself for the marriage state. If going to undertake some hazardous enterprise, he passed through the fire to render himself invulnerable. As the fire sunk low, the girls tript across it to procure good husbands; women great with child might be seen stepping through it to ensure a happy delivery, and children were also carried across the smouldering ashes, as of old among the Canaanites.'

In many places, and especially in south Leinster, young men and women joined hands in couples and jumped together. This probably was nothing more than a mild flirtation, but often the onlookers took it for granted that there was some intention of marriage between the pair, and the wiseacres claimed to be able to foretell the outcome from the way in which the flames flickered as the couple jumped.

For the most part, the jumpers were the boys and young men and the jumping merely an exhibition of bravado in which daring leaps drew applause and there was much rivalry among the jumpers. However, all the reasons given by Wilde, above, are still remembered in tradition, and others, too, are given – jumping through the flames brought health and long life and protected the jumpers from accidents, ailments, epidemic disease and the effects of witchcraft or the evil eye.

The Family Fire

As mentioned above, there was a widespread custom of each household lighting a fire at which ceremonies for the protection of the house and the farmyard, the family, the livestock and the crops were performed. This fire usually was small, no more than one or two furze bushes, or a little heap of twigs, or a sod or two of blazing turf from the kitchen hearth. It was lit in the farmyard, or, at least, close to the house, and as soon as the brief ritual was completed, the fire was allowed to die out, or was quenched, and the active members of the household went off to join the throng at the communal bonfire.

Should there, however, have been a recent death in the family the

144

fire was not lit, and no member of the household went to the 'big' fire. This custom was observed in the case of other festivals also; during the period of mourning for a recently dead relative people did not join in any public merrymaking.

The Growing Crops

All the crops grown on the farm, corn, flax, potatoes, vegetables, fruit-trees, were preserved from harm by the fire, which, it was held, increased the yield, ensured a good harvest and kept away blight, rust and other plant diseases. To ensure adequate protection the fire had to be applied to the fields and this was done in a number of ways.

Where possible the fire was lit where the smoke would be carried by the wind over the more important crops, and the same benefit was gained by those who were lucky enough to have the smoke from the common fire drifting over their fields.

Most people took embers, or ashes from the family fire or from the 'big' fire and threw a portion into each field, or into the four corners of each field.

In places a glowing ember was thrown as far as possible into the growing crop, and if the growth was high enough to hide the glow completely, this was an especially good omen.

Many people took a long-stemmed bush to the fire, lit this and threw it into the crop or carried it through the field. Formerly this was done more elaborately. Special torches made of bushes, of bunches of bog-deal slips, of tightly bound bundles of reeds, or of bunches of straw or oil-soaked rags or sods of turf dipped in oil or grease and borne aloft on poles or pitchforks were lit at the fire and carried around and through the fields and gardens. Often each member of the household had such a torch, and they formed a little procession in making the circuit. The torches were variously called *soip Seáin,* 'cliars', 'wisps' and other local names. Sir Henry Piers saw them in Westmeath in 1682:

'On the eves of St John Baptist and St Peter, they always have in every town a bonfire, late in the evenings, and carry about bundles of reeds fast tied and fired; these being dry will last long, and flame better than a torch, and be a pleasing divertive prospect to the distant beholder; a stranger would go near to imagine the whole country was on fire.'

Amhlaoibh Ó Súilleabháin remarked on them in Callan in 1831:

145

'*Teine cnámh agus sop Seaghain ar gach ardán* – a bonfire and a John's wisp on every height.'

In some places the torches or burning bushes were planted in the ground and allowed to burn out.

If, for any reason, the embers or ashes could not be brought from the fire to the fields on Midsummer eve, the blessing might still be conferred next day by procuring ashes or cinders from the fire and putting these in the crops; this, however, was only a second-best expedient and not at all as potent or as certain as the real ceremony.

There was, for some, an inherent danger in the cinders or ashes in the fields, for it was believed that if these were stolen on the same night by ill-disposed persons, they could be used to cast a spell upon the crops and steal away the 'increase'.

The Cattle at Midsummer

On most Irish farms the milking cattle were not only the most valuable of the livestock, but also the most susceptible of harm both by natural ailment and by magical influence, and over these animals in particular the protection of the Midsummer fire was extended.

If a farmer's field was so situated that the smoke from the communal fire blew over it, then the cows were pastured in that field on Midsummer eve. Equal benefit was obtained from kindling the family fire so that the smoke drifted over the cattle, or by putting lighted brands, embers or ashes from the fire into the pasture fields and paddocks.

Ashes, embers, or charred sticks from the fire might be placed in the dairy to bring good luck and keep milk and butter safe from evil magic. Some people used a charred stick to mark a cross on the dairy door and on the churns and firkins to keep harm away or carried a burning torch or bush around the byre and dairy.

Very often the cows were herded together and driven through the smoke or over the embers of the fire, or between two fires or along a path or through a gap or gate beside which a fire had been lit. The protection of the fire could also be given by touching the animals with a smouldering torch or bush or by holding a burning bush over them. In County Clare the touch on the back with a burning bush ensured that the cows would have healthy calves.

Others singed the cows' hair or strewed ashes from the fire over them. A potent cure for cattle ailments was made by blending with water ashes from the fire, for which intent some of the ashes were carefully preserved. This was a favourite remedy in the northern parts of Ireland for 'elf-shot' animals.

For health reasons some people bled their cattle in the summer, and it was held that Midsummer was the best time to do this. In County Waterford some of the drawn blood was blended with water and with ashes from the fire, and given to the cows to drink.

The Dwellinghouse at Midsummer

The dwellinghouse and its inhabitants could share in the blessing of the fire. In many places it was customary to bring back from the communal bonfire embers or charred fragments of turf or wood and put these on the domestic hearth. Some people kept cinders or ashes from the fire in the house for luck, others because their keeping was believed to ensure a peaceful death to ailing old people. The ashes had curative properties for humans. Mixed with water they were drunk for internal disorders and also used to cleanse and bathe wounds, sores and swellings.

To neglect to bring home an ember from the fire, or to keep cinders or ashes in the house was, for many, to invite unpleasant consequences, as is recalled by a lady who worked as a district nurse on the Aran Islands, and who published a most interesting account of her experiences there. *Glimpses of my Life in Aran*, by B. N. Hedderman, 1917, tells this (p. 95) of a young man who needed treatment for a badly infected finger:

' "Listen to me," I said, "you do not understand the importance of keeping the wound clean," and then I gave a little instruction on germs. He could not understand how they lived in the air, in food, and in water, and most singularly resented his own finger being singled out as an abode for these minute "foreigners".

'His father, who was sitting in a chair in the corner, got up, and shaking a closed fist, with a dozen loud imprecations, exclaimed, "I knew it would be like this; he did not take in a red coal from the fire on St John's night." '

Herb Gathering

About this time of the year, the St John's wort (*Hypericum perforatum*) was gathered for medicinal purposes, and many held that it

147

must be picked on St John's Eve or at least between that day and 'Old St John's Day' or 'little St John's Day' (variously 29 June and 4 July). Other herbs gathered at this season had special virtues; an eighteenth century medical work prescribes for a child who gets fits or spasms while asleep: *An lus mór 's an fothrom do bhuaint eidir dhá fhéil St Seáin agus a mbruith ar uisge trí teorann, a ccur suas a mbuittéal agus a ccumhdach go mbiadh uacaid agat leo . . .* ('foxglove and figwort to be gathered between the two feasts of St John, boiled in the water of three boundaries, bottled and kept until required').

Yarrow (*Achillea millefolium*) was gathered at this season for medicinal use. It was also used in marriage divination by girls who recited while plucking it these words:

> Good morrow, good yarrow, good morrow to thee
> Send me this night my true love to see
> The clothes that he'll wear, the colour of his hair
> And if he'll wed me.

The plant was put under the pillow and the girl dreamed of her future husband.

In east County Cork and in County Waterford the herb variously called '*mugúird*', '*bogúird*', 'mugwort' (*Artemisia vulgaris*) was gathered for medicinal and other purposes. Some kept it in the house for luck, some threw it on the fire for the same purpose. Others kept it in the house, and, as a remedy, singed it and got the patient to inhale the smoke.

Other Midsummer Beliefs and Customs

Fitzgerald and McGregor's *History of Limerick* (ii, 1827, 540–1) mentions the passing of an old custom of Limerick city:

'The tradesmen have laid aside the custom of marching on Midsummer-day, when, arranged under their respective leaders, decorated with sashes, ribbons, and flowers, and accompanied with a band of· musicians, and the shouts of the delighted populace, they proceeded through the principal streets of the city, while their merry-men played a thousand antic tricks, and the day generally ended in a terrible fight between the Garryowen and Thomond-gate boys, (the tradesmen of the north and south suburbs.)'

What seems to be an identical custom in Galway is described in greater detail in Hardiman's *History of Galway*, 295. Here the celebrants were the fishermen of the Claddagh processing through Galway City:

'The Nativity of St John the Baptist (24th June) they celebrate by a very peculiar kind of pageantry. On the evening of that day the young and old assemble at the head of the village; and their mayor, whose orders are decisive, adjusts the rank, order and precedence of this curious procession. They then set out, headed by a band of music, and march with loud and continued huzzas and acclamations of joy, accompanied by crowds of people, through the principal streets and suburbs of the town: the young men all uniformly arrayed in short white jackets, with silken sashes, their hats ornamented with ribbons and flowers, and upwards of sixty or seventy of the number bearing long poles and standards with suitable devices which are in general emblematic of their profession. To heighten the merriment of this festive scene, two of the stoutest disguised in masks, and entirely covered with party-coloured rags as "merrymen" with many antic tricks and gambols make way for the remainder. In the course of their progress they stop with loud cheerings and salutations opposite the houses of the principal inhabitants, from whom they generally receive money on the occasion. Having at length regained their village, they assemble in groups, dancing round, and sometimes leaping and running through their bonfires, never forgetting to bring home part of the fire, which they consider sacred; and thus the night ends as the day began, in one continued scene of mirth and rejoicing.'

Other fishermen celebrated too. Mrs Jeanne Cooper Foster, in *Ulster Folklore*, 53, tells us:

'In most fishing districts, St John's Day is an important date. In some places the boats and nets are blessed, and at Port Ballintrae, Co. Antrim, the salmon-fishermen of the River Bush hold a communal dinner which is considered *the* event of the year. It is known locally as "The Salmon Dinner", and the menu consists of fish-soup, freshly-caught salmon, new potatoes, and *Bushmills* whiskey.'

In many places along the coast this is the time when summer fishing begins, and the period immediately before Midsummer sees boats, nets and other gear being repaired and made ready. Inland, too, the fishermen are expectant, as sea-trout enter many rivers at this period.

In Dublin City the main event was the pattern at St John's Well, Kilmainham, thus described by Weston St. John Joyce (*Neighbourhood of Dublin*, 340–342):

149

'A pattern was formerly held here on St John's Day (24th June), and to accommodate the votaries, a number of tents and booths used to be erected, giving the place the appearance of a fair. As might be expected, an institution of the kind so near a large city, attracted a mixed class of patrons, and the drunkenness and debauchery by which it in time became characterized, made it such a nuisance that efforts were made on several occasions, by the clergy and others, in the eighteenth and nineteenth centuries, to have it suppressed. The observances lingered on, however, and down to about 1835, on each anniversary there assembled in the fields adjoining the road, a number of country carts fashioned into improvised booths in the manner usual at the time, by blankets, patchwork quilts, etc., stretched on arched wattles, while in all directions might be seen turf and bramble fires with pots swinging over them, containing legs of mutton, pigs' feet, bacon, potatoes, cabbage, and other appetising delicacies for the hungry multitude. Around the well collected the votaries with tumblers or horn goblets, mixing whiskey with its saintly waters, or sleeping off the effects of this irreverent mixture.

'In 1538 Doctor Staples, Bishop of Meath, preached to the multitude assembled at St John's Well against the celebrated Archbishop Browne, of Dublin, of which the latter bitterly complains in a letter preserved in the State Papers.

'In 1710, the proceedings at this well having attracted public attention, the Irish House of Commons passed a resolution declaring that the assemblages of devotees here were a menace and a danger to the public peace of the kingdom, and prescribed fines, whippings, and imprisonments as the penalties for these 'dangerous, tumultuous, and unlawful assemblies', which, as Dalton quaintly remarks, was certainly a severer penance than these persons intended to inflict upon themselves.

'Even up to the time of its disappearance, the well was not without a few old pilgrims on St John's Day, some for devotional purposes, and others to procure some of the water, which on the anniversary was believed to possess a peculiar sanctity.'

As may be expected, St John the Baptist is the patron of many holy wells, and at these many patterns and pilgrimages were held on his feast day.

The people of Irishtown, Kilkenny, held high revel on this day, until their portrieve, a certain Thomas Tobin, made an end to the custom, apparently to save money, in 1608. The town clerk entered the following complaint in the minute book of the Corporation of Irish-town:

'Where there hath been, tyme oute of mynde, used by the Portrieve of the Irishtowne to keepe a solemne feaste upon St John Baptist's Eve, with the helpes and aydes of th'enhabitants, for the Burgesses of the Irishtowne; by which feaste none ever tofore toke losse, butt rather gayne, this honest man, by whose means wee know not, did discontinue that good and laudable custom, to what ende, God he knoweth.'

For many families in west Ulster and west Connaught this was a sad occasion, for Midsummer was the time for men to travel as migratory labourers to work in the harvest in England and Scotland. Sons parted with their parents and husbands with their wives and children, and would not see them again until late Autumn or early Winter. Because of this exodus the turf must be saved and the potatoes earthed up before the migrants departed.

Change in the weather was generally expected about Midsummer, the weather sequence for which the farmers hoped being wet weather before the festival and dry after.

About this time the cuckoo ceased to call, and the children were told that he had flown away to Spain.

People who were ill hoped for improvement, and it was generally believed that even those seriously ill, if they survived over Midsummer, would live on at least until Autumn.

Many fairs were held on St John's Day; almanacs of about 1750, before the official acceptance in Ireland of the Gregorian calendar and the consequent change in the dates of fairs, list forty-six towns and other sites at which large fairs were held on this date. As we have noted, fairs were as much occasions of entertainment and merryment as of buying and selling. At a season of the year with long hours of daylight and prevailing fine weather there was no hardship in travelling long distances or in spending a night or two sleeping under a cart or in an improvised shelter. Thus fairs and patterns at this time, and, indeed, throughout the summer, attracted large crowds bent upon enjoyment.

At many of these assemblies it was customary to set up a decorated pole on the assembly ground to form a central point. Nicholas O'Kearney writing for the *Transactions of the Kilkenny Archaeological Society* (i, 1849–51, 378), describes these poles:

'It must be observed that the poles set up on St John's day were always erected where fairs, "patterns", or any other merry-making took place; perhaps the assemblies were originally instituted in consequence of setting up the poles in those places. The midsummer-pole was always called *craebh*, and was dressed with considerable taste with flowers and silk kerchiefs and ribbons; it was generally as lofty as the mast of a sloop, and on its top a small basket of cakes or gingerbread, and a large bunch of parti-coloured worsted garters were tied. The best musician attending the assembly was always selected to perform at the foot of the *craebh*, or pole; and the best dancers vied with one another for the honour of winning the gingerbread and garters – the young man got the garters, and the lady the gingerbread. The winners were held in as high estimation, as if, in days of yore, they had won the first prize at the Olympic games; for they were said – *'gur bhuain siad an chraebh as lár an aenaigh,'* i.e., that they bore away the prize from the whole assembly; and many a sweet Irish ditty resounded their praises, and it was always their own fault if they remained unmarried to contest for the next anniversary prize. It is a pity that the local clergy found excuses sufficiently strong to suppress these innocent amusements – for innocent they certainly were, in the absence of extraneous vice, since the performers knew not the origin of their diversions.'

In several parts of north Connaught and west Ulster the story is told that St John was martyred by being burned alive, and that the Midsummer fires lighted on St John's Eve, 23 June, are in pious commemoration of the saint's death.

Another story current in Connaught was more circumstantial. It told how the Norsemen quartered a rapacious warrior in every house in Ireland and how the Irish plotted to destroy them. The fires lighted at Midsummer were the general signal for attack, and on that evening each household seized and strangled its unwelcome guest. Antoine Ó Reachtúire includes this in his long historical poem *Caisimirt na Sceiche* (Hyde: *Abhráin an Reachtúire*, 1903, p. 308):

> *Preab an Ríoghachta suas i n-éinfheacht*
> *Tugadh focal na faire i mbéal gach aén neach*
> *Lucht faire do thachtadh agus soip do shéideadh*
> *Oidhche Fhéile San Seághain ins gach cearda d'Eirinn*
>
> *(The Kingdom sprang up together*
> *The watchword was given in everyone's mouth,*
> *To strangle the sentinels and to blow wisps*
> *On St John's Eve in every part of Ireland).*

A third story, from County Limerick, is reported by 'Mannanaan Mac Lir' in *Journal of the Cork Historical and Archaeological Society,* ii, 1896, 366–7, and tells of the death of Áine 'a knowledgable woman' who 'used be going with the good people':

'At last, when dying, which was on St John's eve, her friends "the good people" crowded out from every *lios* or *rath* throughout Ireland, they came trooping towards Aine's residence (Knockainey), each one carrying a lighted torch or *cliar* in honour of Aine. And thus it is that a custom which originated in honour of Aine, is still carried on as a remembrance of her, and from this custom she is known as *Aine cliar* ever since."

SS Peter and Paul

Although the Midsummer fire was lit on 23 June, St John's Eve, in most parts of Ireland, there is a large area in the east, stretching from Monaghan to Wexford where the fire was lit on 28 June, the eve of the feast of SS Peter and Paul.

In places, fires were lit on both of these days. As mentioned above Sir Henry Piers noted this in County Westmeath in 1682: 'On the eves of St John Baptist and St Peter they always have in every town a bonfire. . . . .', while Amhlaoibh Ó Súilleabháin saw fires and 'wisps' on both days in Callan, County Kilkenny, about 1830.

Other places with traditions of fires on both days are in Counties· Armagh, Monaghan, Louth, Meath, Longford and Leitrim.

E. E. Evans suggests (*Irish Folk Ways*, 275) that the fire on St Peter's Eve may be due to English influence. This may well be, as the custom was known in the Anglo-Norman settlements of South Leinster at an early date. *The Calendar of Justiciary Rolls, Ireland,* records a case in New Ross in the year 1305 where a dispute arose over the bonfire:

'And Robert Seinde says that the mariners of Wynchelese were not wounded by him. But it is well known that at the vigil of SS Peter and Paul the men commonly staying up at night and making fire in the streets, as is the custom, went to a boat laden with firewood of Thomas Coytif, and took wood from it to make a fire; which Thomas learning, he hurried there, and a contention being stirred there and a great cry raised, Robert Seinde having one servingman with him, turned there to know the cause of the outcry, and met the mariners of Wynchelese, who attacked and beat him, so that he scarcely escaped from them, without his having done them any trespass. And because the mariners likewise wounded his servingman, so that his life was despaired of (in fact, he died within six days), Robert Russell as sovereign of the town, hue and cry being raised, took with him the posse of the town, and fought the malefactors, so that he drove them to their ships, where they remained defending themselves. And he prays that this be enquired. Robert Russell likewise. Let the Sheriff have a jury at the quinzaine of S Michael, nisi prius, etc.'

More than two hundred years later another incident in the same town on the same festival found its way into the official record. In a letter dated 16 July 1538 and preserved in the State Paper Office, London, the Earl of Ormond reported (*Annuary of the Kilkenny and South-East of Ireland Archaeological Society*, Vol. I, part 1, 1855, pp. 35–6):

'This Sainte Petiris Evin laste paste, at Rosse, when the folke of the towne toke ther station aboute the fyrys, and beinge toward the abbay of the freres in their said station, Watkyne Apoell, oon Baker, and three or foure Englishmen, prepensidly retornede from the Suf-frayne and his brethern, and came towarde the condyt of the towne, affermynge that it was to wayshe a hatt of cheries, whiche he hade then in his hande; and the streth being voyde of folke, the said Watkyne and his fellawes dud meth with Cahir McArtes standarthe berrer, and 3 more of the said Cahir's men, beinge at peace, and beholdynge the fyrys, and station of the towne, under a pentice besides the said condite of water, and unawisidly dud drawe ther daggers, and stickide the said Cahirs men with the same, wherby the said standartberer was oute of hande slayne, and the residue beinge wondide to deathe, flede away, and parte of them constraynide to take the river; and when the Suffrain herde herof, he soghte for the said Watkyne and mete him at his dore, eatinge of the said cherryes, who denyede that it was not his dede, and bade the Suffrayne take the offenders; and aftre the Suffrain fonde oute the Englishmen, he pute them to warde, and certifiede Mr Thesaurer and others of the Consaile of the same, who willide the Suffrain to kepe them styll, tyll my Lorde Deputie were retornede; by meanes wherof the said Cahir is at werre with theym, and have lately prayede Old Rosse.'

M. J. Murphy (*At Sleive Gullion's Foot*, 43–4) gives the later date as the local 'bonfire night' and describes the revelry:

'Bon-Fire night took place on the 29th June. This festival, of course, had roots in pre-Christian Ireland, and was simply another instance of a pagan festival being adapted as a rustic celebration in honour of a Christian Saint.

'It was a feast of singing and dancing. Everybody took bog-sods and turf to the place where the fire was traditionally lit, usually on a road in a shallow glen, or on an unused loanen or bye-way. The fire was built first with tinder-dry bog-fir, and the turf piled around it. A huge conflagration resulted, which provided heat and light, though on "Mid-Summer's" night one would expect little necessity for fire-heat; but even Summer nights can be chilly.

'Old men pulled stones from the ditches and used them as seats close to the fire. A form was taken from a nearby house for the fiddler or melodeon player, or perhaps for both. The old people went, too, to tell stories and sing old songs. They sang or recited local compositions, usually satires and comic pieces about the depredations of some local man who was "a heart-scald to he's people and neighbours".

'The young girls were dressed in bibs and brogue boots or shoes. Here they danced all-night in the merry flare of the bon-fire. (In earlier times, dancing took place in Summer on Johnston's mountain, at a level spot near the Tower, or at the Two Big Rocks. They danced on Slieve Gullion, too. These spots are sometimes traceable to-day, since they show a circular plate of green grass amid the heather, trod flat by feet many years ago.)

'When tired or weary, the merry-makers went home, usually with their parents or relatives. It was not an uncommon thing for an old man – or one who had drunk unwisely – to be left alone by the waning bon-fire. One such character said that when he awoke, many of his dead friends were keeping him company on the stones and ditches around. Another said he was awakened by the "Dead Coach" – that unearthly conveyance pulled by horses without heads, driven by headless drivers. Belated vehicles disturbing the night calm even in these days are jocularly referred to as "The Dead Coach".'

However, another writer from the same area, a century earlier (John Donaldson: *A description of the Barony of Upper Fews,* 1838) states that fires were lit on both days in his time.

Here, it would seem, the later date has prevailed over the earlier, but there are indications in other places of a former bonfire on 28 June, as at Kildimo, County Limerick and Leac, County Kerry (*Béaloideas,* 1965, 108).

Thus, in south Leinster there is a firm and long-standing tradition of celebrating Midsummer on 28 June, and not on 23 June on which date it is held in the greater part of Ireland, with border districts in which both days are thus celebrated and there is uncertainty in tradition as to which is the 'real' midsummer. In the border areas, too, and even over wider areas, 28 June is often known as 'Old St John's Day' or 'Little St John's Day'. Our Callan school-master, Ó Súilleabháin, goes even further. For him 24 June is 'St John's Day', 29 June 'Little St John's Day' while 10 July is 'Old Little St John's Day'.

Thus it is evident that there is an ancient clash of tradition, going back at least until the end of the thirteenth century, as to the proper date for celebrating Midsummer, the north, west and south-west of Ireland taking St John's Eve as the 'right day' while the south east preferred the Eve of SS Peter and Paul. That this latter festival was not without honour in ancient Ireland is shown, for instance by an entry for the year A.D. 845 in *Cogadh Gaedhel re Gallaibh, The wars of the Gaedhil with the Gaill* (ed. Todd, 1867, Appendix (A), 227) which reads:

'The foreigners came to Roscrea in this year, on the feast of Paul and Peter, and the fair had then begun, and they were given battle, and the foreigners were defeated through the grace of Paul and Peter, and immense numbers were slain; and Earl Onphile was struck with a stone there, so that he was killed thereby. Some of the men of Mumhain, were fasting to propitiate Paul and Peter the night before. Much evil and distress was received from them and received by them all, which is not written here.'

Here, however, we should note that there is no indication that this was a Midsummer fair, thus it does not upset the theory that the Leinster observance of Midsummer on 28 June may have been an Anglo-Norman introduction.

The various ceremonies to protect household, farm, crops and livestock are associated almost entirely with the fires on St John's Eve; this is also true of the custom of lighting a small family bonfire, while the fires on the Eve of SS Peter and Paul, where they occur, are merely occasions for merry gatherings. Here, again, there may be a difference of tradition, but this is uncertain, as the bonfire custom is weakest in that eastern area where 28 June was the 'right' day, thus the absence of the protective customs here may well indicate a loss of tradition rather than a difference of usage.

Another clash of tradition became evident in parts of Ulster in the early nineteenth century, when the newly founded Orange Order began to celebrate the Williamite victories of the War of 1689–91, the Boyne on 1 July and Aughrim on 12 July, with bonfires as well as with parades and 'marching'. In many places this took the harmless form of rivalry as to the biggest fire and the most noise and music between the

157

'Catholic' bonfire on 23 (or in a small area of south east Ulster on 28 June) and the 'Protestant' bonfire on 1 July or 12 July. Sometimes, however, partisan bitterness led to more ugly deeds, as shown by the following extract from *Abstract of Crime in Ireland 1839*, 140–1:

'Mr Cramer Roberts, Provincial Inspector, says, I was informed by Chief Constable Mansfield that a most atrocious murder had been committed within four miles of Castleblayney.

'It appears a party of about twelve persons, principally boys and children were assembled on the night of the 28th instant, between the hours of eleven and twelve o'clock, around a small bonfire on the hill of Mollyash, in celebration of St Peter's eve. Whilst seated round this bonfire, laughing and talking a party of persons unknown appeared, distant about one hundred yards above them on the hill; shortly afterwards three shots were fired in the direction of this party, by which two persons, Michael Devine, twenty years, and Peter Devine, ten years of age, were shot dead; and two others, Patrick Devine, fifteen years, and Francis Devine, fourteen years of age, were wounded, the former dangerously, the latter slightly. This family of Devines are Roman Catholics, extremely well spoken of by all, even their Protestant neighbours; they are, by all accounts, a most industrious, well-conducted, quiet, inoffensive, and peaceable family, highly respected, and free from all party spirit, as universally admitted by persons of all persuasions and parties.

'A more wanton, unprovoked, premeditated, cold-blooded, and cruel murder has never fallen under my observation, and is clearly characteristic of strong party feeling.'

The Twelfth of July

In *Ulster Folklife*, 1962, 33, R. H. Buchanan writes:

'The celebrations of July 12th, which commemorate King William's victory at the Boyne in 1690, are of a sectarian and political nature; but the processions held by members of the Orange Order in many parts of Ulster make this one of the most colourful and festive days in the local rural calendar. Yet surprisingly enough, we have comparatively little information about its customs and their regional variation. For instance the lighting of bonfires is perhaps one of the most characteristic features of "The Twelfth", especially in Belfast, where the flames of innumerable fires clearly demarcate the Protestant sectors of the city. An amusing comment by John Donaldson provides one explanation of their origin. Writing of the Beltaine and Midsummer bonfires in Armagh in the 1830s, he remarks that these are "kept up in a kind of party spirit, in contradistinction to the British and Caledonian settlers, who, principally on that account, annually commemorate by bonfires on the 1st and 12th July their deliverance from Popish domination by the victories of their ancestors at the battle of the Boyne and Aughrim in 1690".'

Such political occasions were formerly numerous. Barrington, in his *Personal Sketches*, 10–12, humorously sets forth those which were popular some two hundred years ago:

'The fifth of November was celebrated in Dublin for the preservation of a Scottish king from gunpowder in London; then the thirtieth of January was much approved of by a great number of Irish, as the anniversary of making his son Charles the First, shorter by the head; and then the very same Irish celebrated the restoration of Charles the Second, who was twice as bad as his father; and whilst they rejoiced in putting a crown upon the head of the son of the king who could not quietly keep his own head on, they never failed to drink bumpers to the memory of Old Noll, who had cut that king's head off. To conclude, in order to commemorate the whole story, and make their children remember it, they dressed up a fat calf's head on every anniversary of King Charles's throat being cut, and with a smoked ham placed by the side of it, all parties partook thereof most happily, washing down the emblem and its accompaniment with as much claret as they could hold.

'Having thus proved their loyalty to James the First, and their attachment to his son's murderer, and then their loyalty to one of his grandsons, to another of whom they were disloyal, they next proceeded to celebrate the birthday of William of Orange, a Dutchman, who turned their king, his father-in-law, out of the country, and who, in all probability, would have given the Irish another calf's head for their celebration, if his said father-in-law had not got out of the way with the utmost expedition, and gone to live upon charity in France, with the natural enemies of the British nation.

'One part of the Irish people then invented a toast, called "The glorious, pious, and immortal memory of William the Dutchman"; whilst another raised a counter toast, called "The memory of the chestnut horse", that broke the neck of the same King William. But in my mind, if I am to judge of past times by the corporation of Dublin, it was only to coin an excuse for getting loyally drunk as often as possible,. that they were so enthusiastically fond of *making sentiments,* as they called them.'

Saint Swithin's Day

The weather portent of St Swithin's Day is known all over Ireland. Its origin is explained by two different legends, the first of which is given as follows in the *Journal of the Cork Historical and Archaeological Society*, 189, 22–3:

'The fifteenth of July is St Swithin's Day, and the belief that if it rains on St Swithin's Day (Sweeten or Sweeteen [*Suitín*] as he is called in Munster), the succeeding forty days will also be wet, still prevails. The folklore history is as follows: When St Swithin, after being waked, was buried, his monks, who dearly loved him, thought the simple "house of clay" was not befitting their lord abbot, so they determined to build a costly mausoleum which to their minds would more suitably mark his last resting-place on earth, and also show to the world how him they loved while living was venerated even in death. But St Swithin, who during life detested ostentation or display of any kind, besought his divine Master (as it was afterwards revealed to one of his monks) to prevent such a useless expenditure of time and money which might easily be spent with more advantage in relieving the poor and needy. Accordingly when his monks had completed this beautiful and costly mausoleum they named a day (July 15) on which the mortal remains of the saint were to be exhumed and publicly transmitted to their new, and as they considered, more befitting abode. But the prayer of the humble servant of God prevailed, for early on that morning the floodgates of heaven were again, as of old, opened, and one continuous downpour of rain prevailed and thus continued without intermission for the succeeding forty days. The country for miles around was flooded, which gave all parties, St Swithin's included, much concern. Thereupon they all prayed to God to lessen His anger against them, and earnestly besought their good and holy abbot, Swithin, to intercede for them. It was at this period he appeared to one of his monks and revealing to him how displeasing it was to God thus to spend their time in useless display, forbade them ever interfering with his remains thereafter. The command was obeyed, and ever since (as a remembrance of St Swithin) when it rains on St Swithin's Day, the succeeding forty days will be times of anxiety for the agriculturist for ever.'

This, of course, is the medieval English legend of the saint, and there is no doubt that both the belief and the legend came into Ireland from England in the middle ages.

Amhlaoibh O Súilleabháin, in 1828, expressed his scepticism of the prophecy and adverted to the second legend:

'The fifteenth day, Tuesday, that is, St Swithin's Day. Silly people say that if rain falls today that it will fall for forty days; but I think this saying the height of folly and, as rain fell today, I shall watch these next forty days to confute them. I believe they think that it was on the anniversary of this day that the rain began to fall which constituted the Deluge or Noe's Flood. A dark heavy-clouded morning: at half past eight it began teeming rain, which continued unabated for an hour. Scythemen got a thorough drenching.'

Forty days later, on 3 Sept. 1828, he had this to say:

'Not much of the harvest was lost, except in the south of England, where they were cutting it during the St Swithin's rains; that is, from St Swithin's Day, the fifteenth of July, to the twelfth day of August, when the fine weather set in. It is but the height of nonsense to say that, if it rains on St Swithin's Day, it will be raining for forty days afterwards. In Callan (this year), it did only twenty seven days' rain, and, indeed, that was quite enough.'

A paragraph in the *Longford Leader* on 22 Aug. 1942 shows that the belief is long-lived:

'St Swithin's Day has rather justified the reputation of its weather forecast this year, and now everybody is looking forward anxiously to the fortieth day in the hope that new conditions of weather will result. When it rained on St Swithin's Day the incredulous smiled in sympathy with believers in the tradition. Today if they smile it is in anticipation of the end of a dreary forty days which is expected during the coming week – if it is punctual, as it has been in other respects, the changed conditions should arrive by Monday.'

'Hungry July'

It was the ambition of every housewife that the store of food from the previous harvest should last until the new harvest was ripe, and usually there was some anxiety about this, even among 'comfortable' farmers, for a failure of the crops or a delay in ripening or in harvesting because of bad weather might mean short rations. A frequent admonition of a mother to a child who would not finish its meal was 'You might be glad of that before the harvest!'

Not infrequently the store of corn for bread and porridge did run out during the Summer, but for cattle-keeping people, dairy farmers and livestock breeders, this was not serious, as they had meat and soup, milk, curds, cheese and butter to tide them over until the corn was ripe.

If the late summer was a time of anxiety for the farmers it could be a very bitter, even tragic, period for the poor people who had no land or cattle. In the *Dublin University Magazine* there was published in 1841 an interesting series of articles entitled 'Letters from the Coast of Clare', in one of which the author writes as follows (521-2):

'Monday. – A stranger travelling through Ireland in the summer season is often surprised at the plea put forward to excite his compassion, and obtain alms; when perhaps on a lovely afternoon when the sun shines bright, the air is balmy, and all creation revels in enjoyment and plenty, a group of beggars comes up to his carriage, with "Ah, then, your honour, won't you feel for us this hard summer's day; – won't you give us something this hard, cruel, summer's day?"

'A speech like this is incomprehensible to a person unaware of the potato-eating habits of the peasantry, and their natural consequences – who does not know that part of the sweet months of June and July are universally called "the bitter six weeks" from the dreadful privation of food endured by the poor. Their only eatable fails them then; the old potatoes are either all used or unfit for use by that time, and the new –

generally planted late owing to that improvident spirit which no sufferings or experience can forewarn – have not yet arrived at maturity. The misery endured in the interval is inconceivable, and no one that has not witnessed it can have any idea of the incredibly small pittance of food with which the poor peasant contrives to keep "the bare life in him", until plenty arrives again.'

The whole economy of the Irish countryside grew unbalanced in the century from about 1750 to the 1840s. A great increase in the volume of tillage, especially of corn for export, brought a corresponding increase in the numbers of agricultural labourers who had no land of their own except potato plots let to them for a labour rent by the farmers who employed them. Moreover, their lot deteriorated over the period. In 1777 Arthur Young (*Tour in Ireland*, i, 35; ii, 37) observed that almost every labourer had a cow, some two cows, and also some oats or other corn. Fifty years later the labouring class, together with the 'cottier-tenants' who held a little land but not enough to live on without working for wages for part of the year, made up over one-quarter of the whole population, and were reduced in their standard of living to subsistence-level dependence on the potato.

An official enquiry into the condition of these people, the *Poor Law Inquiry* of the early 1830s, amply corroborates, for almost every district in Ireland, the account from the coast of Clare given above. For instance, this from County Meath. (*Parliamentary Papers* xxx, 1836, 16:)

'Privation (the usual allowance of potatoes being curtailed by one-half or two thirds) was the common lot of almost all labourers only occasionally employed, but numerous families were obliged to live on a few pennyworths of meal, weekly, (which they begged or borrowed during that time), made up into a kind of soup by boiling it with the weed commonly called *prassagh* in Ireland, and *charlock* (wild mustard) in England. This plant is decidedly unwholesome, and when eaten in the manner just described, is said to render the skin nearly as yellow as its own flower. To such an extent is this practice carried in seasons of scarcity that the clergy were obliged to forbid the eating of this weed; and in some cases the priests and farmers set persons to prevent them from gathering it.'

The period of shortage might vary in length, from place to place and from year to year, from a fortnight to two months. A witness to the *Poor Law Inquiry* at Dromahaire, County Leitrim stated:

'Those who can afford to have an opinion as to the quality of their

164

potatoes, consider that they begin to deteriorate about the beginning of June, and that they have become positively unwholesome by the end of the month; however, the poor stick to them as long as they last, and that is in general until the middle of July.'

Another witness, from East Galway, told how those who were a little better-off bridged the gap in their potato diet by having spared some oatmeal from the last harvest, but deplored the sad state of those who had no corn, (*Parliamentary Papers*, xxx, 1836, 2–3):

'There is a general opinion that after *Garlick Sunday* (the first Sunday in August) the kind of potatoes most in use, viz. "lumpers", have acquired an unwholesome quality; after that day, those who can afford it cease to make these their sole food, and substitute oatmeal in some degree, and use their deteriorated potatoes for feeding pigs. However, there are many cottiers who have no alternative but continuing to eat them or procuring others on credit at a high price.'

That the coming of the magic date 'Garlick Sunday' – of which more anon – did not entirely end the shortage is shown by another witness to the same *Inquiry* this time at Murrisk, County Mayo, (*Parliamentary Papers* xxx, 1836, 5):

'The digging of the potatoes for daily use commences after Garlick Sunday, but not to such an extent as to prevent a great rise in the price.'

The month of July comprised the worst period of shortage, and hence it was widely known as 'Hungry July', *Iúl an Ghorta, July an Chabáiste,* (because those who had it ate a great deal of cabbage as a substitute for other foods), 'Staggering July' and similar names. Our Callan schoolmaster, Amhlaoibh Ó Súilleabháin, in remarking on this in his diary (27 July 1830), again remarks on the pallid complexion of the hungry.

'July of the Famine this month is called now: Yellowmonth is its proper name in Irish and it is an apt name; for if the cornfields are yellow, the faces of the poor are greenish yellow, because of the livid famine; for they are subsisting on green cabbage and other inferior odds and ends of a similar character.'

As might be expected, the farmers who could afford to do so, tried to lessen the sufferings of the poor to the best of their means, and to a really astonishing degree. The *Poor Law Inquiry* (*Parliamentary Papers* xxx, 1836, 106) remarked: 'The quantity given in this way by farmers, small occupiers and often by the labourers themselves is incredible', while another Parliamentary Paper (1830, vii, p. 46) gives the value of this bounty from the farmers to the poor as one million pounds in a year, the equivalent of ten millions or more in our money – truly an incredible figure. But even the comfortable farmers were feeling the pinch of shortage as last year's stocks of provender ran out, and the coming of the new harvest was, very naturally, an occasion for rejoicing by everybody in rural Ireland, rich and poor alike, for we must remember that in the period before the harvest began there was little or no work for the wage-earning labourers. The threshold of plenty was the festival of Lúnasa, which began the harvest.

In ancient Ireland the festival of the beginning of the harvest was the first day of Autumn, that is to say, it coincided with 1 August in the Julian calendar. This has continued in recent tradition, insofar as *Lúnasa* or Lammas-Day was still taken to be the first day of Autumn; the gatherings and celebrations connected with it were, however, transferred to a nearby Sunday, in most parts of Ireland to the last Sunday in July, in some places to the first Sunday in August.

There appears to be a twofold reason for this change. In the first place, the coming of the harvest, with its urgent rush of work and its uncertain weather, made working days precious. In the second place the customs and celebrations of this festival, as we shall see, involved large gatherings, not merely of one family or a few neighbouring households, but of the people of whole parishes or even wider areas. Thus a Sunday was a much more suitable occasion than an ordinary working day.

One effect of this change of date was a corresponding change of name. The old *Lúnasa* was, in the main, forgotten as applying to the popular festival and a variety of names substituted in various localities, such as *Domhnach Chrom Dubh, Domhnach Deireannach* (Last Sunday), Garland Sunday, Hill Sunday and others to be mentioned later.

The First of the Harvest

Everybody hoped to have the first crops ready for gathering at the traditional date which began the harvest. To cut any corn or dig any potatoes before this day came was considered improper; it was against custom and was taken generally as evidence of bad husbandry and extravagant housewifery.

As regards oats and the earliest maturing potatoes, the hopes of harvest by the end of the July were usually fulfilled except in a very bad year. Where only a part of the crop was ready, some of it was garnered in honour of the occasion, and even when it was still unripe at least a small portion of it was taken.

The newly-gathered crop provided the main dish at a festive meal in honour of the day, and this was the first food eaten from the new harvest. Over the past two centuries or so, the meal consisted of new potatoes, garnished, according to the means of the household, with cabbage, fish, fowl, bacon or fresh beef or mutton.

Here and there, however, the memory of an older custom survives, by which the festive dish came from the new corn, which, according to tradition, should be reaped on the morning of the day, and made into bread or porridge before evening. The ordinary sequence of operations in preparing grain for food is reaping, threshing, winnowing, drying, grinding and sieving, but this may be speeded up on occasion by the process known as 'burning in the straw' which combined the results of threshing, winnowing and drying in one swift operation. In this, the whole sheaf, or the ear end of the sheaf was set on fire; thus separating the grain from the straw, burning away the chaff and hardening the corn, all at once. It only remained to shake or wipe the grain clean of ashes before grinding it in the quern. In his story *Séadna* ch. 30, An tAthair Peadar Ó Laoghaire describes how food was quickly prepared for an unexpected visitor:

'She went out into the haggard, to the best corn-stack that was there, and pulled two good sheaves from the middle of the stack. She brought the two sheaves in. She swept the hearthstone and washed and dried it; then she lit a bogdeal splinter and burned the sheaves on the hearthstone. Only the straw and the chaff were burned, however; the grain was not burned but finely dried, far better than on the flagstone of the mill. Then she gathered up the dried oats and took it outside and let the wind blow through it so that the ashes of the straw and chaff were thoroughly cleaned out of it. When it was nice and clean she brought it in and put it in the quern and ground it. She then passed it through a coarse sieve and again through a fine sieve so that not a bit of chaff remained in it. She then put the meal in a wooden bowl and stirred some fresh cream into it and put a spoon in the bowl and gave it to Séadna. He ate it, and thought he had never eaten nor even tasted better food, it was so wholesome and tasty, so rich and full of energy.'

That this method of rapidly separating the grain from the straw and chaff was formerly a common practice in Ireland is shown by the fact that in 1634 the Dublin parliament passed 'An Act to Prevent the unprofitable Custom of Burning of Corn in the Straw' (10 & 11 Charles I, ch. 17) which prescribed fines and imprisonment for those who 'doe for a great part instead of thrashing, burn their corn in the straw, thereby consuming the straw, which might relieve their cattel in winter, and afford materials towards the covering or thatching of their houses; and spoiling the corn, making it black, loathsome and filthy'.

The practice is mentioned by many writers in the seventeenth and eighteenth centuries, but by the nineteenth it had become obsolete and was done only on rare occasions.

Another welcome feature of the festive meal was fresh fruit. Those who had currants or gooseberries in their gardens, and this was usual even among small-holders in Munster and South Leinster, made sure that some dish of these appeared on the table. Those who lived near heather hills or woods gathered *fraocháin* ('fraughans', whortleberries, blueberries) which they ate for an 'aftercourse' mashed with fresh cream and sugar. Similar treatment was given to wild strawberries and wild raspberries by those lucky ones who lived near the woods where these grow.

Outdoor Gatherings

In very many localities the chief event of the festival was not so much the festive meal as the festive gathering out of doors. This took the form of an excursion to some traditional site, usually on a hill or mountain top, or beside a lake or a river, where large numbers of people from the surrounding area congregated, travelling thither on foot, on horseback or in carts and other equipages.

Often the gathering place was somewhat remote, to be reached by climbing hill tracks or scrambling over rough country. For the young and active this added to the enjoyment of the outing – for instance it gave the young men the opportunity of helping the girls over the rough places and of showing off their agility and boasting of their prowess. It also meant that the older people and the smaller children, not able to travel the rugged ways, did not join in the outing. This meant less restraint on the merriment of the robust and energetic.

Many of the participants came prepared to 'make a day of it' bringing food and drink and musical instruments, and spending the afternoon and evening in eating, drinking and dancing. The young men engaged in tests of skill and strength, in sports and games. The girls picked wild flowers and made them into garlands and nosegays. Almost always there were wild berries to be picked and enjoyed.

Gatherings on Hills

In H. S. Swan's *Romantic Inishowen*, 103, Mr James E. O'Donnel describes such a gathering:

'One of the old customs of Inishowen consisted in all, or nearly all, the grown-up boys and girls of the six surrounding parishes meeting on Heatherberry Sunday at the spring well called Súil-a'-Tobair near the top of Slieve Snaght (the highest mountain in the peninsula). Heatherberry Sunday was the Sunday before the "Gooseberry" fair day of Buncrana (26th July). Met ostensibly for the purpose of gathering heather-berries, the boys and girls when they came together on the mountain, turned the event into a social occasion. They danced, frolicked, sported and generally enjoyed themselves. Amongst the games played were Leap frog and Rounders, but "Duck" was the most popular game. As a sequel to these chance meetings and mountain-top flirtations many weddings resulted. The period of courtship usually continued from Heatherberry Sunday till "Runaway Sunday" or "Galloping Tuesday" as the Sunday before Lent and Shrove Tuesday were popularly called. A country wedding was then generally a big event. It ended with feasting and merrymaking and a "Ceilidhe" lasting into the small hours of the morning. The origin of Heatherberry Sunday (which was not confined to Inishowen) is lost in the mists of antiquity. But fashions have changed, and this old custom has in recent years almost entirely died out. I myself was for many years a regular attendant until the year 1909.'

Another typical hill outing was that still remembered in tradition in the 1930s by old people around Knockfeerina in County Limerick. Knockfeerina is a ridge of over a mile in length; it is not very high, 948 feet at its summit towards its eastern end, but as it rises abruptly from the Limerick plain it is a notable landmark. The young people of the locality gathered for the celebration on the level top of the ridge to the west of the conspicuous hump which forms the summit, and here they played games, flirted, danced and sang, ate and drank the dainties which they had brought with them, and picked *fraocháin* (whortleberries) and flowers, some of which they laid on the small cairn called the 'strickeen' at the summit which covered the reputed entrance to Donn Fírinne's underground palace. In the evening a great bonfire was lit near the 'strickeen'.

A gathering on the Laois – Offaly border is described by Helen Roe in *Béaloideas,* ix, 31:

'On the last Sunday in July the people of Mountrath, Trumera, and the surrounding districts go up on the Slieve Bloom Mountains, on to the slopes of Ard Erin. They bring with them food, and spend the day on the mountain.

'There are all kinds of games and trials of strength, and in the evening they kindle big fires, and the young men run races round the fires, and the more daring of them leap over the fires. In this district, this Sunday is called Height Sunday.'

There were many such hill and mountain gatherings. Máire Mac Néill, in her *Festival of Lughnasa* enumerates 78 hills on which these assemblies were held; nine in Connaught, fifteen in Leinster, fifteen in Munster and thirty-nine in Ulster.

In addition to these there are heights on which the merry secular gatherings took on at some period in the past a religious character and became pilgrimages or patterns.

By far the most widely known of these is Croagh Patrick. The great quartzite cone of the 'Reek' as it is popularly known, rises abruptly from a mountain ridge on the southern shore of Clew Bay in County Mayo; the summit, 2,510 feet high, is only a mile and a half from the edge of the sea. Along the ridge and leading up to the summit are two rough tracks, one from the eastern end and one from the western. Up these tracks the pilgrims have come on 'Reek Sunday', the last Sunday in July, for over a thousand years, to honour Ireland's patron saint, to obtain heavenly merit and to perform penance, on the spot where, according to traditions already recorded in the seventh century, the saint fasted for forty days and nights. This account adds (*Tripartite Life of Saint Patrick,* ii, 323):

'For God had said to all the saints of Ireland, past, present and to come: O Saints, go up above the mountain which towers and is higher than all the mountains that are towards the setting of the sun, to bless the people of Ireland, that Patrick might see the fruit of his labour; because the company of all the Irish saints came to him to visit their father.' Thus, already twelve hundred years ago the 'saints' are enjoined to go on pilgrimage to the top of Croagh Patrick.

Other accounts, increasing in number as the years go on, testify to the popularity of the pilgrimage, although the date is not definitely given until the year 1432, when a Papal letter granted a relaxation of canonical penances to those who made the pilgrimage to the top of Croagh Patrick on the Sunday before the feast of St Peter's chains (that is to say the last Sunday in July) and gave alms for the support of the chapel on the summit, to which a great multitude resorted on that day. (*Calendar of Papal Registers, Papal Letters,* Vol. VIII, p. 440.)

Thackeray wrote of the pilgrimage in 1843; in his *Irish Sketch Book,* chapter xxi, he describes the scene, expressing horror at the severity of the penance and disgust for the 'superstition' of the misguided papists.

Towards the end of the nineteenth century this great pilgrimage almost came to an end because of lack of ecclesiastical favour. However, when in 1903 Dr John Healy became Archbishop of Tuam, he had an oratory built on the top of the mountain, so that the pilgrimage Masses could be fittingly celebrated there. Since then the number of pilgrims has increased year by year; in 1969 it was estimated that 60,000 people took part in it. One reason for the increase is the ease of modern transport. Pilgrims now come from all over Ireland, brought by special trains and omnibuses and hundreds of motor cars, although many still travel thither on foot in the old way. Most of the pilgrims climb the track from the east, setting out in the dark so as to reach the top shortly after dawn, many fasting since the previous day, many in their bare feet. They pause at a number of 'stations', points on the track where prayers are recited. On the top of the mountain there are Masses and sermons, and Holy Communion is given.

Formerly many of the returning pilgrims engaged in dancing, singing and other amusements, as well as eating and drinking, when they returned to the foot of the mountain. This is no longer the case, although vendors of sandwiches, lemonade and other refreshments are in attendance to provide for the weary pilgrims on their way down the mountain track.

Three other mountains formerly had pilgrimages at this time, Mount Brandon in County Kerry, Slieve Donard in County Down and Church Mountain in County Wicklow. These, however, were attended only by people from the immediate locality, and were very far from attaining the fame of Croagh Patrick; all three have fallen into disuse.

Gatherings at Lakes and Rivers

Another favourite gathering place at the Lúnasa festival was beside a lake or a river. Máire Mac Neill (*Festival of Lughnasa*) lists 13 of these, nearly all in the north midlands – four in County Meath, three in County Westmeath, two in Tyrone and one each in Counties Cavan, Galway, Leitrim and Mayo.

These waterside gatherings differed little from those on the hills. There were the same singing and dancing, eating and drinking, picking of wild flowers and fruit.

One interesting custom was the driving of cattle and horses into the water. This is mentioned in the 1680s by Piers in his *Description of the County of West-Meath,* 121–2:

'On the first Sunday in harvest, viz. in August, they will be sure to drive their cattle into some pool or river, and therein swim them; this they observe as inviolable as if it were a point of religion, for they think no beast will live the whole year thro' unless they be thus drenched; I deny not but that swimming of cattle, and chiefly in this season of the year, is healthful unto them as the poet hath observed:

Balantumque gregem fluvio mersare salubri.

Virg.

'In th' healthful flood to plunge the bleating flock, but precisely to do this on the first Sunday in harvest, I look on as not only superstitious, but profane.'

Wakefield in his *Statistical Survey of Ireland,* 1812 also adverts to this, and like Piers, ascribes it to 'superstition', that useful pigeon-hole for whatever an author despises because he cannot understand it. Wakefield says (ii, 625):

'August 7th, 1808. From Castletown Delvin to Lord Sunderlin's, at Baronstown, the people are all catholics, and regular in attending places of worship. They are, however, much addicted to superstitious notions, and make their horses swim in some of the lakes on Garlick Sunday, that is, the second Sunday in August, believing that this will render them healthy during the rest of the year.'

In places, boys mounted the horses and raced them through the lake or river. A lively description of this by one, 'J.L.L.', under the title 'The Pattern of the Lough' and describing the gathering at Lough Owel in County Westmeath in the year 1818, appeared in the *Dublin Penny Journal*, 7 Feb. 1835, part of which reads thus:

'We must come to the province of Leinster, where, I believe, above all other parts of this island, the patterns are still most frequently held. On the banks of the beautiful *Lough Ouel* or *Houel*, situated within two small miles of the town of Mullingar, there is still a pattern held on the first Sunday in August, called among the country people, the "Pattern of the Lough"; and the Sunday on which it falls is as marked among the festivals of the year as Easter Sunday or Christmas Day, and usually referred to by the title of "Lough Sunday". The tents are usually pitched on the Saturday previous, in a field adjoining to that in which the great crowd collects; and the principal attraction is the swimming of horses in the lake. Early on the Sunday morning, the multitude assemble from all quarters of the country: some for the purpose of amusement, or meeting friends who live at a distance; others to settle the preliminaries of a marriage contract; a great many, because it is the custom, and because others go; but the greater number to meet and fight the people of an adjacent barony, or to revenge some real or imaginary quarrel or insult. Swimming horses in the lake is a favourite feat, and affords much amusement to the spectators. It is also attended with considerable danger; and scarcely a year passes but some life is lost on the occasion. Matches are made; and as none but the most resolute young men, and the most expert swimmers, dare engage in the exercise, the sport becomes very exciting. Yet accidents more frequently occur from the terror and want of capability in the animals, so unused to such immersions and such efforts, in an element of which they are much in dread, than in the want of resolution, presence of mind, or agility in the riders.'

He goes on to tell of a swimming race between five horses, during

18 Swimming race on Garland Sunday (Hardy: *Legends, Tales and Stories of Ireland*, 1837)

which one horse was injured by colliding with the boat which marked the turning point, and both horse and rider were drowned.

In the *Ordnance Survey Letters for County Mayo*, II, (pp. 142–3 in the typescript copy) an account is given by one of the Surveyors, T. O'Connor, of the customs observed in the early years of the last century at Lough Keeran near Bohola in County Mayo:

'At this Lough, which is a small pool in a bog to the left of the road leading by the old church to Bohola, and nearly opposite the ruin, there is usually a patron on the Sunday commonly called Garlic Sunday, but *recte* Garland Sunday; a name assumed from the circumstance of Ceres, the Goddess of corn, being worshipped on that day, on which garlands made of the stalks of corn with the ears on were, it is said, worn in her honour. This Sunday is in Irish called *Domhnach Chrom Dubh*, Crom Dubh's Sunday.

'The people, it is said, swim their horses in the lake on that day, to defend them against incidental evils during the year, and throw spancels and halters into it, which they leave there on the occasion. They are also accustomed to throw butter into it, with the intention that their cows may be sufficiently productive of milk and butter during the year The *Clad Ime* – (lump of butter) thrown in at a time, does not be more than a quarter of a pound weight. After the crowds have gone away, the poor who have not the necessaries of life, otherwise than by obtaining them by alms from liberal or charitable persons, assemble and carry off as much of the butter as they can gather out of the lake. There was formerly a tree at this place, around which the people were in the habit of fastening by a noose, cords (*buaracha*) that were used in tying cows.

'The Roman Catholic bishop of the diocese, in which the parish containing the old church and Lough is situated, got the tree cut down in order to prevent the people from getting on with such ceremonies.

'The priests have dissuaded the people from getting on with their ceremonies at the lake, so far that they are altogether giving them up. The stations are still practised on the patron day, but the people are ceasing from throwing butter into it or going, on with their other practises at it.'

It is unfortunate that here the writer does not make it clear whether the making of 'garlands made of the stalks of corn' is a custom of that part of Mayo, or his memory of some description of a ceremony of Classical religion.

The custom of swimming horses and cattle may have formerly been more widespread. Thomas J. Westropp mentions (in *Journal of the Galway Archaeological and Historical Society*, ix, 64), 'The driving of horses, ridden by naked boys, into the sea at places on Galway Bay, on Garland Sunday' but gives no further information.

Other 'Lúnasa' Customs and Beliefs

This was a favourite time for patterns at blessed wells and other local shrines. In this it resembles other great festivals, but a number of these, held upon heights, are apparently connected with the hill gatherings. In *The Festival of Lughnasa*, Máire Mac Neill lists and describes thirteen of these, as well as eighty blessed wells venerated at this time; of these latter, however, many seem to have no direct connection with the festival of the beginning of the harvest.

It was also a favourite time for the holding of fairs. In this regard, we should remember that certain ancient *Oenacha* or fair-assemblies were held at Lúnasa. The *Metrical Dindshenchas* (ed. Gwynn, III, 2–5) has a long poem describing the Fair of Carman, the great crowds, the presence of Kings and nobles, the religious ceremonies, the buying

175

and selling, the coming of foreign merchants, the musicians and other entertainers, the sports and games. Another Lúnasa fair was that of Tailtiu (the modern Teltown, County Meath) of which the Annals of the Four Masters record that so great was the throng at the fair in 1168 that the line of horses and vehicles was six miles long. (*Annals of Ireland,* ii, 1168).

These assemblies have long since ceased to be held. That at Teltown continued as a small gathering of the local country people until some time in the eighteenth century. That at Carman disappeared in the Middle Ages, and even its site is now not definitely known. D. A. Binchy has shown (*Ériu,* xviii, 113–38) that the political significance of these gatherings has been overestimated. They were, however, notable occasions for trading and popular entertainment.

A number of fairs still held or until recently held at this season bear names like 'Lammas Fair', 'Gooseberry Fair', 'Bilberry Fair'.

The most notable of the survivors is the Fair of Puck at Killorglin, County Kerry, formerly held on 1–2 August but now on 10–12 August, which combines trading and 'all the fun of the fair' for all of County Kerry and even of places much farther away.

'Before the first of August, fruit cakes called *bairín breac* are made'. This remark by Coquebert de Montbret, a Frenchman visiting County Galway in 1791, is another example of the festive dish, but it should be considered together with cake ceremonies, similar to the cake-dance at Easter described above, at Lúnasa gatherings at Drong Hill and at Cnocnadtobar, both on the south side of Dingle Bay in County Kerry. At both of these hill gatherings a special cake was on display, the honour of dividing it being given to some young couple about to be married, or to the couple who danced best.

Divination to foretell the future was carried out at this time, and as might be expected at the all-important harvest season, this was mainly forecasting of weather. Floods were expected, and their course and volume were forecast and carefully observed. For instance, a paragraph in the Cavan newspaper *The Anglo-Celt* on 31 July 1943, observes: 'Old residents say that there is no danger of Lammas flood this year, as such occurs only in a year when there is flooding in May'.

Many other weather signs, such as the appearance of distant hills, were considered. In County Limerick the dome of Knockfeerina was a weather portent over a wide area. If it looked blue and distant, then a fine harvest was expected; if it appeared green and close at hand the worst was feared.

176

In most parts of Ireland, certainly in places where the Irish language survived, the figure of Crom Dubh was associated with the festival. He was portrayed as a wizard or pagan chieftain who opposed St Patrick and, in many legends was overcome by the saint. Other legends of Patrick's defeat of demons and pagan potentates are associated with many of the festival sites. In County Limerick Donn Fírinne, the mysterious being who lived in state with his fairy followers under Knockfeerina, was active at this time and the appearance of fairy creatures on the hill caused no surprise. Donn rode upon the wind and ruled the weather; he and his host battled with other fairy rulers for the crops, and the potatoes of the area whence came the defeated side were blighted.

On the whole, the numerous usages and beliefs which heralded the harvest spring directly from the supreme importance of this season in the lives of the people. However, such customs as the offerings of flowers and fruit at the 'Strickeen' on Knockfeerina or the garlanding with flowers of the largest pillar stone, formerly called *Rannach Chrom Dubh* in the great stone circle at Grange beside Lough Gur may possibly be survivals of pre-Christian religious ceremonies.

Cork Harbour Ceremony

Writing about the castle at Blackrock, in his *Researches in the South of Ireland*, 211–12, Crofton Croker goes on:

'Here the mayors held an Admiralty Court, being appointed by several charters Admirals of the Harbour, a right which they annually assert on the first of August, when the mayor and corporation sail to the entrance of the harbour, and perform the ceremony of throwing a dart into the sea, as a testimony of their jurisdiction.'

This is confirmed by a record in the city council book which reads:

'30 May, 1759. Resolved. That Mr Mayor do provide an Entertainment at Blackrock Castle 1 August next, and that the Mayor and the other proper officers of the Corporation do go in their boats to the Harbour's mouth and other parts of the channel and river to exert their ancient rights to the government thereof, and that the Mayor and other high officers do land at convenient places in the said harbour and proceed to high water mark in evidence of the right of jurisdiction granted by Charter to the Corporation in all Creeks and Strands within the Harbour as far as high water mark.'

177

The Assumption

Féile Mhuire 'sa bhFomhar, The Festival of Our Lady in the Harvest, being a holiday in the middle of the farmer's busiest season was doubly welcome because fine weather gave the opportunity of excursions and other outdoor pursuits. In west Limerick and north Kerry servants and workpeople always included in their bargain with their employers the stipulation that 'the Fifteenth of August and the Races of Listowel' were to be holidays. In most parts of Ireland within reach of the coast, an excursion to the seaside was part of the enjoyment of the '15th of August' and many people maintained that a bathe in the sea on this day was especially beneficial to health.

Another health-giving ritual was the drinking of three large mouthfuls of sea water which was famed, *inter alia*, as an aperient. Indeed in seaside resorts in County Waterford the local inhabitants distinguished between two kinds of visitors at this season. Day-trippers were nicknamed 'oalishers' and those who stayed for several days 'gaybricks', the explanation of the names being the Irish phrase with which the visitors greeted each other; on the first day they asked – '*Ar ólais é?* (Have you drunk it?)' and on subsequent days '*Ar dh' oibrigh sé?* (Has it worked?)'.

In parts of the north of Ireland, where Orangemen paraded on 12 July, their political opponents, the Ancient Order of Hibernians and similar groups, held rival marches on 15 August, often to be distinguished from those of the Orange Order only by the emblems displayed and the music played, while both occasions were all too frequently marked by disturbances of the public peace.

However, the main activity in rural Ireland on 15 August was the holding of 'Patterns' at the numerous local shrines of the Blessed Virgin Mary. These were a combination of religious exercises and secular amusements, and are described below.

178

Saint Bartholomew's Day

This festival, on 24 Aug. which up to 1778 was, for Catholics, a holiday of obligation, was something of a landmark for growers of corn, because the corn harvest should be well advanced by that date. Traditionally, this was the day when flails were made ready to thresh the harvest, and if a high wind – injurious to ripe corn – came about this time it was said to be 'Beairtlí na Gaoithe' ('Bartholomew of the Wind') preparing his flail to thresh the laggards' corn still standing in the field.

The Pattern Day

There is scarcely a parish in Ireland in which, in former times, the day of the local patron saint was not celebrated by a 'pattern' (Irish *Pátrún*, English Patron). The festivities began with religious devotions at the shrine of the saint. It is probable that in pre-Reformation days these religious ceremonies were held at the parish church under the direction of the clergy. This was ended by the wholesale confiscation and destruction of churches in the century and a half between the 1540s and the 1690s, in which Ireland was devastated again and again by wars which were mainly of a religious character. By 1700 hardly a parish church remained in Catholic hands and organized catholic ceremonial had almost entirely disappeared, and Patron Day ceremonies survived as gatherings of the local laity at the ruin of the church or monastery, or, perhaps most frequently, at the holy well. Devotions at these places usually consisted of the making of 'rounds', the devotees walked around the shrine a certain number of times, reciting certain prayers, the ritual varying somewhat from one shrine to another. Part of the devotion at a holy well was the drinking of its water; ; the bathing or washing of sores and affected members in search of a cure was also usual, and different shrines were famed for the cure of different ailments. Pilgrims usually left at the shrine some token of their visit, in some cases coins placed in a box, in others pieces of cloth hung up, in others almost any small object which they happened to have about them. The traditions, rituals, legends and customs associated with holy wells and similar shrines are very numerous and varied, and many of them are much older than the religious calamities mentioned above, older perhaps in some cases than christianity itself. It is clear, however, that the disappearance of formal public ceremonial among Catholics in Ireland as a result of the religious wars and the Penal Laws, gave added importance to the gatherings of the laity at

19   Pattern Day at Mám Éin, County Galway (W. H. Bartlett, 1842)

these 'Patterns', while the absence of clerical direction gave much greater freedom both in unorthodox forms of devotion and in secular amusements.

Ecclesiatical authorities tried to keep these matters under control. For instance the Synod of Tuam in 1660 (the year of the Restoration of Charles II, when the rigours of Cromwellian persecution of Catholics were being relaxed) decreed as follows:

'Prohibentur tripudia, tibicines, symphoniae, commisationes et alii abusus in visitatione fontium et aliorum Sacrorum locorum, maxime tempore indulgentiarum.'

(Dancing, flute-playing, bands of music, riotous revels and other abuses in visiting wells and other holy places are forbidden, especially at times of indulgence).'

The regulation goes on to say that on no account must a visit to one of these shrines be regarded as a substitute for attending at Mass on a holiday of obligation.

The Penal Laws of the early eighteenth century also legislated against patterns. The infamous 'Act to prevent further Growth of Popery' (VI Anne 3), as well as prohibiting 'the riotous and unlawful assembling together of many thousands of papists to the said wells and other places' and prescribing a fine of 10/- on all who met at wells and 20/- on vendors of 'all ale, victuals or other commodities' with a public flogging in default of payment, enjoined on all magistrates the demolition of 'all crosses, pictures and inscriptions that are anywhere publickly set up, and are the occasion of any popish superstitions'. It is probable that this law caused the destruction of such embellishments as may have existed at wells and other shrines, but in the suppression of patterns it was in the main ineffective, not least because it depended for enforcement on the local gentry who, except for the occasional religious bigot, usually turned a blind eye on this comparatively harmless local custom. The patterns continued to flourish through the eighteenth and on into the nineteenth century.

Thomas Crofton Croker attended one in Gougane Barra in 1813 and gave a detailed description of the devotions and revels in his *Researches in the South of Ireland.* Having seen it all he had supper in a tent:

After having satisfied our mental craving, we felt it necessary to attend to our bodily appetites, and for this purpose adjourned to a tent where some tempting slices of curdy Kerry salmon had attracted our notice. In this tent, with the exception of about half an hour, we remained located from half-past seven in the evening, until two o'clock the following morning, when we took our departure for Cork.

'After discussing the merits of this salmon, and washing it down with some of "Beamish & Crawford's Porter" we whiled away the time by drinking whiskey-punch, observing the dancing to an excellent piper, and listening to the songs and story-telling which were going on about us.

'As night closed in, the tent became crowded almost to suffocation, and dancing being out of the question, our piper left us for some other station, and a man, who I learned had served in the Kerry militia, and had been flogged at Tralee about five years before as a White-boy, began to take a prominent part in entertaining the assembly, by singing Irish songs in a loud and effective voice. These songs were received with shouts of applause, and as I was then ignorant of the Irish language, and anxious to know the meaning of what had elicited so much popular approbation, I applied to an old woman near whom I sat, for an explanation or translation, which she readily gave me, and I found that these songs were rebellious in the highest degree. Poor Old King George was execrated without mercy; curses were also dealt out wholesale on the Saxon oppressors of Banna the blessed (an allegorical name for Ireland); Buonaparte's achievements were extolled, and Irishmen were called upon to follow the example of the French people.'

Amhlaoibh O Súilleabháin took his children to the local pattern in July, 1829:

'The twenty-sixth day, Sunday, feast-day of St James, that is, Patron day at St James Well, close to Callan. A fine sultry sunny thin clouded still day. "No breath there of wind, to stir tree-top or flower". It is a proper summer's day, and it is badly needed, for yesterday and the day before were so cold, almost, as March days. My three youngest children and myself went to the Patron. There were gooseberries and currants and cherries for children: ginger bread for grown girls: strong beer and maddening whiskey for wranglers and busybodies: open-doored booths filled with lovers: bag-pipers, and "risp-raspers" (fiddlers) making music there for young folks: and pious pilgrims making their stations around the well. My children and myself left the Well at six o'clock. Well dressed respectable people were moving about in crowds every-where.'

The same mixture of piety and pleasure was noted by Mason at Kilrush, Co. Clare (*Parochial Survey*, II, 459):

'Easter Monday is a great holiday here; and multitudes go into Scattery Island this day for the purpose of performing penance on their bare knees, round the stony beach and holy well there. Tents are generally erected in the island on this occasion, and oftentimes more whiskey is drank by the pilgrims, than is found convenient on their return in crouded boats.'

In *Journal of the Cork Historical and Archaeological Society*, 1896, 331 we read:

'at this date (August 15) a very large "patron" was formerly held at "Our Lady's Well" in the townland of Castleharrison, and parish of Ballyhay, about three miles south of Charleville. The "patron day" was abolished in the first quarter of this century through the exertions of the local Catholic clergy, consequent on this "patron" being turned into "a meeting place" for the vile system of faction fighting, which then disgraced our province.'

W. St. J. Joyce has a similar tale to tell of the pattern at Tallaght, County Dublin in his *Neighbourhood of Dublin*, 203–4.

'St Maelruan's patron, or "pattern", was every year celebrated here from a remote period on the 7th July, but in later years the original Saint's name was lost sight of altogether, and replaced by the corrupted form, "Moll Rooney", under which title the "pattern" continued to be annually held, until it came to be such a nuisance, owing to drunkenness and debauchery, that it was suppressed in 1874. The proceedings consisted in making a kind of effigy, supposed to represent the saint, and carrying it about from house to house in procession, headed by a fiddler or piper. The occupants of each house then came out as they were visited, and danced to the music after which a collection was made to be spent on drink. Few went to bed that night; many slept in ditches on the way home, and drinking, dancing and fighting went on intermittently till morning. Another item in the performance in recent times was to visit the grave of an old village piper named Burley O'Toole, who had expressed a dying wish to that effect, and to dance and fight around his grave.

'The degeneration of this patron is unfortunately only typical of others throughout the country, which explains why so many of them have been discontinued through the influence of the clergy and others.'

Although it is true that many of these local celebrations had degenerated into debauchery, it is also unfortunately true that in the course of the nineteenth century, when Victorian 'respectability' had for many of both clergy and laity assumed the sanctity of moral law, many quite harmless customs were discouraged or forbidden because they offended the sanctimonious.

The later eighteenth and earlier nineteenth centuries covered a period when the Catholic laity was regaining middle-class status, and much of the code of behaviour which seemed to them appropriate to their new condition was borrowed from their middle-class Protestant neighbours who were not merely largely puritan but also largely out of sympathy with the manners and modes of the 'peasantry'. Thus was lost much of the gaiety of the Irish countryside, not least in the observance of calendar custom, and Sir William Wilde could note in his *Popular Irish Superstitions*, 17:

'One of our most learned and observant Roman Catholic friends has just written to us, in answer to some queries relative to superstitions – "The tone of society in Ireland is becoming more and more 'Protestant' every year; the literature is a Protestant one, and even the priests are becoming more Protestant in their conversation and manners. They have condemned all the holy wells and resorts of pilgrims, with the single exception of Lough Derg, and of this they are ashamed: for,

20 Donnybrook fair (Hall: *Ireland*)

whenever a Protestant goes upon the Island, the ceremonies are
stopped! Among all the affectionate mentions of his dearly-beloved
father made by John O'Connell, he had not the courage to say 'The
Lord rest his sowle'. I have watched these changes with great interest." '

Were Sir William alive today he might note, with a return of
self-respect and self-confidence, somewhat of a popular revival of
country things – ballads, music, dancing and to some extent calendar
custom.

Sir William, however, did not lay all the blame for this blighting of
rustic gaiety at the doors of the self-righteous. He admits (he was
writing in 1849) that the Famine had deeply affected country life (id.
14–15):

'The old forms and customs, too, are becoming obliterated; the
festivals are unobserved, and the rustic festivities neglected or forgotten; the bowlings, the cakes and the prinkums (the peasants' balls
and routs), do not often take place when starvation and pestilence stalk
over a country, many parts of which appear as if a destroying army had
but recently passed through it. Such is the desolation which whole

districts, of Connaught at least, at this moment present; entire villages being levelled to the ground, the fences broken, the land untilled and often unstocked, and miles of country lying idle and unproductive, without the face of a human being to be seen upon it. The hare has made its form on the hearth, and the lapwing wheels over the ruined cabin. The faction-fights, the hurlings, and the mains of cocks that used to be fought at Shrovetide and Easter, these twenty years, and the mummers and May-boys left off when we were a gossoon no bigger than a pitcher. It was only, however, within those three years that the *waits* ceased to go their rounds upon the cold frosty mornings in our native village at Christmas; and although the "wran boys" still gather a few halfpence on St Stephen's Day we understand there wasn't a candle blessed in the chapel nor a breedogue seen in the barony where Kilmucafauden stands, last Candlemas Day; no, nor even a cock killed in every fifth house, in honour of St Martin; and you'd step over the brosnach of a bonfire that the childer lighted last St John's Eve.'

Michaelmas

It would appear that the feast of St Michael the Archangel (29 September) had no especial significance under the older Irish system of time reckoning. The coming of the Anglo-Normans, however, and the establishment of their legal customs over a great part of Ireland gave Michaelmas an important place in the calendar. A glance at any collection of ancient Anglo-Irish deeds or charters will show that in grants, settlements, contracts, payments of rent, and so on, the dates of legal consequence were Easter and Michaelmas. In several towns, Michaelmas was the day of the Mayor's election; thus, in 1699 John Dunton wrote of Drogheda (McLysaght: *Irish Life in the XVII Century,* 390):

'It is governed by a mayor, two sheriffs and aldermen, and they have a custom that as soon as ever their mayor is sworn on Michaelmas-day in the morning an account of it is sent by an express to Dublin, which in four hours or less conveys it thither, though I could never learn the origin of it, yet they say here that the Lord Mayor of Dublin is not to be sworn until he hears the Mayor of Drogheda is.'

In Kilkenny the election of the Mayor at Michaelmas was celebrated by bull-baiting, as we learn from John Prim in *Trans. Kilkenny Archaeological Society 1852,* 326:

'But although bull-baiting, in order to make way for cock-fighting was excluded from the category of polite recreations in Kilkenny in the beginning of the eighteenth century; it still remained a much affected pastime with the lower classes, the butchers, however, keeping the direction and arrangement of the sport amongst themselves, as they supplied the animal whose torture was to amuse the mob. In this way it survived to the present generation, a bull being baited regularly every Michaelmas Day, on the occasion of the swearing of the new mayor into office and some mayors even contributing money towards increasing the festivity, in order to make themselves popular with the butchers' fraternity – always considered a very important ally on occasions of political excitement. The original bull-ring was in the neighbourhood of St Francis' Abbey, where the locality is still termed "The Ring"; but the modern bull-baiting always took place in St James' Green, and the last time the savage spectacle was there witnessed was so late as the 29th September, 1837.'

In certain areas Michaelmas had some importance in payment of rent, letting of grazing, repayment of loans, hiring of servants and other such transactions. More usually the autumn date for minor contracts of this kind was November Day, but here and there landlords and others in power tried, with varying success to substitute Michaelmas for this. A county Limerick tradition tells of the people's resentment of the landlord's attempt to make this change and of efforts to avoid it.

Michaelmas marked *Fomhar na nGéan*, the goose harvest, when geese hatched in the spring were ready for the market. By far the most popular Michaelmas custom in Ireland was the eating of a goose for dinner on this day. Farmers' wives who had large flocks (the care and disposal of fowl being women's business) made presents of geese to friends and often gave them to poor families too. This was one of the days when, according to tradition, farmers killed an animal and gave portions of meat to the poor. That this custom may be of some antiquity is suggested by a passage in Keating's *Forus Feasa ar Éirinn;* the passage is summarized as follows in *Journal of the Kildare Archaeological Society*, v., 447:

'Geoffrey Keating in his *History of Ireland* (pages 342–5 of the London edition of 1723) relates at length a legend of how St Patrick was the means (through the intercession of St Michael) of restoring to life Lewy, the young son of Leary, Monarch of Ireland, in the fifth century. The young prince's mother, Aongus, was so overjoyed at having him restored to her alive, that she placed herself under a solemn vow, to bestow annually on the poor on Michaelmas Day one sheep out of every flock she possessed, in honour of the Archangel. And it was ordained by law that all the Christian converts in the kingdom should follow the queen's example. And in obedience to this injunction arose the custom of killing St Michael's Sheep called in the Irish language Cuid Mhichíll, observed to this day. For it is most certain that every family, upon the nine-and-twentieth of September, which is the anniversary festival in honour of St Michael, at least of the ordinary sort of people, kill a sheep, and bestow the greatest part of it upon relieving the poor.'

In some instances it appears that a rent of geese was paid at Michaelmas, thus in the early fourteenth century the burgesses of the town of Forth, County Carlow, rendered each Michaelmas ten geese or twenty pence in lieu thereof. (*Calendar of Justiciary Rolls 1305-7*, 346). In parts of the west and south-west Michaelmas marked the end of the fishing season, and the fishing boats and gear were stowed away for the winter.

In east Munster and south Leinster where most farms had orchards, about Michaelmas was considered the proper time for picking the apples and for making cider which formerly was a popular home-brew in those areas. It was also one of the periods when down was plucked from live geese for the filling of mattress and pillows.

At Tramore, County Waterford, the summer holiday season was closed with a curious ceremony. The custom of 'going to the sea' is old in this area; merchants from the towns as well as farming families have been coming to Tramore for more than two hundred years, with the result that many local people derived much of their livelihood from this custom, lodging-house keepers, owners of bathing-machines, vendors of fish, 'say-grass' (dilisc), periwinkles and other marine delicacies, and many others. On the feast of St Michael, these people marched in a body to the edge of the sea and threw in an effigy named 'Micil', as a jocose hint to the great Archangel that his festival meant financial loss to them.

For those who followed that sport, the hunting season began at Michaelmas, as Mason noted in his *Parochial Survey*, at Kilrush:

'On the 29th September, (Michaelmas day,) the harvest being generally secured, hunting commences. Plenty of hares are to be had in all parts of the union, and particularly in the bogs of Shragh. Foxes are scarce, and keep chiefly in the cliffs.'

The End of the Harvest

Ripe corn must be gathered in without undue delay lest the grain be shed from the ears or the crop damaged by bad weather or by disease. Thus a degree of urgency was normal at harvest time, especially before the coming of the harvesting machinery. Everybody was called out to help, men and women, young and old, master, workpeople and neighbours.

At other times each group had its own work, the men in the fields, the women in the house, the children at school. Only at harvest time were they all together engaged in the same work, and with fine weather and the promise of abundance it was only natural that there were jokes, pranks, and general merriment, with the anxious farmer unwilling to damp the high spirits but trying to ensure that these did not hold up the work.

The last bit of corn in the last of the farmer's fields was the visible symbol of the end of the harvest, and the cutting of this last bit was, all over Ireland, attended with some ceremony.

Usually a small portion, enough to make one sheaf, was left standing while the rest of field was fully finished, then all the workers gathered to see it cut. It was generally said that some living creature, a small animal or bird was to be found in the last of the standing corn. This was often actually the case, as frogs, corncrakes, partridges and such small creatures drew back before the advancing reapers until finally making a dash for safety. In most cases the creature was, or was said to be, a hare, and 'putting the hare out of the corn' meant finishing the harvest – 'have you put the hare out yet?' 'We'll have her put out before the night!'

Often, before the last piece was cut the workers raised a shout or made noise to 'put out the hare', and if a farm nearby still had standing corn, the hare was said to go there; 'we sent you the hare' was the quip thrown at the farmer whose harvest was late.

People remembered the old tale of the hag who turned into a hare to steal the cows' milk, and they also spoke of putting out the hag or *cailleach,* who was driven from farm to farm until she reached the field of the last man in the parish to cut his corn. Then she could go no farther, and the unfortunate tardy one had to support her for the year. In many parts of Ireland the last sheaf itself was called the *cailleach* or hag.

The manner of cutting the last sheaf varied from one district to another. In places as far apart as Antrim and Down in the north-east and Limerick and Tipperary in the south-west the reapers stood back a short distance and threw their reaping hooks in turn at it. To cut it in this way needed both luck and skill and the worker who succeeded in cutting the last stalks was loudly cheered. Where both luck and skill failed, the one whose hook fell nearest – or in some places farthest – was thus chosen to cut it. Where scythes were used, the workers might be blindfolded in turn and each allowed one or more sweeps with the scythe until it was cut. In many places in east Ulster the bit of standing corn was bound into a sheaf or ornamentally plaited before the cutting contest.

The last sheaf was held by many to affect the destiny of its cutter, but opinions differed as to whether the outcome would be good or bad luck. Generally in the midlands the owner of the field, or in some cases the youngest present, was chosen, in other districts lots were drawn to decide. Some held that whoever cut or bound it would die unmarried. In County Carlow the girls were asked each to have a stroke at it with a reaping hook, and she who felled it at one blow would be married within the year.

The last sheaf was usually tied in an ornamental fashion and carried from the field by a chosen bearer, most often by the one who had cut it. Pranks were played on the bearer, a very widespread one being the throwing of water on bearer and sheaf. In County Leitrim this was said to prevent drought during the next year. In County Clare holy water was sprinkled on sheaf and bearer.

Usually the bearer, accompanied by all the workers, brought the sheaf into the farmyard or to the door of the dwelling-house, and there presented it to the owner or the owner's wife, asking for a treat, either drinks there and then or the promise of a harvest feast. The sheaf might be hung around the housewife's neck, with a jocose threat to choke her if the treat were not forthcoming, or tied to the body or legs of the owner with similar threats.

191

Sometimes the sheaf was 'bought' by the farmer or his wife paying out a sum of money so that the workmen could treat themselves to drinks at the local tavern.

The 'Clousúr'

In county Kerry, and especially on the small farms of the Dingle Peninsula the end of the harvest was known as *an clousúr* (from Latin *clausura*, closure, conclusion). When the harvest work was completely finished, the oats stacks thatched and secured and the potato pits properly made, the menfolk of the family brought their harvesting implements, spades and reaping hooks, into the kitchen and threatened to burn them in the fire unless the women provided them with a festive meal. Usually they went through the pantomine of laying one or more implements on the fire, whereon the women rushed to save these from being burned, and promised that the meal would be ready that evening or on another suitable evening. The same custom appears to have been known formerly in parts of Connaught also.

21 Harvest *cailleach*, County Leix (National Museum, Dublin)

The reaping hooks used in Ireland in the past had smooth blades, which were sharpened as required during the reaping. Not everybody could produce a perfect cutting edge on a scythe or a reaping hook, and those who had this 'gift' were duly proud of it. There was even a charm, *ortha an fhaoir*, the 'edge charm', which might be recited to induce a reluctant implement to take a keen edge. A good worker always resharpened his implement at the conclusion of the day's work, and at the final conclusion of the harvest the scythes and hooks were finely sharpened before being stored away with their edges protected by pieces of wood or a wrapping of straw rope.

Gleaning

In parts of Counties Kildare and Meath the first Sunday after 15 August was known as *Deascán* Sunday (*deascán* = gleaning). On that

192

day the gleaning of the cornfields was done by the farmers with their families and work people. The farmer's wife prepared the midday meal in picnic fashion, to be eaten in the field in an interval of the gleaning in which everybody took part. The gleaned corn was made into sheaves in the ordinary way and added to the corn already gathered.

22   Harvest knot, County Armagh (National Museum, Dublin)

The Harvest Home

The successful gathering of the harvest was usually followed by a 'harvest home' – a feast given by the farmer for his workers both paid and voluntary.

In the small farms of the north and west of Ireland where the total number of workers did not exceed a dozen or so, the feast was usually held in the farmhouse kitchen, while in the larger farms of the south and east with many more workers it was more likely to be in the great corn barn. In either case the last sheaf was prominently displayed, and at the dance which usually followed the feast, the girl who had tied the sheaf was led out first by the farmer or by his eldest son.

Naturally the size and quality of the feast varied according to the circumstances of the givers. On a small farm it was usually simple with a few drinks, while on a large farm there might be an abundance of rustic delicacies with a corresponding flood of liquid réfreshment. A lively account of one of these latter is given by Patrick Kennedy in *The Banks of the Boro*, 110–12, the period is about 1815:

'Mrs Greene, and her daughters and her servant-maids, and a few helpers, had been engaged from breakfast time in getting the mighty dinner ready – kitchen and parlour fires, and one or two in an outhouse, being fully occupied. The barn had been cleared out the day before, and in the course of the present morning was made as spruce as besoms and brushes could make it, and enlivened by two rows of tables, covered with clean table cloths, and furnished with dishes and well-arranged rows of plates, knives, forks, etc. Several fine bunches of full-eared wheat were suspended from the "collar-beams", chairs were settled at the ends of the tables, and the sides furnished with forms and stools, and those who were only used to see the place in its litter of straw, grain and sheaves, were delighted with its now neat and orderly appearance.

'Our festival took place when the gloomy weather of October was approaching. The invited were informed that dinner would be ready soon after two o'clock – a sufficiently late hour for working men accustomed to noontide for their principal meal. Some minutes before the hour specified, groups of labourers and small landholders were seen approaching; and on the lawn, and in the big yard, and even in the haggard, collections of threes, and fours and fives, might be seen in Sunday dress, high stiff shirt-collars, well-greased shoes, clean grey stockings, and brushed hats, striving to look unconcerned, but all the while uncomfortable in their best clothes, and somewhat disturbed by unwonted idleness at an ordinary hour of labour. Mr Dick Greene and his two fine young sons, Brian Roche, Charley Redmond, and Edward O'Brien, with some other farmer-folk of the better class, were in attendance as honorary guests, and these moving from one group to another, kept up their spirits near to the healthy spot, till the large dishes of potatoes, and meat, and cabbage were seen pouring out of the back door, and crossing the yard to the barn. Then was heard the clang of the bell from its little campanile over the stable, and the junior members of the family, our dear old friends under Mr O'Neill, Charlotte and Martha, and Rebecca and Richard, to whom this was a genuine gala day, and who had been playing tricks on every one in their exuberance of spirits from an early hour now acted as whippers-in, collecting and hurrying this or that shy person from lawn and haggard, and all the out-lying purlieus, till the chairs and forms were filled, and mighty slices of bacon or roast beef reposing on beds of white cabbage, began to be distributed by our "big farmer", and Mr Samuel his son, and the young men already named.

'The Mistress of the mansion had no great trouble with the solid portion of the entertainment once the seats were taken. The good cup-potatoes, in ordinary cases forming a wedge whose broad back rested on the table, were here supplied in large dishes. The quantity of these, and of the sides of bacon, and rounds and ribs of beef first laid down needed no renewal. Instead of the ordinary noggin of milk which each guest was in the habit of seeing at his right hand, he found a jug or big mug full of good home-brewed beer, such as a Dublin epicure could not obtain in his habitat at any price. No need of waiters hurrying to and fro to attend to the wants of the guests. Every carver generally supplied to his own clients as much meat and cabbage at once as he could consume; the potatoes were there in abundance, and black-jacks stood at intervals to supply the mugs or jugs with the appetizing draught.

'The good natured frolicsome children desired no better fun than running with these jacks when they began to get low to the beer barrel at the end of the building, filling and carrying them to their stations, generally pulling the ear of the person to whom they handed the vessel, if they found the eyes of father or brother turned away, and indulging in hearty outbursts of childish merriment – the sweetest sounds in creation. The son of the house and other carvers, seated at the ends and sides of the tables, kept a sharp eye on their neighbours, to see that they were freely honouring their meat, and drink; and if they saw anyone failing to make progress, sometimes threatened to report them to the master, who occupied himself in moving from post to post, and attending to the general comfort of the convivial gathering.'

Kennedy goes on to tell how, at the end of the meal, all the guests trooped out into the farmyard and the garden for a while, to find on their return that the barn had been cleared for the dance. Large bowls of punch were provided, healths were drunk, and the music and dancing, interspersed with solo items from notable local performers, continued until a late hour.

In the southwest the end of the potato harvest was celebrated by the giving of a 'stampy party' for the workers and helpers, so-called because the main dish was cakes of 'stampy', a bread made from grated raw potatoes, squeezed dry and mixed with flour and various flavourings. This was followed by a dance.

In parts of east Ulster, where the flax crop was of major importance, the end of the 'lint-pulling' – the flax harvest, was often celebrated by a harvest supper.

23 Harvest knot, County Armagh (National Museum, Dublin)

Harvest Knots

In certain areas, as part of the harvest celebration, small ornamental twists or knots of plaited straw were made and worn as a sign that the harvest was completed. Sometimes, this was done more or less casually about harvest time; frequently, however, the knots were specially made for the harvest 'home' or dance and worn on that occasion. Usually, they were made in two types, a more elaborate plait, with the corn ears still attached, worn by the women and a less ornamental twist, although made with equal skill, by the men.

In *The Ulster Journal of Archaeology*, 1942, 2, T. G. F. Paterson tells of these in County Armagh:

'Last autumn a friend asked me if I had noticed that harvest-knots were more in evidence than in former years. At the same time he queried as to why it should be so. I could only suggest that the revival might be due to the large acreages under corn and the consequent gossip amongst the older people as to harvesting customs in the days before mechanical reapers and binders came into general use.

'I was intrigued by the report, and on investigation I found it was an actual fact. In Armagh city on market-days in September-October I met many young men from the districts around the town, with such knots in their button-holes. That decided me to look farther afield. To my surprise and pleasure I discovered them in evidence in practically every parish from Loughgall and Grange, north of Armagh city to Killevy and Creggan, the two most southern of our county parishes.

'There are various types, some more ornate than others. In days past the girls wore their knots in their hair, and it was usual for them to incorporate the heads of the grain, whereas the men wore simple knots without any such appendages. It is clear however that the harvest-knots, though worn at the cutting of the calliagh, were not made specially for that ceremony. There is indeed ample evidence that they were worn on or before the actual cutting of the corn and for some time after, and that they were formerly exchanged between the sexes as a token of admiration or love, a custom fast dying out, hastened no doubt by the fact that machinery now does the work of lifting and binding, tasks undertaken almost exclusively by the womenfolk of half a century ago.'

And he notes:

'One young man, wearing a handsome and rather unusual knot, on being questioned as to who made it, replied "my sister". In conversation, I learned that he lived near, whereupon I said, "I shall call and have your sister teach me to make that particular knot". He then became much confused, and eventually confessed that it was "a gift from a girl".'

The custom of making these knots has a very interesting geographical distribution. They were found in localities in four main areas, namely east County Cork, eastern Offaly and Laois, north County Dublin and a wide area of Ulster, with concentrations in County Armagh and east County Donegal.

There is no doubt that this custom, which is well known and widespread in England and Scotland, was brought into Ireland, probably at various times, by peasants from Britain who were 'settled' in Ireland during the various plantations. Thus the instances in east county Cork may be connected with newcomers in Elizabethan times, perhaps in the aftermath of the Desmond defeat. Those in Laois and Offaly are surely a relic of Queen Mary's plantation of that area, and those of Ulster of the seventeenth-century planters, while north County Dublin has a strong element of population derived from the Anglo-Norman adventurers of late medieval times.

24   Harvest knot, County Donegal (National Museum, Dublin)

The Disposal of the last Sheaf

In most cases, as we have seen, the last sheaf was brought home and set up in the house or barn during the feast. Its further disposal varied from place to place.

Generally it was hung up in the house or in the barn or byre until it was replaced by the new sheaf at the following harvest. In some houses in County Armagh T. G. F. Paterson observed that sheaves were preserved year after year (*Ulster Folklife* ix, 62).

In County Donegal, we are told, some people made crosses from the last sheaf on St Brighid's Eve, while in County Galway it was sometimes made into 'bobbins' for the roof-ridge of the house. Some held that it had curative powers, and gave it to sick animals or calving cows, while the grain from it, burned to ashes and made into an ointment, would cure skin ailments.

People in Offaly ground the grain and added it to one of the harvest supper dishes. In Laois the grain might be thrown to the fowl and the first cockerel to reach it marked down for killing on St Martin's Eve. Others fed it to the horses, to increase their strength or to the fowl to ensure the supply of eggs.

The use of a sheaf of corn to find a drowned body is well known. The sheaf usually with a lighted candle set on it was laid on the water at the spot where the unfortunate victim had fallen in, and allowed to drift with the current until it came to rest where the body could be found. Some held that only a last sheaf had this virtue, or that it was far more efficacious than any ordinary sheaf.

A more sinister use of the last sheaf is remembered in some areas of North Leinster. This was the horrible ceremony known as 'burying the sheaf' and was, in effect, an attempt at murder by magic. A last sheaf had to be stolen. Then it was given the victim's name – some said that it had to be 'baptised in the name of the devil'. Next it was 'killed' by stabbing or striking and then buried. As it decayed in the earth, so the victim went into decline and finally died. He could only be saved by finding the sheaf, digging it up and burning it.

It is with relief that we turn from this gruesome practice to the pleasant and pious one of using some of the last of the harvest to decorate the church for the Harvest Thanksgiving which is held by Protestant congregations in many parts of Ireland. T. G. F. Paterson tells us about this in County Armagh. (*Ulster Journal of Archaeology*, 1944, 108):

'In certain districts where the population is mostly of Scotch and English descent, I saw some decorated plaits commonly called "Dressed Calliaghs", a type that finds a place in the harvest decorations at the annual Church Festival following the gathering in of the crops.

'Apart from the appearance of the "Dressed Calliagh" at Harvest Services, it is customary in some parishes to make beautifully-shaped miniature corn ricks for the same Festival, at which they usually occupy a conspicuous place. The ricks are indeed works of art, the building of them requiring deft fingers and an eye for proportion, besides an expenditure of patience in shaping and thatching. I saw two such ricks this year: one in Derrynoose and the other in Mullavilly parish.'

Samhain

The ancient festival of *Samhain*, the first day of Winter is traditionally kept on 1 November, the Feast of All Saints, and the vigil of this day, *Oíche Shamhna*, Hallow E'en, Hollantide, is celebrated all over Ireland with feasting, merrymaking and divination.

This is a description of how the day was kept in the western part of County Limerick at the end of the last century:

'In this West Limerick hill country I have heard the names *Oíche Shamhna* or *Oíche na sprideanna* applied to the Eve of November the first. I met old people who remembered the name *Sean-Shamhain* but they could not definitely give the exact day. Sixteen miles to the east I heard it called *púca* night and Snap-apple night near Rathkeale.

'It was called *púca* night and *oíche na sprideanna* (spirit night) because of the old people's belief that both the fairies and the ghosts of the dead were active then.

'November day and eve were regarded by old people as undoubtedly one of the leading festivals of the year. In the Rathkeale area the *púca* was supposed to spit on and blight blackberries and other fruits. Children were forbidden to touch them from that date lest the blight should affect themselves.

'Our ancients looked on the night as the end of the year's growth, and fairies were let loose to visit every growing plant and with their breath blast berries and hedge-rows, field blossoms, ragworts and late thistles. Our elders saw evidence of a great festival in the food offerings left near doors of houses often outside, some of these being the last portion of the potato or corn garden of which a small part was left in the ground for the fairy host to ensure their favour for the coming year. Many elders do not know to whom these offerings were given. Vessels were filled with water in more recent days and left as offerings.

'Holy water was sprinkled on animals that night with blessings.

200

Nowadays we have church offerings for the Holy Souls. Old shop-keepers in selling snuff or tobacco give a little *tuille* in honour of the departed.

'In mid Limerick candles were formerly lighted on the night after November 1st, one for each deceased relative at a window of the room where death occurred. I saw a case where the candle was placed in the window facing the grave-yard and left lighting all night. I heard of another case where a candle in a lantern was left lighting all night on the grave of the loved one.

'Here in the West the custom is well nigh lost. Yet the belief that the dead can return on this night is firmly rooted still. "Go to the churchyard gate if you have courage" said old Dicky Ned to me nearly forty years ago "and you will meet there the friend you love," – referring to a dear friend who had died some time before.

'Another old friend, in Rathkeale, told me of the last woman who was hanged in public in Limerick. This lady had killed her husband, with the intention of marrying a certain young man. She relied on her influence with Barrington of Murroe to shield her. She even went to his place in Wicklow till the danger should pass.

'It was all in vain: the crime was too glaring. She was arrested, tried and condemned. The date of the execution was fixed. Some days before she sent for the young man, who had no hand in the dreadful deed. He visited the woman. Very coolly she told him she would come to marry him on November Eve.

'She was duly executed: it was remarked that in her last moments she paid the greatest attention to dress wearing a pair of fashionable brogues with silver buckles.

'Neighbours remarked that when the young man went at night for a walk the sound of those brogues was always heard on the road beside or after him.

'The last day of October came and the young man, as in a trance excited, dressed himself carefully in the evening and towards midnight listened for the steps outside. They came to the horror of his friends in the house and like one enraptured he broke away from his sister and brother, who heard the steps of two persons fading in the distance.

'Next day he was found drowned.

'On this night those who injured during life some departed one dreaded meeting the offended soul. I well remember how on at least three separate occasions a certain man called on me in the afternoon of November 1st to walk home with him. He had imbibed a little

201

strong drink and on the way, on each occasion, he recounted how years before he had wronged a "widow-woman" leading her to believe that the cow he sold her was in calf. For this deception the unforgiving widow periodically way-laid him on All Souls Eve. This local wide-spread fear probably gave rise to the custom (now happily extinct) of pretending to be ghosts with a hat of ancient days or shawl of a grandmother to frighten some young relatives. I know of this having been done.

'Many well known divinatory customs of an amusing kind were carried on formerly much more than at present. Old and young formerly took part in these games. Among these were the roasting of beans and nuts. The girl who placed the bean watched where this would leap, some ambitious youth perhaps making a wide front on the landscape. Melted lead passed thro' a key formed shapes suggestive of future destiny in the water – a gun, a spade, a coffin, a scissors, an awl, a ship or boat or even the tall hat of a clergyman each indicative of some vocation. Many a maiden and many a youth secretly spread shift or shirt before a fire and watched from some safe coign of vantage to see who would turn these articles late at night. The reel of thread was cast into a lime kiln to find out who would wind it up again. A snail in the hollow between two plates was supposed to trace some plan of a future for the person who put it there.

'This very morning I called on an old lady in Athea who told me that as a girl, one November Eve, she ate up a salt herring in three bites in the hope that her future husband might appear to her in a dream, offering her a drink of water. When she confessed this high crime, the parish priest said *Ná raibh eagal' ort go dtachtfadh an dial thú?* ("Were you not afraid that the devil would choke you?")

'Often the divination and other games, snap-apple, ducking for apples and coins in a tub, were carried out by a group of young people who gathered in some houses where the owners were sympathetic to the fun.

'At the gathering there was a little feast where cream pancakes, stampy, apple cakes, nuts and black-berry pies figured. A ring concealed in one of the cakes foretold a marriage next "sherofe" or a tiny boat of wood pre-figured a journey to Skellig rocks and single blessedness.

'Often, in coming to and going home from this gathering young jokers took the wheels from carts and placed them on the house-top. Cabbages taken from a haggard were to all seeming stolen by a

202

neighbour. Often a man sleeping off his drunkness by the roadside arrived home with painted face or coat of many colours.

'As regards weather forecasts, a stake was put standing at the junction of two streams, upright and sunk in the mud. The elders professed to deduce from its appearance next day (Nov. 1st) how the winter weather would turn out. The moon on the Eve was also a guide.

'On this Eve more than at any other festival the fairy hosts were supposed to muster their best in the forts and lisses. Most old people thought that there were more malevolent spirits abroad on the Eve of November than at May Eve or St John's Eve.

'Many people took steps to protect themselves and their property and livestock. A plain cross of wood was often fixed overhead on the thatch inside the housedoor to keep off evil spirits. I heard of no straw cross thus used. The cross I was told was often placed on the ground outside in front of the door. Holy water was generally sprinkled on the door. Often where some farm animal died as a result of a visit from some fairy of evil at Hallow-E'en in previous years holy water would be scattered or a rude cross affixed to the stable door. If animals show illness or restiveness on Nov. Eve people often spit on them to banish if present some mischievous sprite. I heard a few stories of old people who when young on this Eve saw in a rath or fort some of their departed friends disporting themselves with the fairies. On this night those who wished to invoke the help of evil spirits must find a briar which was rooted at both ends and crawl through it while making their un-hallowed request. Among the things which could be thus obtained were the power to "colour" playing cards and to work those *piseóga* by which a neighbour's profit might be stolen. One local story told of what happened when a character called Rake O'Neill did this.

'Rake sought a long time for a double rooted briar and finding it at last crept under it on Hallow E'en in the Devil's name to obtain his wish. Being music-crazy he asked for the gift of perfect music. He was astonished to find on the ground as he turned round after this feat – a fiddle. He took up the violin and found it had only one string. He tried to fit it out with the usual number but always failed. Another odd thing was that it would only play one tune which everybody declared was the *ceól-sidhe* (fairy music) which filled every listener with delight. The parish priest objected to the sensations this music gave rise to and he ordered Rake to bring him the fiddle so as to exorcise the evil one, whereupon Rake took his fiddle to England where he met a Frenchman who took him to France where for thirty years he played the tune each night to a charmed audience at the royal court. When Rake died it was found that as the priest gave him absolution the fiddle-string snapped with resounding force, and bow and violin fell asunder.'

Feasting and Merrymaking

Hallow E'en was a night when the housewife must open her cupboards and spread a little feast for the family. Even the poorest household must have something special for supper in honour of the night, and here, as on other festivals, more prosperous neighbours ensured that a present of milk, butter, vegetables and other ingredients of the feast, passed to their poorer friends as well as to their workpeople.

The vigil of the Feast of All the Saints has for many centuries been a day of abstinence, that is to say, a day on which no meat was eaten. Thus the traditional dishes on Hallow E'en did not include meat.

A favourite food was colcannon ('pandy', 'champ'), that is mashed boiled potatoes mixed with cooked green cabbage and chopped raw onion, seasoned with pepper and salt. In some households this was served in a large common dish, around which the whole family sat, each armed with a spoon. In both cases a hollow was made in the middle of the colcannon and a large pat of butter put in. This soon melted, and each spoonful was dipped in it before going into the mouth.

'Stampy' (cakes made from a blending of grated raw potato and flour, flavoured with sugar, carawayseeds and cream), 'boxty' (similar cakes, but with mashed cooked potato), oatcakes and batter pancakes were favoured too, as were dumplings, apple-cake, blackberry pies, puddings of various sorts. 'No shraft without a wedding' says the proverb 'and no Hollantide without a pudding'.

In 1831, Amhlaoibh Ó Súilleabháin entered in his diary:
'The thirty first day, Monday. November, or Hallow Eve. A fine, dry, cloudy, day: a gentle south west wind. I spent the night sociably and comfortably, eating apples, drinking tea, roasting nuts, drinking "punch" and eating "apple pie". Thus I ended up the autumn season.'
– showing how a worthy and sober schoolmaster joined in the revelry.

Children get gifts of apples and nuts for the occasion from friends and relatives, and various games are played with these, the old, traditional fruits of the countryside.

General Vallencey, in *Collectanea de Rebus Hibernicis*, xii, 460–1, tells us that:

25   Hallow E'en (*The Book of Days*, 1864)

'Every house abounds in the best viands they can afford: apples and nuts are devoured in abundance; the nut-shells are burnt, and from the ashes, many strange things are foretold . . . They dip for apples in a tub of water, and endeavour to bring one up in the mouth; they suspend a cord with a cross-stick, with apples at one point, and candles lighted at the other, and endeavour to catch the apple, while it is in a circular motion, in the mouth.'

These games, already old two hundred years ago, continue in popularity. They were described in *Journal of the Kildare Archaeological* Society, 1908, p. 448:

'(a) A half-barrel was placed on the floor, and nearly filled with water; silver coins were thrown in, and large apples set floating on it; boys, stripped to the waist, with their hands tied behind their backs, then endeavoured to take up the former with their lips, and the latter with their teeth; and what they landed they were allowed to keep.

'(b) Two sticks fastened together, cross-fashion, with their ends pointed, were slung by a cord from a rafter or beam. An apple and a lighted candle, alternately, were stuck on the ends of the sticks, and they were sent spinning round. The game was now for a boy to bite a piece out of the apple, without getting a mouthful of the candle.'

They are still familiar to most Irish children. Some are content with a simpler form of the hanging apple, with just one apple on a string. Others, fearing the danger of burns to the smaller children, substitute potatoes for the candles, and much merriment is caused by a contestant taking a bite from one of these instead of from an apple.

In a west Kerry version a box, stool, churn or similar object is placed under the hanging apple. Each player has a short stick in one hand and, keeping the other hand on the box or stool runs around it seven times as rapidly as possible and then tries to strike the apple with the stick. Success here wins the apple, but the dizziness induced by running around usually caused the player to miss, and often the onlookers must scatter wildly to avoid the blow.

These games give the night some of its popular names. 'Snap-Apple Night', 'Ducking Night', 'Nut-crack night', *Oíche na n-úll*.

Samhain – Beliefs and Customs

Samhain, 1 November, was the first day of winter and the end of the farmer's year. All his crops, all his livestock had to be secure for the hard season to come. Corn of all sorts, hay, potatoes, turnips, apples must by now be harvested and stored with ricks well made and well thatched and tied. Dry cattle and sheep were moved from distant moorland and mountain pastures and brought to the fields near the farmstead. Milking cows were brought into the byre for the winter and hand-feeding with stored fodder began. In the South-east of Ireland, where this crop was grown, winter wheat had to be in the ground by this date.

Turf and wood for the winter fires must have been gathered, and lucky was the household which had in store a pile of bog-deal, the sweet-smelling, clear-burning roots or stems of ancient pine trees found in cutting turf.

'Everyone has debts at Hallow E'en' says the proverb, and this was a time of general settling-up. Workmen were given their wages, rents were paid and the hire of conacre-tillage and grazing was settled. In the days before the festival, and in many places on its eve, fairs and markets, such as the famous 'Snap-apple Fair' in Kilmallock, were held.

206

Nor was general activity confined to humans, for the denizens of the other world were abroad too, and, however great the fright, nobody would really be surprised to meet with the *Púca*, or the Black Pig, or that horrible headless apparition, the *dallachán*, or to awake in the night and find the returned dead of the family seated around the kitchen hearth.

Thus 'Lageniensis' records, in his *Irish Folk Lore*, 1870, 219:

'It is considered that, on All-Hallows' Eve, hobgoblins, evil spirits, and fairies, hold high revel, and that they are travelling abroad in great numbers. The dark and sullen Phooka is then particularly mischievous and many mortals are abducted to fairy land. Those persons taken away to the raths are often seen at this time by their living friends, and usually accompanying a fairy cavalcade. If you meet the fairies, it is said, on All-Hallows' Eve, and throw the dust taken from under your feet at them, they will be obliged to surrender any captive human being belonging to their company. Although this evening was kept as a merry one in farmsteads, yet those who assembled together wished to go and return in company with others; for in numbers a tolerable guarantee, they thought, was obtained from malign influences and practices of the evil spirits.'

People travelling on this night could easily be led astray by the fairies. To counteract this, the late wayfarer should carry a black-handled knife or have a steel needle stuck in his coat collar or sleeve. If by chance he was led astray, he might disguise himself by turning his coat inside-out, on which the fairies would no longer know him and divert their attentions elsewhere.

On this night, anybody throwing out water should call out *Seachain!* (beware!) or *chughaibh an t-uisce!* (water towards you!), to enable the ghosts and fairies to step aside and avoid being splashed.

Many people, in passing by ring-forts and other abodes of the fairies, heard sounds of revelry within, and November Eve, like May Eve was fraught with danger of fairy abduction.

Children were told that the *púca* went about on this night spitting or urinating on all wild fruits, which must not be eaten henceforth; this was a practical way of preventing the small ones from eating damaged and decayed fruits.

With all this unseen activity precautions had to be taken. In many places, crosses, less elaborate than those for St Brighid's Eve, were made and set up. In the *Journal of the Kildare Archaeological Society*, 1908, 450, we read that:

'It was customary, too, on this Eve to weave a cross called a "Parshell". This was done by laying two little sticks, seven inches in length, cross-ways; then starting at their junction by weaving a wheaten straw under one arm, over the next, and so on (adding a fresh straw as the other was used up) until about an inch from the ends of the sticks, when the straw-end was made fast. The "Parshell" was fixed over the dwelling-house doorway on the inside, with the object of warding off ill-luck, sickness, and witchcraft for a twelvemonth. A new one was made on the following All Hallows Eve, and put in place of the old one, which was shifted to another part of the house, or to the

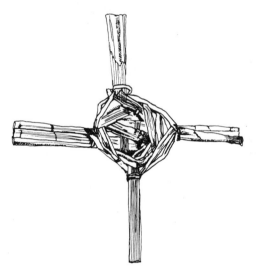

26 Hallow E'en cross, County Mayo (National Museum, Dublin)

cow-stable, the following words being used in removing it:- "Fonstaren-sheehy".'

Infants and children were protected by sprinkling holy water on them, and by putting iron or a dead ember from the fire in the cradle.

Elizabeth Andrews, in *Ulster Folklore,* 96, gives a tradition from Derry:

'The fairies, being believed to be fallen angels, are especially dreaded on Hallow Eve night. In some places oatmeal and salt are put on the heads of the children to protect them from harm. I first heard of this custom in the valley of the Roe.'

As regards the coming into the house of the souls of its dead, Patrick

Kennedy recalls a memory of Wexford about 1820, in *Evenings in the Duffrey*, 92:

' "Glory be to God," said one of the old women, "wouldn't it be an awful thing if the souls of all the people that ever lived in this house were now sitting on the shelves of the dresser and the bars of the bacon-rack, and everywhere they could find a seat, and looking on at what we're doing. Some people do be saying that happens on every All Saints' Eve". Bedad, a good many in the company got rather disturbed, and looked one side and the other, and only every thing was so bright and cheerful, they'd, I'm sure, be frightened enough.'

Most people, however, regarded the night of 2 Nov., All Souls Day, and not that of Hallow E'en, as the time of the visit of the dead, and of prayers and other ceremonies for their rest; these are described below, under that date.

There are traditions of the lighting of bonfires. In his *Irish Folk Lore*, 218, "Lageniensis" speaks of this custom as already obsolete.

'Bonfires were formerly kindled at this time, as well as at Mid-summer. When the embers had partially burned out, those who assembled were accustomed to cast them about in various directions, or sometimes at each other, with no slight danger to those who were not skilful in parrying or escaping from the burning brands. Among men and boys this was regarded as an amusement only, however dangerous it might prove to individuals; but it is thought to have been connected with former Druidic or Gentile incantations. The high streets or market squares of towns and villages, or fair-greens and cross-roads in the country places, were usually selected for kindling this Samhan pile.'

The custom, however, still is to be found in places, and particularly in Dublin City, as is shown by this newspaper report, in *The Sunday Press*, 1 Nov. 1970:

'Hallowe'en provided one of the busiest nights this year for Dublin firemen last night, Gardai spent several hours touring the city keeping bonfires under control and preventing youths and children taking materials from business premises for the fires.

'Between 6 p.m. and 8.30 p.m. Dublin Fire Brigade headquarters handled more than 120 calls from the public and Gardai to deal with bonfires out of control. At one stage 10 units were on continuous bonfire duty.

'The Gardai had their share of work. Youths took tyres from premises in Leinster Street and the East Wall for bonfires. Children left crackers on roads to be detonated by passing cars.'

Hallow-E'en Guisers

A familiar sight in Dublin city on and about October 31 is that of small groups of children, arrayed in grotesque garments and with faces masked or painted, accosting the passers-by or knocking on house doors with the request: "Help the Hallow E'en party! Any apples or nuts?" in the expectation of being given small presents; this, incidentally, is all the more remarkable as it is the only folk custom of the kind which has survived in the metropolis.

27 Hallow E'en mask, County Wicklow (National Museum, Dublin)

A couple of generations ago, in parts of Dublin and in other areas of Ireland, the groups would have consisted of young men and grown boys, who often travelled considerable distances in their quest, with consequently greater reward. The proceeds were usually expended on a "Hallow E'en party," with music, dancing, feasting and so on, at some chosen house, and not merely consumed on the spot as with the children nowadays.

General Vallencey, (*Collectanea de Rebus Hibernicis* xii, 1783, 459–60) tells us that:

'On the Oidhche Shamhna, (Ee Owna) or Vigil of *Saman*, the peasants in Ireland assemble with sticks and clubs, (the emblems of laceration) going from house, collecting money, bread cake, butter,

210

cheese, eggs, &c. &c. for the feast, repeating verses in honour of the solemnity, demanding preparations for the festival, in the name of St Columb Kill, desiring them, to lay aside the *fatted calf*, and to bring forth the black sheep.'

Here the worthy General's referring to the sticks carried by the men (probably to deter hostile dogs) as "emblems of laceration" is merely his romantic imagination searching for anything which might, no matter how remotely, be attributed to some supposed ancient religious rite.

Irisleabhar na Gaedhilge, ii, 370, states that in parts of County Waterford:

'Hallow E'en is called *oídhche na h-aimléise*, *"The night of mischief or con"*. It was a custom in the county – it survives still in places – for the "boys" to assemble in gangs, and, headed by a few horn-blowers, who were always selected for their strength of lungs, to visit all the farmers' houses in the district and levy a sort of blackmail, good-humouredly asked for, and as cheerfully given. They afterwards met at some rendezvous, and in merry revelry celebrated the festival of *Samhain* in their own way. When the distant winding of the horns was heard, the *bean a' tigh* prepared for their reception, and got ready the money or *builín* (white bread) to be handed to them through the half-opened door. Whoever heard the wild scurry of their rush through a farm-yard to the kitchen-door – there was always a race amongst them to get possession of the latch – will not question the propriety of the word *aimiléis* applied to their proceedings. The leader of the band chaunted a sort of recitative in Gaelic, intoning it with a strong nasal twang to conceal his identity, in which the good-wife was called upon to do honour to Samhain. Though I heard it frequently in my young days, I forget the words. Perhaps some reader would supply them, and give further information respecting a curious custom evidently a relic of the olden time.'

A contributor to *An Claidheamh Soluis*, 15 Dec. 1906, 5, gives an example of these verses, from Ring, County Waterford:

'*Anocht Oidhche Shamhna, a Mhongo Mango. Sop is na fuin-neogaibh; dúntar na dóirse. Eirigh id' shuidhe, a bhean an tighe. Téirigh siar go banamhail, tar aniar go flaitheamhail. Tabhair leat ceapaire aráin agus ime ar dhath do leacain fhéin; a mbeidh léim ghirrfiadh dhe aoirde ann agus ciscéim choiligh dhe im air. Tabhair chugham peigín de bhainne righin, mín, milis a mbeidh leamhnach 'n-a chosa agus uachtar 'n-a mhullaigh; go mbeidh sé ag imtheacht 'n-a chnocaibh agus ag teacht 'n-a shléibhtibh, agus badh dhóigh leat go dtachtfadh sé mé, agus mo chreach fhada níor bhaoghal dom.'*

'("Oh Mongo Mango, Hallow E'en to night. Straw in the windows and close the doors. Rise up housewife, go inside womanly, return hospitably, bring with you a slice of bread and butter the colour of your own cheek, as high as a hare's jump with a cock's step of butter on it. Bring us a measure of thick fine sweet milk, with new milk below and cream above, coming in hills and going in mountains; you may think it would choke me, but, alas! I am in no danger.")'

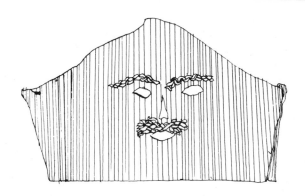

28 Hallow E'en mask, County Wicklow (National Museum, Dublin)

Another example of some thirty lines from Kinsale, County Cork, is given in *Irisleabhar na Gaeilge*, xvi, 157. It ends:

> *Seo, a mháighistreás,*
> *Cuarduigh do phócaí*
> *Agus tabhair rud éigineach do sna buachaillíbh,*
> *Agus scaoil chun siubhail iad;*
> *Nó buail mé féin idir an dá shúil*
> *Le píosa leath-choróineach.*

('Now, mistress, search your pockets, and give something to the boys, and let them go on their way. Or hit me between the eyes with a half-crown piece').

There is no doubt that General Vallencey's reference (above) to St Colmcille, the fatted calf and the black sheep, comes from a nonsense rhyme of this kind.

Another description of this custom, from east County Cork, is given

212

by W. Hackett, in *Transactions of the Kilkenny Archaeological Society*, 1852-3, 308:

'Not many years since, on Samhain's eve, 31st October, a rustic procession perambulated the district between Ballycotton and Trabolgan, along the coast. The parties represented themselves as messengers of the Muck Olla, in whose name they levied contributions on farmers; as usual they were accompanied by sundry youths, sounding lustily on cows' horns; at the head of the procession was a figure enveloped in a white robe or sheet, having, as it were, the head of a mare, this personage was called the *Láir Bhán,* "the white mare", he was a sort of president or master of the ceremonies. A long string of verses was recited at each house. In the second distich were distinctly mentioned two names savouring strongly of Paganism, the archaeological reader will understand what they were. Though they did not disturb the decorum of the assembly, they would not have been permitted to be publicly uttered elsewhere; for those people, and, indeed, all our peasantry are very free from any coarse expressions. The other verses purported to be uttered by a messenger of the Muck Olla, in which it was set forth, that, owing to the goodness of that being, the farmer whom they addressed had been prosperous all his life, that his property would continue as long as he was liberal in his donations in honour of the Muck Olla; giving a very uninviting account of the state into which his affairs would fall should the Muck Olla withdraw his favour, and visit him with the vengeance certain to follow any illiberal or churlish treatment of his men. Whether it was owing to the charm of the poetry or the cogency of the appeal, the contributions were in general on a liberal scale, every description of gifts was bestowed, milk, butter, eggs, corn, potatoes, wool, etc. To distribute the accumulated store, it was the regular practice for a sort of rural merchant or two to await the return of the group and purchase the whole stock, distributing his share to each according to a conventional arrangement of their respective ranks. These scenes were enacted at night. Could such contributions have been levied in the open day, aided by physical force and the use of weapons? In such a case the "laying waste the country round" becomes an intelligible expression. Could the Muck Olla have been a deity, exhibited, as in Egypt of old, as a living animal? Can the rural merchant be a substitute for some lingering druid, who maintained his ground long after the establishment of Christianity?'

The last sentences here are worthy of General Vallency at his most imaginative, when the mysterious 'Muck Olla' was probably a nonsense-rhyme phrase (possibly *macalla*, echo?) and the strong savour of Paganism merely some earthy rustic pleasantry.

The hobby-horse figure, the *Láir Bhán* (White Mare), we shall meet again on St Stephen's Day. There are some other traditional memories of horse figures in Hallow E'en merry-making. For instance, the writer of these lines recalls a Hallow E'en game of his childhood in west County Limerick in which two children 'acted' a horse, the first was masked and made up the head and forelegs, the other, holding to the waist of the first, was the back and hind legs, the whole covered by a rug. Our elders called this figure *Capall an tSúsa*, 'the rug horse'.

The young men or children who went around thus on Hallow E'en were called 'guisers', 'vizards', 'hugadais', *'buachaillí tuí'* and other names. In more recent times, say sixty years ago, they were still active in parts of east Ulster, mid and south Leinster and east Munster, with some traditions of former existence elsewhere.

Games, Dares and Pranks

In his *Caitheamh Aimsire ar Thorraimh* (translated as *Irish Wake Amusements*) Seán Ó Súilleabháin has listed and described a long series of amusements, ranging from storytelling and singing, through card-playing, riddles and tongue-twisters, contests of strength, agility and dexterity, horse-play and practical jokes, to formal and set games of many kinds, which were customary at wakes long ago. He points out that many of these amusements were practised on other occasions, too. Hallow E'en was one such occasion.

As we might expect, the type of game played on Hallow E'en depended very much upon the composition of the company gathered to celebrate the feast. In a household of father, mother and younger children, one would naturally expect to see only small children's games, while a group of elderly people would engage in a game of cards or in storytelling, reciting poems or 'drawing down old times'.

In a group of adolescents and young adults, however, more lively games, of the type of 'blind man's buff', 'shuffle the brogue' or 'four corner fool', or tricks and contests of skill and strength were usual.

If the night were fine these young people were sure to carry the fun out of doors and romp through the farmyard or the village street.

A favourite pastime was the issuing of dares – challenges to do some daring or difficult feat, such as, for instance, leaping over a milk-churn or climbing a barn roof or a high tree. Because of the weird atmosphere

214

induced by divination, ghost stories, accounts of apparitions and fairy manifestations and so on, a frequent dare was to go to some reputedly eerie place, a graveyard, a ruined castle or a haunted house. Sir Jonah Barrington, in his *Personal Sketches*, 107–113, tells of a boyhood experience of his own, which happened about 1775. He was, he admits, reluctant to take part in 'trying any unnecessary experiments or making any superstitious invocations, particularly on All-Hallow Eve, or other mysterious days, whereupon a sort of bastard witchcraft is always practised in Ireland'.

He goes on:

'Hence I was universally ridiculed on those anniversaries for my timidity; and one All-hallow Eve my father proposed to have a prayer-book, with a £5 bank-note in it, left on a certain tomb-stone in an old Catholic burial-ground quite apart from any road, and covered with trees. It was two or three fields' distance from the dwelling-house; and the proposal was, that if I would go there at twelve o'clock at night, and bring back the book and a dead man's bone, many of which latter were scattered about the cemetery, the note should be mine; and, as an additional encouragement, I was never after to be charged with cowardice. My pride took fire, and I determined, even though I might burst a blood-vessel through agitation, or break my neck in running home again, I would perform the feat, and put an end to the imputation.'

Braving the dark he returned with the prayer-book the banknote and a large femur, which, in an excess of bravado he threw on the supper table, amid the shrieks of the ladies, and boasted that he would lay it at the head of his bed while he slept. But, awakened by a noise, he was terrified to see the bone dancing about the floor of his bedroom, until:

'A loud laugh at the door clearly announced that I had been well played off upon by the ladies for my abrupt display of a dead man's bone on the supper table. The whole of the young folks entered my room in a body with candles, and after having been re-assured, and nourished by a tumbler of buttered white wine, I obtained by degrees knowledge of the trick which had occasioned a laugh so loud, so long, and so mortifying to my self-conceit.

'The device was simple enough – a couple of cords had been tied to the bone, and drawn under the door, which was at the bed's foot, and by pulling these alternately the conspirators kept the bone in motion until their good-humoured joke had well-nigh resulted in the loss of their kinsman's reason.'

One of the company might be challenged to 'get the fern seed', a powerful charm which would make its bearer invisible. Énrí Ó Muirgheasa wrote in *Béaloideas,* 1930, 331–2:

'But in my youth the belief in the potency of the fern-seed was strong in Farney, Co. Monaghan. My recollection is that it was collected on Oidhche Shamhna or Hallow-eve, and there was a regular ceremony for the purpose.

'The hardy individual who essayed this dangerous task had to repair alone shortly before midnight on Hallow-eve to the solitary place where the ferns grew, with a number of pewter plates – nine or thirteen, I forget which – all regularly laid or imposed over one another, and having a sheet of white paper or linen between the two lower ones. These were held under the fern, and precisely at midnight the seed was dropped, and so great was its enchanted power that it passed through all the plates except the lowermost one, where it got caught on the linen or paper.

'This was then folded up and carried in the pocket of the adventurer, who thereby could render himself invisible. In this respect the Farney belief agrees with the English rather than the continental one. But it was not for the mere pleasure of making himself invisible the seed was obtained, but in order that the possessor could, unobserved, enter houses, search rooms, plunder treasures and indirectly get gold, thus agreeing with the continental folk-belief.

'Another point of agreement was that in Farney they said that all the powers of the world of darkness and evil were mustered to frighten off the temerarious individual while in the act of securing the seed. They could not touch him, but yells, screams, thunders, whirlwinds, lightnings, and the actual appearance of fiends, all conspired to shake his nerve. They told of one person who, while waiting for the seed to fall, got such a fright that he became demented, and, though subsequently half-cured by the parish priest, he continued "simple" or half-witted for the rest of his life.'

Another daring feat was to go to the graveyard, find a skull, and pull a tooth from it with one's own teeth, thus becoming master of an infallible cure for toothache.

Often the dare was to play a trick on some individual known to be cranky or hot tempered, to knock on his door and run, to climb on his roof and pour water down his chimney, to blow pepper through his keyhole, and then to escape by running off. Often, too, a booby-trap was combined with this – the angry householder, rushing out, was deluged by a can of water balanced over his door, or fell into a tub of water or over some obstacle placed in his way.

Usually such pranks were played on persons generally held to be mean or otherwise unpleasant. In places the victims were those who refused to contribute to the guisers, who might revenge themselves by returning later and quietly tying the door so that the occupants could not come out, and then throwing the cart-wheels on to the roof or the plough into the manure heap, or rebuilding the corn-rick over the reaping machine or painting inscriptions on the house walls with tar. One stingy farmer kept the whole parish amused for days by his efforts to chase away a 'strange' horse, which was later revealed, by a shower of rain, to be his own horse disguised by a coat of whitewash.

A well-known prank was to waylay some returning toper and paint his face or clothes, or take his cart apart and re-assemble it inside his house or unharness the animal, thrust the shafts through a gate and re-tackle the animal again. The full flavour of these jokes came only with the return to consciousness of the inebriated one.

Sometimes groups of young people went around playing tricks on everybody, running along a village street and beating on every door with rods or cabbage stumps, or bombarding them with cabbage heads or turnips rifled from neighbouring gardens.

Other pranks were suggested by the belief that spirits were abroad. The wandering about of the fairies and goblins gave rise to their impersonation by groups of boys and young men bent on mischief. Houses and farmyards were visited by these 'spirits', dressed in weird garments, and with masked or blackened faces. They howled and moaned at the windows or down the chimney or set up a carved turnip head made ghastly by a lighted candle within.

Children were threatened with awful visitations if their behaviour was bad, and sometimes a disguised elder came to the door demanding that the child who had been naughty, or had not learned its lessons should be given up to be carried away to the fort or other local reputed dwelling of the fairies.

Pranks of these kinds were played almost everywhere in Ireland on Hallow E'en. Usually they were of the more innocuous kind but this was an occasion when almost anything might happen, and when much was forgiven which at other times would be gravely censured and its performers punished.

217

Weather Divination

Hallow E'en weather divination like that of other festivals, was simple. The wind was observed at midnight, when its direction indicated the prevailing wind during the coming season, and its strength told of storms or calm weather in the course of the winter.

If there was a moon, it gave weather omens; if clear it meant fine weather, if clouded the degree of this foretold a like proportion of rain, while clouds racing over the moon warned of storms to come.

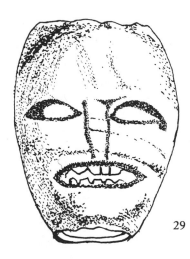

29 "Turnip ghost", County Donegal (National Museum, Dublin)

A stick thrust into the river bank showed whether the water was rising or falling. Some read the omen as telling of winter floods, others as indicating whether the prices to be obtained for farm produce would be high or low during the coming year. Some people maintained that a plough-coulter and not a stick should be used as a mark on the river bank.

Divination Games

Games and pastimes in which divination played a part were sure to be performed in any household which included young people. The best known of these, and the most popular to-day, is the inclusion of certain objects in the *bairín breac* (the large fruit cake), a ring, a small silver coin, a button, a thimble, a chip of wood, and a rag were mixed in with the dough in making the cake, and foretold the finder's future.

218

The ring meant early marriage, the coin wealth, the button bachelorhood and the thimble spinsterhood while the chip of wood revealed that the finder would be beaten by the marriage partner and the rag meant poverty. Some put in a pea and a bean to tell of future poverty and wealth. A little religious medal indicated that the finder would take holy orders or enter a convent.

In some households, the ominous objects were put, not into a cake but into the dish of colcannon or champ which formed the main dish. M. J. Murphy (*At Slieve Gullion's Foot*, 45) says:

'A marriage ring was often mixed in the champ. Here boys and girls gathered round a pot on the floor, and armed with big spoons, tried to be first to get the ring in their mouths. The winner would be married ere next Hallow Eve. This game, however, was most amusing. Little chivalry or decorum was observed in the eagerness to get the ring, and the champ went over hair and eyes and ears as well as into the mouth.'

Sometimes a little circle of withy was used instead of a wedding ring.

Two other games are described in *Journal of the Kildare Archaeological Society*, 1908, 448:

'Two hazel-nuts, walnuts, or chestnuts, or even two grains of wheat, were selected and named after some boy and girl who were supposed to be courting. They were then placed side by side on a bar of the grate, or in the turf-ashes, and according as to whether they burned quietly, or jumped apart from one another, so would be the future before them.

'Four plates having been set down on a table, water was poured into one, a ring placed on another, some clay in the third, and in the fourth was placed either some straw, salt, or meal. A person would then be blindfolded and led up to the table, and into whichever plate he or she placed their hand, so would their future turn out. The water signified migration, the ring marriage, the clay death, and the fourth plate prosperity. On re-arranging the order of the plates, others would be blindfolded and led up in like manner.'

In County Kerry two beans were named for couples, first heated and then dropped into a vessel of water, with the words:

'Píosam, pósam,
Lánamha phóire,
I méisín uisce,
I lár na teine,
Is tá mo lánamha pósta.'

219

('Píosam, Pósam
A pair of beans
in a dish of water
in the middle of the fire
And my pair are married')

If both beans sink at once, then the named pair are sure to marry and live in harmony. If one sinks and one floats, they will not marry, if both float they will marry and quarrel. *Folklore,* 1893, p.361–2 has a note from Laois by Miss A. Watson which tells of another very popular game:

'When we were children Hallow Eve was always an occasion for practising mysterious rites, the end and aim of each being to foretell the future. The first thing always was to get an old iron spoon, filled with lead in scraps; this was held over a hot fire till it melted. Then a key, which *must* be the hall-door key, was held over a tub of cold water, and the hot lead was poured through the wards of the key. The lead cooled in falling through the water, and when it had all settled in the bottom of the tub, the old nurse proceeded to read its surface. I don't know whether there was originally one especial story of the 'willow pattern' description, but I do know that the many I have heard all bore a family likeness. There was always a castle with a tower here, and a narrow window there, and a knight riding to the door to deliver a beautiful lady who was imprisoned there. And of course the lady was the round-eyed child who was listening with bated breath, and who was eventually to marry said knight. (If anyone likes to try the experiment, he will find that the lead falls in wriggles like snakes, with no possible pretensions to any shape or form.)'

This is, of course, a child's version of the game. Usually the leaden shapes were taken to represent the trade or profession of the future husband, a hammer for a smith, a scissors for a tailor and so on. Some said that the key should be taken for the occasion without the owner's knowledge or consent, others that it should be a widow's door key.

Lady Wilde, in *Ancient Legends of Ireland,* 111, describes another divination game:

'Another spell is the building of the house. Twelve couples are taken, each being made of two holly twigs tied together with a hempen thread: these are all named and struck round in a circle in the clay. A live coal is then placed in the centre, and whichever couple catches fire first will assuredly be married. Then the future husband is invoked in the name of the Evil One to appear and quench the flame.

'On one occasion a dead man in his shroud answered the call, and silently drew away the girl from the rest of the party. The fright turned her brain, and she never recovered her reason afterwards. The horror of that apparition haunted her for ever, especially as on November Eve it is believed firmly that the dead really leave their graves and have power to appear amongst the living.'

Still another, once popular in County Meath, was known as 'Shaving the Friar'. A small pile of ashes was built up in a pyramid shape, and a small stick was put standing up in the middle of the pile. Then each player took a small piece of wood and raked away a small portion of the ashes, saying 'Shave the poor Friar, and draw a little nigher', until the stick falls down. The player who caused its fall will, in one version, be the first to die, in another no divination was involved, and it became a forfeit game instead, in which the loser had to kneel down until he guessed the name of one of a series of objects – household utensils and so on – held behind his back.

Marriage Divination

Besides the divination games there were many tricks carried out by individuals and in private to divine marriage prospects.

The County Clare school-master, Bryan Merryman, in the long Irish poem *Cúirt an Mheadhon Oidhche* which he wrote towards the end of the eighteenth century, puts into the mouth of one of his female characters an account of the methods which she used in attempts to divine the identity of her future husband, which may be translated thus (lines 287–306):

> 'No trick of which you'd read or hear
> At dark of moon, or when it's clear,
> At Shrove or Samhain or through the year,
> That I've not tried to find my dear!
> Under my pillow I've kept all night
> A stocking stuffed with apples tight,
> For hours a pious fast kept up
> Without a thought of bite or sup.
> My shift I'd draw against the stream
> In hope of my sweetheart to dream.

221

The stack I'd sweep without avail.
Left in the embers hair and nail.
The flail against the gable laid.
Under my bolster put the spade.
My distaff in the oast would lie.
I'd drop spun yarn in the lime-kiln's eye.
Flax seed upon the road I'd fling.
A cabbage head to bed I'd bring.
There is no trick of these I mention
That I've not tried for the Devil's intention!'

All of this young lady's devices were widely known in Ireland. In addition to the apples, the cabbage head and the spade, other things which might be put under the pillow or under the head of the bed to induce a dream of the future partner were *bairin breac,* or the first spoonful of colcannon from the supper dish and the last left on the plate, both put into the girls left stocking and tied with her right garter, or nine ivy leaves with the words:

'Nine ivy leaves I place under my head
to dream of the living and not of the dead,
to dream of the man I am going to wed,
and to see him tonight at the foot of my bed.'

The young lady's pious fast was intended to induce thirst, so that she might dream of her future husband offering her a drink of water. A salt herring eaten at bedtime, or heavily salted porridge, or a spoonful of mixed flour, salt and **soot** were held to be equally effective.

Drawing one's shift against the stream was a preliminary to drying it. Some believed that it should be wrung out on the river bank, on which the figure of the lover will be seen on the opposite bank, or his face reflected on the water. Others said that it must be hung up to dry, and the watching girl would see her future husband turning it during the night. Sometimes a young man would dip and dry his shirt in this way to see his future wife.

'Sweeping the stack' was sweeping around the base of the corn stack with a broom three times in the hope that on the third circuit the future partner would appear or his name be spoken aloud. Another version omits the sweeping and claims that to walk around the stack three times was sufficient.

222

Hair and nail clippings dropped into the last embers of the fire was another powerful charm to induce a dream of the husband or wife to be. The flail and the spade, essentially masculine implements, were sure to bring a vision of the chosen man, while the *cuigeal*, the distaff from the spinning wheel, placed in the corn-drying kiln would have a like result.

Dropping a ball of woollen thread into the pit of a limekiln and winding it back slowly was a sort of fishing. If the thread caught, the girl asked who was holding it, and voice of the future husband should answer. In another version of this charm the ball of yarn was dropped out of the girl's window. General Vallency, in *Collectanea de Rebus Hibernicis*, xii, 460, says that the *Pater Noster* was recited backwards while winding in the wool.

Bravest of all was the girl who made her way to the crossroads as the night wore on and there sprinkled flax seed on the road or laid a *súgán* across it, for at the very hour of midnight her future husband would be seen stepping across it.

If an apple is peeled in one long strip and the peel allowed to fall upon the ground, it will form the initials of the future husband, and if an apple is eaten before a mirror his face is seen looking over the girl's shoulder. Lady Wilde tells of a tragic sequel to this, in *Ancient Legends of Ireland*, 110:

'And a lady narrates that on the 1st of November her servant rushed into the room and fainted on the floor. On recovering, she said that she had played a trick that night in the name of the devil before the looking-glass; but what she had seen she dared not speak of, though the remembrance of it would never leave her brain, and she knew the shock would kill her. They tried to laugh her out of her fears, but the next night she was found quite dead, with her features horribly contorted, lying on the floor before the looking-glass, which was shivered to pieces.'

If the face is washed but not dried before going to bed, the lover will appear in a dream, proferring a towel.

Ashes, raked from the fire and spread evenly over the hearthstone may be found in the morning to bear footprints or other significant marks, while if a little flour is spread smoothly on a large plate or dish, and a live snail dropped into it, the creature's progress through the flour will spell out initials or other letters which carry a message of hope or disappointment for future marital bliss.

A number of small scraps of paper were each marked with a letter of the alphabet, and these were floated face downwards on a basin of water. In the morning they should be found to have sunk to the bottom, and those which have turned over to show the letters will show the initials or spell the name of the future spouse.

A daring girl might take a mouthful of water, and holding it in the mouth without swallowing, creep close to the door or window of a neighbour's house and listen until the name of a young unmarried man was mentioned in the conversation by somebody within, when by virtue of the charm this youth would become her husband. A grain of wheat held between the teeth was believed by some to be equally potent.

Three stalks of corn pulled from the stack at the dead of night could also tell their tale. The first two were discarded, but the state of the third ear would surely reveal, by its form and size, how rich and how handsome would be the destined husband or wife.

A head of cabbage, pulled up by the root gave much information on the crucial marriage question. A. J. Pollock, in *Ulster Folklife*, 1960, 62, gives a version from County Down of this very widespread custom:

'The girls were blindfolded and sent out in pairs, hand in hand, to the garden or field and told to pull the first cabbage they found. Its size and shape – whether it was big or small, straight or crooked – would indicate the shape and stature of their future spouse. If much earth adhered to the root they would have plenty of money; if there was only a little they would be poor. The taste of the "custoc", i.e. the heart, would tell them his temper and disposition, according to whether it was sweet or bitter. Finally the "runts" or stems were hung above the door; each was given a number and the name of a boy friend, for example Barney might be the name given to the third runt. If Barney was the third person to enter the house on the night, this was considered to be a good omen.'

Other versions go further and say that if the young man indicated in the charm can by some means be induced to eat part of the same cabbage head, he will inevitably lead the girl to the altar.

Another charm from County Down, but widely known elsewhere, is given by the same writer (*id.* p. 63):

'If none of these charms worked you could always try to "winnow three wechts of nothing", the wecht being the skin of a winnowing tray. You had to go alone to a barn, open both doors and take them off their hinges. This was important, for the Being that would appear might otherwise shut the doors and do you harm. You then took the wecht and went through the motions of winnowing corn in a strong wind.

This was repeated three times, and on the third occasion an apparition would pass through the barn, in at the "windy" door and out through the other. The face would be that of your future husband, and the clothes he wore and the tools he carried would tell you both his occupation and station in life.'

A similar charm, to be carried out by a young man, is given in the *Journal of the Kildare Archaeological Society*, 1908, 449:

'A boy would go to a barn and sow oats along its floor, in the name of the devil, from one end to the other. Having done that, he would go to the door, open it, and expect to see the fetch of his future wife standing outside. Instances have been known where, in place of the fetch, a coffin has appeared, and this foretells to the beholder that he will not be alive on that night twelve-month.'

R. H. Buchanan (*Ulster Folklife*, 1963, 68) gives a further charm from County Down:

'In many parts of Co. Down salt was used in another way. Here the girl would sprinkle salt on the four corners of the bed and repeat the following verse:

'Salt, salt, I salt thee
In the name of God in unity.
If I'm for a man or a man for me
In my first sleep may I see him,
The colour of his hair, the clothes he'll wear
The day he weds with me.'

Marriage divination by means of little ladders and spinning wheels, as noted on St Brighid's Eve, was also, and perhaps more generally, practised on Hallow E'en, which was above all others the proper season for such activities. Rose Shaw, in *Carleton's Country*, 57, refers to this custom in the Clogher Vallery of county Tyrone:

'Also they had made wee ladders with rushes cut in the Three Counties Hollow, and they would hang the ladders above their beds that night – a sure way for a girl to see "himself" walk up the ladder in her dreams.'

Before leaving the subject we may mention two others, although this does not exhaust the full catalogue. Both are from County Longford and are given by Cáit Ní Bhrádaigh in *Béaloideas*, 1936, 268-9:

'Put three knots on the left garter, and at every knot say:

225

> 'This knot, this knot, this knot to see
> The thing I never saw yet.
> To see my love in his array
> And what he walks in every day,
> And what his occupation,
> This night may I in my dream see.
> And if my love be clad in green,
> His love for me it is well seen.
> And if my love be clad in grey,
> His love for me is far away.
> And if my love is clad in blue,
> His love for me is very true.

'Go to bed, place the knotted garter under your pillow, and you will see your future husband in a dream.

'Cut nine stalks of yarrow with a black-handled knife. When all are gone to bed say:

> 'Good morrow, good morrow, my pretty yarrow!
> I pray before this time to-morrow
> You will tell who my true love shall be.
> The clothes that he wears, and the name that he bears,
> And the day that he'll come to wed me.'

The black-handled knife in this last example is a well-known charm against fairies and other uncanny visitors. Such protection was not unwelcome, for in all these divination charms there is, in tradition, an uncomfortable sense of dabbling with unseen and potentially malevolent powers.

Some death divination was practised too. A note in the *County Louth Archaeological Journal*, 1910, 323, reads:

'The above customs closely resemble the following one still practised in Farney and probably other parts of Ireland: On Hallow-eve night each member of the family gets an ivy leaf without spot or stain and immerses it in a glass or cup of water where it is allowed to stand over night. In the morning, if the leaf is still spotless, the person who set it in the water is sure of life at least until that day twelvemonths, but if the leaf is found spotted in the morning the person it represents will surely die during the ensuing year. Such, at least, is the belief. Some leaves undoubtedly become spotted when allowed to stand some time in water, probably owing to bacteriological causes.'

226

Another is given by R. H. Buchanan in *Ulster Folklife*, 1963, p. 68:

Another Mourne custom, which was also recorded a century ago in Armagh, was to fill a thimble full of salt and turn it upside-down on a plate. "Stacks" of salt were made for each person, left overnight, and if one should have fallen by next morning the person so named would die within the next twelve months.'

All Souls' Day

The second of November is the festival of All the Souls of the Faithful Departed, and, in accordance with ancient church practice, prayers for the repose of the souls of the dead were recited on this day.

A widespread belief was that dead members of the family returned to visit their old home on this night, and that care should be taken to show that their visit was welcome. Thus Rose Shaw tells us from County Tyrone (*Carleton's Country*, 21):

'All Souls Eve is sacred to the memory of the departed. After the floor has been swept and a good fire put down on the hearth, the family retires early, leaving the door unlatched and a bowl of spring water on the table, so that any relative who had died may find a place prepared for him at his own fireside. On that one night in the year the souls of the dead are loosed and have liberty to visit their former homes.'

In parts of County Limerick a table was laid with a place for each of the dead, and the poker and tongs placed in the shape of a cross on the hearthstone.

Many people lit one candle for each dead member of the family when evening prayers were being said. In some cases the candles were quenched when the prayers were ended, in others they were left to burn out. Many people made visits to the graveyard where their relatives were buried, to pray for their souls and clean and tidy the graves; some placed lighted candles on the graves while praying.

The belief that the souls of dead kinsfolk could come to the aid of the living at this time was current. The present writer, as a child, asked an old storyteller in County Limerick 'if he wasn't afraid to go into the haunted house?' and got the reply 'In dread, is it? What would I be in dread of, and the souls of my own dead as thick as bees around me?' In much the same strain, a tradition from County Kildare, recorded in the *Journal of the Kildare Archaeological Society*, V, 451 asserts that:

'It is said that on this one day in the year the souls of the dead are allowed to re-visit their native districts: and if only human eye had the power to see them, they would be observed about one on every side "as plenty as thraneens in an uncut meadow".'

Martinmas

In his *Parochial Survey* Mason records that in the Athlone area:

'On the eve of St Martin, (who is one of the greatest saints in their calendar,) on the 11th November, every family of a village kills an animal of some kind or other; those who are rich kill a cow or a sheep, others a goose or a turkey; while those who are poor, and cannot procure an animal of greater value, kill a hen or a cock and sprinkle the threshold with the blood, and do the same in the four corners of the house; and this ceremonious performance is done to exclude every kind of evil spirit from the dwelling where this sacrifice is made, till the return of the same day in the following year.'

This is one of the festivals on which there was a traditional distribution of portions of meat by the more prosperous people to their poorer neighbours. Amhlaoibh Ó Súilleabháin, in his Diary, comments upon this custom in County Kilkenny in 1830:

'The tenth day, Wednesday, Martinmas Eve. A morning of fierce teeming rain, with a howling south west wind: torrents scouring down Green Street: birds quiet under shelter of the trees and bushes. It is usual to shed blood, on Martinmas Eve; this is to say, blood of goose or gander, hen or cock, pullet or chicken, duck or drake, fat porker or great and good beef, big wether or bleating kid; blood of sprightly lamb or gentle sheep or ragged goat or of some other good meat. It is a good old custom, which ought to be kept up, wherever no butcher's meat is to be had. Every strong farmer, and every country gentleman ought to kill a sheep or a beef or a porker, and share it with the hovel dwellers of the neighbourhood, and with God's poor. Today, the poor wandering labourer has his back to the bush; perhaps without breaking his fast.'

In 1828 the same diarist had noted:

'The eleventh day, Tuesday. St Martin's Day. No miller sets a wheel

230

in motion today; no more than a spinning woman would set a spinning wheel going; nor does the farmer put his plough-team to plough. No work is done in which turning is necessary. I do not know what this means, if it means anything.'

For County Wexford in the 1820s, Patrick Kennedy confirms this (*Banks of the Boro,* 364) and adds further detail:

'A Wexford legend says that on one recurrence of this festival, November 11, the people in all the boats plying about the Wexford line of coast were warned, by an apparition of the saint pacing along the waves, to betake themselves to the harbours. All who neglected the advice perished in a storm that ensued the same afternoon. In our youth, no Wexford boat would put to sea on that saint's festival, no miller would set his wheel a-going, no housewife would yoke her spinning wheel. Occasionally when a goat or sheep was ill, and seemed likely to die, its ear was slit, and itself devoted to St Martin. If it recovered, it was killed and eaten on some subsequent 11th of November. It would not be sold in the interim for ten times its value.'

Towards the end of the nineteenth century the practice in County Kildare is noted in *Journal of the Kildare Archaeological,* v., 451:

'No wheel was allowed to turn, or plough to work, before 12 noon on St Martin's Day. This applied equally to the spinning-wheel as to the cart or mill-wheel.

'On this day, too, a cock was caught, killed in an out-office, and while bleeding, brought into the dwelling-house, and its blood allowed to drop in the four corners of the house, so as to ensure a prosperous year. The body of the bird was afterwards cooked, and partaken of by the whole household.

'The mild, close days that so often follow a brush of hard weather, about the middle of November, are known as St Martin's Summer.'

In recent traditional practice and memory all of these beliefs and customs of St Martin's Eve and Day were known, with some local variation, over a very large area of Ireland comprising all of Connaught, all of Munster except for south County Kerry and south-west County Cork, all of south and mid Leinster, and a few places in south-west Ulster.

There is no doubt that the custom is ancient. A reference to it in an Irish manuscript (Rawlinson B. 512, in the Bodleian Library, Oxford), which appears to have been written about 1500, is quoted by Whitley Stokes in the *Tripartite Life of Patrick;* Stokes's translation reads as follows:

231

'The tale of the Martinmas pig here below. Martin, it is he that conferred a monk's tonsure on Patrick, wherefore Patrick gave a pig for every monk and every nun to Martin on the eve of Martin's feast, and killing it in honour of Martin, and giving it to his community if they should come for it. And from that to this on the eve of St Martin's feast everyone kills a pig, though he be not a monk of Patrick.'

The killing of a pig is again mentioned in an Irish vocabulary written by Donal O'Davoren in 1569:

'Lupait i. ainm in bainb marbthar im fhéil Mártan, agus dom doich is don tiagerna doberar. (Lupait is the name of the young pig which is killed at the festival of Martin, and my opinion is that it is given to the Lord).'

Henry Morris suggests (*Béaloideas*, ix, 233) that these early references to pigs rather than other animals being killed at Martinmas merely indicates that the pig 'was then the commonest small domestic animal, and in size it could be accommodated to the size of the family party'.

It seems clear that there is a connection between the Martinmas killing and the killing of animals fattened by the harvest plenty to provide the winter's meat supply; this was a well known feature of medieval farm economy, when fodder was scarce and had to be reserved for the milking, breeding and working stock.

As to the legends and traditions regarding the origin of blood-spilling and work prohibitions, especially those banning the turning of wheels, these have been discussed by Seán Ó Súilleabháin in *Studies in Folklore*.

Christmas

Preparing for Christmas

Of all the Christian festivals, Christmas was considered by the Irish people to be the most important, and preparations for its proper celebration began many days in advance.

There was spiritual preparation. From the beginning of Advent the more piously inclined added prayers to their usual morning and evening devotions, repeating them in quiet moments throughout the day. Children were urged to say additional *Paters* and *Aves*, and to keep a tally of these; some earnest youngsters might boast of as many as 5,000 such prayers before the coming of the festival.

Everybody, even the most obdurate, was expected to go to church and "do his duty" at this time, and the hard cases, whose absence at other times of the year was conspicuous, were jocularly known as "the hardy annuals" because of their unwonted devotion at this time.

Some days before the festival there was a general and thorough cleaning of house and farmyard. The men cleaned and tidied all the outbuildings and the yard, entrances, passageways and surroundings, and then white-washed the dwelling house both inside and outside, and usually at least the outside of all the barns, byres and other outbuildings.

Meanwhile the women were busy inside the house, sweeping, washing and cleaning. A major laundering operation included all washable garments and household linen. Tables and chairs were scrubbed with sand, while pots, pans and delf were scoured until they shone. And woe betide the miscreant who tramped in with muddy boots or sullied the housewife's work with dirty fingermarks.

The welcome task of providing the decorations usually fell to the

233

children who for some time past had been making careful note of holly, ivy, bay and other evergreens for cutting and bringing home on Christmas Eve.

Holly with berries was especially prized, as were long fronds of ivy which might be used as garlands. Some children were given starch or whiting by their mothers, with which they whitened the ivy berries for added gaiety. Loose holly, ivy and bay or laurel leaves were strung on twine by the aid of a packing needle, or sewn to pieces of linen to form patterns or seasonal mottoes. The children had saved any pieces of coloured paper which came their way, and these were cut with scissors into various shapes for added adornment.

In the later nineteenth century pedlars and other 'travelling people' spread readymade paper decorations and printed 'mottoes' through the countryside, or these were bought in the towns as part of the Christmas shopping.

In parts of Munster a small cross made by tying holly sprigs to two crossed pieces of wood formed a central feature of the decoration.

Mistletoe is of comparatively rare occurrence in Ireland, but where it is found, for instance in south County Wicklow or near Limerick, it was used in decoration. The custom of kissing under the mistletoe was known only in a few places, such as County Armagh, where, we are told, a girl would hang a sprig over the door and then kiss the first unsuspecting young man who came in; by custom he then had to buy her a Christmas present.

Shortly before Christmas some members of the family went to the nearby town to 'bring home the Christmas'; this was usually on the day of the Christmas market – called the *Margadh Mór*, the 'Big Market' in most parts of Ireland. To this the country people brought butter and eggs, hens, geese and turkeys, vegetables and other farm produce, and with the money obtained for these, made their Christmas purchases of meat, dried fruits, spice, sugar and tea, candles, tobacco, whiskey, wine and beer, toys and sweets for the children, new clothes and household gear. Shopkeepers made presents to their customers; these 'Christmas boxes' usually consisted of seasonal dainties, such as fruit cakes, drinks – the size of the present nicely proportionate to the amount of the customer's business.

Country people brought gifts of bacon, fowl, eggs, potatoes and so on to their friends and relatives in the towns, while these reciprocated with presents of 'town goods', while children were sure to have coins slipped into their hands or pockets. At the market good will and high spirits

30 Giving the Christmas present (William Brunton, 1854, by courtesy of University College, Dublin)

prevailed. Business in the taverns was brisk and the air was loud with the calls of the owners of street stalls and sideshows.

Prosperous farmers usually killed an animal, a bullock, a calf, a pig, or a sheep some days before Christmas, and sent portions to their friends, not forgetting their workpeople and their poorer neighbours to whom they gave meat, eggs, butter, milk and other foods to augment the Christmas table.

In those areas where the practise was traditional the makers of *poitín*, home-made whiskey, were busy, even though this activity has been forbidden by law for many decades. In west Connaught at least a quart of *poitín* was laid in by each householder on pain of public displeasure at his parsimony.

Care was taken to have a plentiful supply of fuel, and most households had obtained a special log of wood or bogdeal, *bloc na Nollag* for the fire. Many farmers sent fuel to poor neighbours. Chimneys had already been cleaned, usually by pulling a prickly bush up and down the flue by means of a rope.

Mason's *Parochial Survey* tells us of Culdaff, Co. Donegal:

'Previously to Christmas, it is customary with the labouring class to

235

raffle for mutton, when a sufficient number can subscribe to defray the cost of a sheep.'

This was a widespread custom. The raffle was usually protracted, often lasting several evenings, as the usual method of finding the winner was an eliminatory series of games of cards.

In the north midlands and in south Ulster the men of a locality often clubbed together to hold a 'join' at a selected house. Each man contributed a small sum, which was spent upon liquid refreshments by the aid of which a pleasant evening of talk, song and storytelling was enjoyed. Such 'joins' might be held at anytime within ten days or so of Christmas.

31 Nativity scene, on a slab at Termonfeckin, County Louth
(From a Photograph by the author)

Christmas Eve

Christmas, in Ireland, was very much a family festival, when sons and daughters who were working away from home were expected to return to spend at least a couple of days in their parents' house. Christmas Eve was the usual time for this reunion, and the young men and women who were employed in towns or with farmers within reach of home finished their work by midday on the Eve, and made their way home before night-fall if possible. Usually they brought little presents to father and mother, and to younger brothers and sisters. Those who could not come were expected to write, and many a poor family looked forward to the 'American letter', which was sure to contain not only good wishes, but also a present of money, often a substantial one.

Christmas Eve was spent mainly on the last preparations for the festival, in the final sweeping and cleaning and, especially in preparing the festive food for the next day's dinner, traditionally the most plentiful and elaborate of the year.

Roast or boiled beef seems to have been the most popular old-time Irish Christmas dish. This is remembered in the spiced beef which is still eaten at Christmas, although to a much less extent than formerly, in Dublin and other towns. The farmers as we have seen, made presents of meat to their workers and to the poor of the locality. Often this was corned beef from the animals killed at Martinmas. As meat was a rare luxury for the poor, these gifts were thus all the more welcome on festive occasions.

Beef was still the main Christmas meat in many parts of Ulster until well within living memory; a boiled ox-head was, we are told, a favourite dish in Armagh, Tyrone, Monaghan and other parts of the north.

Among the more prosperous farmers of Leinster and Munster the dinner usually included fowl – chicken or a goose – as well as bacon and mutton or beef and all of these, as well as cakes, puddings and pies, were made ready on Christmas Eve for the final cooking next day.

'Cutlin pudding' was made on Christmas Eve in County Wexford. First a thick porridge of wheaten meal was prepared, then sugar, dried fruits and spices were added, and the whole was made into a ball as big as, or bigger than, a football, and wrapped in a greased cloth ready for boiling.

William Penn, passing through Cork at Christmas in 1669 (*My Irish Journey*, ed. I. Grubb, 1952) remarked 'December 25. Was Pie Day, none could be got to work'. In the Ballyshannon area of County Donegal there is a tradition of 'Christmas pies in the shape of cradles, decorated with strips of pastry to represent the manger of Bethlehem'.

In almost every part of Ireland the Christmas candles were lit at nightfall on Christmas eve, usually with some little ceremony or at least with a brief prayer. In west County Limerick it was done thus:

'On the eve of Christmas, shortly after dark, the man of the house set in the principal windows large candles purchased in the town, fixing each one in a sconce made from a turnip or a piggin filled with bran or flour. One candle for the house holder, one for his wife, and one each for the grandparents who lived with them. Little ones often put up tiny candles of their own, often coloured. A bit of holly set off each candle. Some households left the candles burn all night, putting them out on leaving the house before dawn for the first mass. But many careful households put them out before all retired to rest to avoid the danger of fire. One big candle was known as *coinneal mór na Nollag*. The candles were lit about six o'clock and the *angelus* was then said by the members of the household.'

In many places three candles were lit in honour of the Holy Family. In Cork, in 1842 Mr and Mrs Hall (*Ireland*, 1, 25) noted a three-branched candle lit on Christmas Eve, 'without question to commemorate the Trinity', as they surmised, and allowed to burn until midnight. The custom of getting the youngest child – with help from an older person if necessary – to light the principal candle is widespread.

If the principal candle should be quenched without apparent reason before the proper time, this was a bad omen. This was noted by Mason in his *Parochial Survey*, in Shruel parish, County Longford:

'A large candle is lighted on Christmas night, laid on a table, and suffered to burn out. If it should happen, by any means, to be extinguished; or more particularly if it should (as has sometimes happened) go out without any visible cause, the untoward circumstance would be considered a prognostic of the death of the head of the family.'

The lighting of candles is usually explained as being done to show that Joseph and Mary, who found no room at the inn in Bethlehem, would be welcomed to the house. In many places the welcome was extended, thus:

'On Christmas eve it was the custom in west Limerick, not only to leave the doors open and a candle burning in every window in the house, but in addition to leave a table set for three people "to have a proper welcome before the Travellers to Bethlehem". A dish of water was left on the window ledge to be blessed by the "travellers" and then kept for curative purposes.'

While in County Armagh we are told (*Ulster Folklife*, 1957, 11) 'On Christmas-eve you put on a good fire before you go to bed, sweep the floor, put bread on the table and keep a candle lit and the door unbarred.'

Others held that such preparations were to welcome deceased members of the family returning to the old home on Christmas Eve. Some households lit a special candle for one of the family who had died since last Christmas. After dark, in many places, the children were taken to some hill or high point to see the whole landscape lit up by the candles in the windows.

Christmas Eve was observed as a fast day. Many people took no food at all until the main meal, which consisted traditionally of stockfish, such as hake, cod or ling, with white sauce and potatoes.

The fast, however, did not last until midnight, for soon after the candles were lit, and when all preparations had been completed, the celebration of Christmas proper began by the cutting of the rich Christmas cake and the production of tea, punch and other beverages. Sweets and apples were given to the children, and the whole family sat around the fire in high good humour until it was time for night prayers and bed. The holy character of the season was not forgotten; the children were told that an angel stood on every spike of the holly leaves, adoring the Divine Infant, and that no prayer was left unanswered on this night of all nights. Even to die at this time was blessed, because heaven was open to all on Christmas Eve.

In Dublin city small wreaths of holly, yew or other evergreens are still sold just before Christmas. These are taken to the cemeteries and laid on family graves on Christmas Eve or Christmas Day, and especially on the grave of a relative who had died during the year.

In mid-County Limerick the old German custom of firing a salute from shotguns at noon on Christmas Eve was kept up by the Palatines until recently; the present writer heard it being done in 1935, when the name 'Grüssenschuss' was still remembered by old people in the district.

At midnight on Christmas Eve, according to a belief held in most parts of Ireland, the cows and donkeys kneel in adoration of the Christ Child, and at that moment, too, they have the gift of human speech. Nobody, however, should spy upon their devotions, much less speak to them at that sacred moment. They should, however, be shown every kindness, given a generous feed of sheaf corn or branmash, and many people decorated the byre and the stable with evergreens and lit a lantern there on Christmas Eve. Sometimes the children tied sprigs of holly to the cows' horns.

The cock is overwhelmed with joy at Christmas and will crow at unusual times; to hear him crow at midnight was a particularly good omen.

The weather on Christmas Eve was significant. Cold weather, with frost or snow was welcomed, as this indicated a mild spring and an absence of illness; 'A green Christmas makes a fat churchyard' says the proverb. When it snowed on Christmas Eve the children were told that geese were being plucked in heaven. And a new moon on Christmas Eve was a very lucky omen.

Christmas Day

Christmas day was for the most part spent in the home and 'a quiet Christmas' was every's ambition. This was very much a family festival and nobody should enter another's house on this day unless specially invited to do so.

As many of the family as possible went to church services. Most Catholics went to early mass, not least because preparations for the feasting must begin early. Usually the dawn had not yet come when people set out for church, and many lighted their way with lanterns or torches. When leaving the church, some people took wisps of straw from the Crib to bring luck and blessing.

On returning from church the womenfolk busied themselves with cooking the Christmas dinner while the men and boys remained out of doors, usually taking part in some sport or pastime. Hurling ('caman' or 'shinny' in places) seems to have been the most popular of these from Kerry to Antrim. Tomas O'Crohan describes this on the Great Blasket:

'On Christmas Day there was a match in which the whole village was engaged. Two were appointed, one for each side, as leaders. Each of these called in turn until all present on the strand were divided. Hurleys and a ball we had. The match was played on the White Strand, without stocking or shoe, but out to the neck whenever the ball went into the sea. For the twelve days of Christmas no man on the Island could drive a cow to the hill from pains in the back and the bones, two with blackened shins, another limping for a month' (*An tOileánach*, 150).

In parts of Donegal the young men brought their hurleys to church, and, service over, began the hurling match at the church gate, each party trying to carry the ball into its own townland. In west County Limerick a special ball was made for the Christmas hurling, in the core of which was a small tin box containing a pinch of loose shot. The impact of a hurley on this ball sounded much louder than with an ordinary ball.

In many districts the favourite game was hunting hares with greyhounds or harriers. In Monaghan and other parts of Ulster there

240

were shooting matches; each competitor paid an entrance fee, which provided a prize for the winner.

The Christmas dinner was the biggest and most elaborate meal of the year and the housewife took pride in setting a generous table before appetites sharpened by hurling or hunting, and all the more welcome as Advent was a fasting season in Ireland until 1917. A widespread custom was the drinking of three sips of salted water before dinner; this was held to be conducive to good health.

After dinner the family sat around the fire in pleasant conversation. The children played, while anybody who could entertain with a song, a tune or a story was sure to be called upon to exhibit this talent.

To hear the crickets chirping behind the hob on Christmas Day was regarded as a sign of good fortune for the coming year.

In a few places in the north east of Ireland Christmas was not observed at all by the descendants of certain Scottish puritans; Mason's *Parochial Survey*, mentions this around Maghera, County Derry:

'On Christmas-day the English and Irish, after resorting to their respective houses of worship, spend the rest of the day in festivity. The dissenters, not considering it an holiday, follow their usual occupations.'

Waits

A description of life in Kilkenny in the early nineteenth century gives the following account of a Christmas custom formerly well known in that and other towns (John Hogan: *Kilkenny*, 416):

'Calling the "Waites" – This Charley, the sweep, had a second business on hand, and was, I believe, the last who professed the trade in this city. This avocation, was termed at that time "Calling the Waites", which consisted in the following performance being gone through on every night for a fortnight before Christmas:—Charley, accompanied by his retinue of young negroes, including blind Foley, the piper, each provided with a lantern, started from his house at St Rock's each night at twelve o'clock, and proceeded to the house of his nearest client, when the performance commenced by a stave from the piper on his organ, after which Charley stepped forward and thus addressed the family inside:—"Good morrow, Mr Byrne; good morrow, Mrs Byrne; Good morrow, all the young Byrnes; past twelve o'clock; a fine frosty morning". Next the twelve urchins in black performed to a peculiar air on the bag-pipes a dance around their master in a fashion or style something approaching to an Indian hornpipe after which the party set out to the house of their next engagement. This ceremony was performed at the house of every respectable family in the city without distinction of class or creed; and if by any inadvertence a house was passed over, the owner received the omission as a slight on his family. On St Stephen's Day, Charley, the twelve young blacks, accompanied by Foley and the bag-pipes, visited each of his clients. The custom on this occasion was that Charley and his staff should drink "A Happy Christmas and a Merry New Year" in each house of his clients, and receive as a fee for his attentions an old half-crown (2s. 8½d.), and as the hospitality of the time exceeded that of ours, the sweep, the piper, and the young blacks were frequently carried home towards night, as they themselves were not able to "carry their liquor".'

The same custom is mentioned in Mason's *Parochial Survey* in the little town of Ballymahon, County Longford:

'For some weeks before Christmas, several musicians, generally pipers, serenade the inhabitants of Ballymahon about an hour or two before day-break, calling out, in the intervals, the hour of the morning, and stating whether it is cold, wet, frosty, or fine. This is called going about with "The waits"; and those who give themselves this trouble expect to be paid for it in the Christmas holidays, when they go about in the day light playing a tune, and receiving the expected remuneration at every door.'

This custom has survived into recent times in a few western towns, such as Ballinrobe, Carrick-on-Shannon, Ballyhaunis, and Castlebar, following exactly the same routine. Singers or musicians went about for some days before Christmas, serenading the townspeople and calling out greetings by name. Some days later they made the rounds again knocking at every door and receiving small gifts.

A similar practice was known in County Cavan, where the young men and boys provided themselves with horns, formerly cows' horns, later pint or quart bottles from which the bottoms had been removed. Going to the tops of the little hills in which the area abounds they blew salutes to Christmas, answering each other from hill to hill. On the morning of Christmas day they blew loud salutes to waken the people for early mass, and often accompanied groups on their way to church, still blowing cheerfully and helping old people and children over rough roads and paths.

Amhlaoibh O Súilleabháin notes this Christmas morning call in Callan in 1828 – 'the twenty-fifth day, that is, Christmas Day. The moon shining before daybreak from a sky without cloud or mist, welcoming the good Child Jesus. A big drum being beaten at five o'clock; flutes and fifes being played by the youths of the town.'

This custom survived well into the present century in some towns and villages of Leinster.

The singing of carols – Christmas hymns – was known in some towns. In Kilmore, County Wexford, a traditional group of carols – a different one for each of the twelve days of Christmas – is still sung in Church. Local tradition says that these songs are more than two centuries old, and that the leader of the singers has always been a member of the Devereux family.

Saint Stephen's day

Over the greater part of Ireland St Stephen's Day is still remembered as the day for 'Hunting the Wren' although the custom itself has died out in many areas.

Mr and Mrs Hall, visiting Cork about 1840, described it thus (*Ireland*, i, 23–5):

'For some weeks preceding Christmas, crowds of village boys may be seen peering into the hedges, in search of the "tiny wren"; and when one is discovered the whole assemble and give eager chase to, until they have slain, the little bird. In the hunt, the utmost excitement prevails; shouting, screeching, and rushing; all sorts of missiles are flung at the puny mark; and not unfrequently, they light upon the head of some less innocent being. From bush to bush, from hedge to hedge, is the wren pursued until bagged with as much pride and pleasure, as the cock of the woods by the more ambitious sportsman. The stranger is utterly at a loss to conceive the cause of this "hubbub", or the motive for so much energy in pursuit of "such small gear". On the anniversary of St Stephen (the 26th of December) the enigma is explained. Attached to a huge holly-bush, elevated on a pole, the bodies of several little wrens are borne about. This bush is an object of admiration in proportion to the number of dependent birds, and is carried through the streets in procession, by a troop of boys, among whom may be usually found "children of a larger growth" shouting and roaring as they proceed along, and every now and then stopping before some popular house and there singing the Wren song.

'To the words we have listened a score of times, and although we have found them often varied according to the wit or poetical capabili-

243

ties of a leader of the party, and have frequently heard them drawled out to an apparently interminable length, the following specimen will probably satisfy our readers as to the merit of the composition:

> The wran, the wran, the king of all birds,
> St Stephen's day was cot in the furze
> Although he is little his family's grate,
> Put yer hand in yer pocket and give us a trate.
> Sing holly, sing ivy – sing ivy, sing holly,
> A drop just to drink it would drown melancholy
> And if you dhraw it ov the best,
> I hope in heaven yer sowl will rest,
> But if you dhraw it ov the small
> It won't agree wid de wran boys at all.

'Of course contributions are levied in many quarters, and the evening is, or rather was, occupied in drinking out the sum total of the day's collection.'

Patrick Kennedy, writing of Wren Boys in Wexford (*Banks of the Boro*, 233–4) tells us that, in the public esteem:

'... many degrees under the Mayboys and mummers, were the wrenboys, who in our youth flourished in the eastern portion of the county. No doubt we have seen and been among parties of boys who lost much time on St Stephen's Day, in searching for a little dhruleen (wren) through the furze bushes, generally without success; but on the solitary occasion when the chase was successful, and we had secured the lifeless body of the poor little thing (it was accidentally killed) in a holly bush, we only serenaded our own families and Father Murphy's niece. She insisted on treating us to some beer. The most courageous of the party ventured to taste it but incontinently spluttered it out, and took to his heels. None of the others was found hardy enough to try its flavour.

'The professional artists used by some means to secure a live wren, and fasten it by a string to the twig of an ivy or holly bush, and, enlivened by the strains of an ear-piercing fife, invade the quiet of strong farmers' houses, and dance, and shout, and sing the well known legend beginning:

> The wran, the wran, the king of all birds,
> On St Stephen's day was caught in the furze, etc.

32 Hunting the Wren, Cork (Hall: *Ireland*)

'Then hands were taken, and steps performed round the bouchal na dhruleen, who capered away in his best style, shaking the bush and the poor prisoner in unison. They generally succeeded in extracting drink or money; and the day's labours ended with a carouse for detailing the mysteries of which we have no relish.'

Later in the same century the ritual in County Kildare was as follows (*Journals of the Kildare Archaeological Society*, v, 452):

'Saint Stephen's Day.

'This is the day on which the "Wran-Boys" go their rounds. For a day or two previously the wren has been hunted and knocked over with stick or stone. Two or three of them are tied to a branch torn from a holly-bush, which is decorated with coloured ribbons. On St Stephen's Day small parties of young boys carry one of these bushes about the country, and visit the houses along the road, soliciting coin or eatables. At each house they come to they repeat a verse or two of a "song" which commences –

> The wren, the wren, the king of all birds,
> On St Stephen's Day, was caught in the furze;
> Though his body is small, his family is great,
> So, if you please, your honour, give us a treat.
> On Christmas Day I turned a spit;
> I burned my finger: I feel it yet,
> Up with the kettle, and down with the pan:
> Give us some money to bury the wren.

'The song varies in different localities, but all versions appear disjointed, and in no way refer to St Stephen's Day, nor to the object of killing the wren.

'In some cases the wren-boys carry round little toy-birds on a decorated bier, and they themselves have ribbons and coloured pieces of cloth pinned to their clothes.

'If they receive no welcome at a house, and are told to "be off out of that" there is the danger of their burying one of the wrens opposite the hall-door, through which no luck would then enter for a twelvemonth. Eventually, at the end of the day, each wren is buried with a penny.'

It is noted by Helen Roe in Laois in the 1940s (*Béaloideas*, ix, 29–30)

'In all parts of the county the wren boys go their rounds on St Stephen's Day. During the past thirty years this custom has undergone many changes. Formerly, the bush, usually a holly tree, was decorated with a few rags and the dead body of a wren. It was only carried by boys, and the first group of boys to visit a house bearing the wren-bush were considered to bring luck for the coming year, and in consequence were suitably rewarded. Later comers were not so fortunate. As a result, it was customary to come very early, while it was still dark, and sing outside the house. After twelve noon the bushes were thrown away.

'Nowadays it is comparatively rare to see a bush with a dead bird, but the other decorations have become much more elaborate – coloured paper, ribbons, tinsel bulbs, silver and coloured streamers, etc.

'Children of both sexes now go round, as well as grown young men. These lads are usually masked with comic faces, and wear a sort of fancy dress, and are dressed as women. They bring with them very often melodeons or mouth-organs, and render versions of the more popular fox-trots and film songs of the day.

'Hardly anyone now seems able to remember more than a few lines of the rhyme, which used to be chanted in full. There is no time limit, but they begin much later – about ten in the morning – and go on until late in the afternoon.

'The wren boys also go about in groups by bus from village to village.

'The following represents all of the wren boys' song that I can recover. It is recited in a high nasal whine at great speed, which renders it almost unintelligible, and also helps to disguise the children's ignorance of what they are saying:

> The wran, the wran,
> The King of all birds
> On St Stephen's Day,
> was caught in the furze
> And though he is little
> His family is great;
> So rise up, landlady,
> And give us a treat.
> Up with the kettle
> And on with the pan;
> Mr. So-and-So is a gentleman.
> We hoosed her up,
> We hoosed her down,
> We hoosed her into

So-and-So town.
We dipped her wing
In a barrel of beer,
Then rise up landlady
And give us good cheer.
Up with the kettle,
On with the pan
Give us an answer
And let us be gone.
Give us something new,
Give us something old.
Be it only silver
Or copper or gold.
It's money we want
It's money we crave;
If you don't give us money
We'll bring you to the grave.
So up with the kettle
And on with the pan
For Mr. So-and-So is a gentleman.'

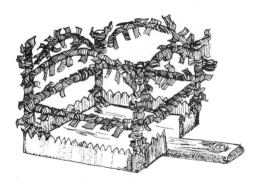

33 Wren box, County Galway
(National Museum, Dublin)

Except in the northern part of Ulster, from Donegal to Antrim, the Wren hunt and procession was known all over Ireland in more or less the form described in the accounts given above. A group of young people went about in disguise or fancy dress claiming that they had captured or killed a wren and requesting help to bury it. They sang a verse explaining their quest, and also provided other entertainment by dancing, singing and playing music. The money collected was spent on food and drink to be consumed later at a 'Wren Party'.

Some groups of wren boys buried the wren at the end of their rounds, and sometimes the wren was buried in front of a house where a contribution had been refused.

Traces of what appears to have been a more elaborate ritual are, however, occasionally to be found. Generally in Munster where the custom survives most strongly, the 'boys' are headed by a 'Captain' who is dressed in quasi-military style and carries a sword. Two other characters frequently included were the *amadán* (jester) who carried a bladder on a stick, and the *óinseach* (female jester) – a boy disguised in women's clothes. This pair kept the onlookers amused by quips, pranks and buffoonery while the other 'boys' sang and danced to entertain.

A note in *The Graphic* (Jan. 1894, 8) 'With the wren Boys at Dingle' reads:

'The Wren Boys, having killed a wren tie it to a holly bush on a pole. Two of them decorate their heads and shoulders with straw and wear masks with single eyeholes. These also carry large bladders tied to sticks with which to clear the way. Two others also masked, dress in petticoats and are supposed to represent dancers; six more carry flags, while one plays a fife and another a drum.'

Part of the Dingle ceremony appears to have been a mock battle between a group with wooden swords and another group armed with bladders on sticks; named individual characters among the combatants, such as 'Sir Sop' and 'Sean Scott' seem to indicate even more elaborate ritual formerly.

Around Tralee and in the Dingle Peninsula the wren boys usually had a *láir bhán* ('white mare'), a hobby-horse. Made with a wooden frame covered by a white sheet, this had a carved wooden horse-head and dangling legs. The boy who bore it on his shoulders could, by means of strings, make the jaws snap and the hind legs kick up, and persons who crowded too closely, or who did not instantly contribute, were menaced by teeth and hooves.

The verses sung or recited by the wren boys vary considerably from place to place, and often these are confused with those of the mummers and with other Christmas rhymes.

Patrick Kennedy's reference to the low esteem in which the custom was held in Wexford is borne out in other places. Amhlaoibh Ó Súilleabháin remarked in Callan in 1828:

'The rabble of the town going from door to door, with a wren in a holly bush, asking for money, in order to be drunk late this evening. It is a bad custom to give it (money) to them.'

249

In Cork in 1845, the mayor, Richard Dowden, forbade 'the hunting of the little bird on Saint Stephen's Day by all the idle fellows of the country'. In many places the proceedings were rowdy and sometimes the 'boys' were drunk before the end of the day. Sometimes, too, rival groups of wren boys met and fought, especially when one group invaded the territory of another.

On the other hand, in those areas where the custom still flourishes, it is usually conducted with decorum, and the visits of the wren boys are met with at least good humoured tolerance. In places the failure of the boys to visit a house would be taken as an insult to the occupants; however, a household of which a member has died during the year is not visited.

Usually, in the south west of Ireland, the proceeds of the collection made in their rounds by the larger groups are spent some days later in providing food and drink to be consumed at a 'Wren party' to which a large number of guests may be invited.

A very widespread custom in Ireland was the observing of St Stephen's Day as a fast day; this was said to ensure good health during the coming year, although cynics held that abstention from food on this day was a natural consequence of overeating on Christmas Day.

In many places St Stephen's Day was given over to outdoor sports such as horse-racing, beagling, coursing and fowling, while in former times, cock-fighting and bull-baiting were favourite pastimes in parts of Ulster and Leinster.

The Mummers

A visitor to Cork in 1685 reported as follows (T.C.D. MS 1206), quoted in Alan Gailey: *Irish Folk Drama*, 8):

'Last evening there was presented the drollest piece of mummery I ever saw in or out of Ireland. There was St George and St Denis and St Patrick in their buffe coats, and the Turke was there likewise and Oliver Cromwell and a Doctor, and an old woman who made rare sport, till Belsibub came in with a frying pan upon his shoulder and a great flail in his hand thrashing about him on friends and foes, and at last running away with the bold usurper, Cromwell, whom he tweaked by his gilded nose – and there came a little Devil with a broom to gather up the money that was thrown to the Mummers for the sport. It is an ancient pastime, they tell me, of the Citizens.'

In more recent times, over the past 150 years or so, similar plays

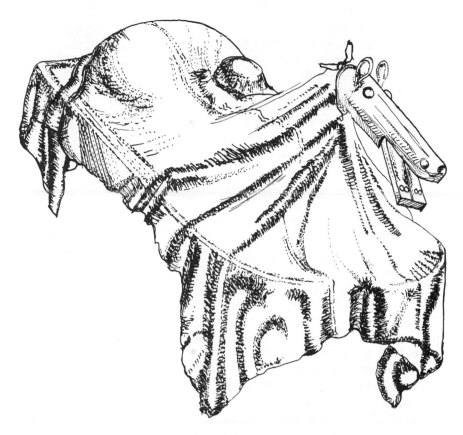

34   Hobby-horse (*láir bhán*), County Kerry (National Museum, Dublin)

were performed by groups of local boys in many parts of Ireland. These plays were always in verse and almost invariably the main theme was a combat between two heroes, the fall of one of them and his revival by a doctor.

A typical performance, recorded in Donabate, County Dublin, in 1952, runs thus:

The action begins with the entry of a martial figure in a gay uniform with a beribboned soldier's hat, a sash and a sword. He speaks:

Here I come, Rim Rhyme,
Give me room and give me time
For myself and many more

251

Tired of the road, and all footsore
We fought our journey, every inch.
Prepared to murder, at a pinch
He who tries us to oppose
We'll split his skull and punch his nose
If you don't believe what I have said
You may take it from me you'll soon be dead.
The one above all I'd hate to be
Is that white-wigged man from o'er the sea
The Sasanach who'd raise my gorge
So, enter in, my brave Prince George'

(Prince George enters. He, too, is gaily dressed):

'Here I come, a gallant prince,
And for no mortal will I wince,
Draw your sword and I'll draw mine.
Draw your breath while I draw the line.
Thus far, and not another foot
Or through your throat this blade I'll put.
Deeds of valour, deeds of fame
Are associated with my name.
Come who will his skill to try
Take it from me, that man will die.
England for ever will Ireland enslave;
I'll soon put our enemies into the grave.'

Rim Rhyme:

'Come on, you gallant boaster
Till I give you a roaster.
For good old Ireland's glory,
I'll make you sore and gory.
What brought you here at all, you clown?
We never heard of your renown
Soon they'll hear in England dread
that another of their sons is dead.'

(They fight, Prince George falls.)

Prince George:

'Send and get a doctor quick!
You struck me not by skill but trick.
When he comes, if he can't cure
You'll be punished, you may be sure.'

(Enter the Doctor, in tail-coat and top hat, carrying a large valise).

Prince George:

'Oh Doctor, Doctor, cure me dear
And richly I will meet your gear.
What can you cure? Can you cure at all?
Don't let me like a soldier fall.'

Doctor (taking bottles, knives, saws, etc. out of his bag):

'Cure I can, for a noble fee.
From your complaint I'll set you free.
I can cure by day and night.
I can diagnose by sight.
The plague it is no plague to me
Get it, kind sir, and I'll set you free.
Even the evil hoxy-poxy
I can alleviate by proxy.
Let me apply my stethoscope;
Then I'll know if there is hope
Open your mouth! Put out your tongue
Have you a pain in either lung?
How is your bel—— I mean your tummy?
Inclined to heave? or rather rummy?
I know the symptoms one and all.
You just got shocked from a sudden fall.
I attended a woman of ninety eight
Who fell off her bike and broke her pate.
For her it was a great disaster,
But I cured her with my famous plaster.
I have in the waistband of my breeches
A cure for anything that itches.

Even he who's poor or rich
Is bound sometime to get the itch.
Buy my cure, it has no match,
But I'll guarantee that you won't scratch
So you cannot rise with a pain in your back?
Come lend a hand, my good friend Slack.'

Next comes in a figure in tattered clothes. In one hand he carries a
violin and in the other a griddle. Tied to his back are three effigies
made of clothes stuffed with straw, one large and two small. He helps
the Doctor to set Prince George on his feet; then he faces the audience
and speaks:

'Hear I come, poor Slick Slack,
My wife and family on my back,
Five fingers on the fiddle,
And five more on the griddle.
Brave I am, there is no doubt,
Well known here and round about.
Above board, and on the level.
I'm the man that bet the Devil.
If you don't believe my drivel
Enter in, Little Divil.'

Enter Little Divil. He is dressed in black and his face is blackened:

'Here I come, little Divil.
Despite my name you'll find me civil.
Chewing tobacco and spitting quid
Is the very worst thing I ever did.
So up, good people and give us a hand
To put a good coffin on Jenny the Wran.'

Enter Joe the Butcher. He wears a striped apron and carries a
carving knife and a steel:

'Joe the Butcher, here I come.
The tricks of the trade are under my thumb
I can skin an old cow from her head to her heel
With no other aid than my knife and steel

254

I'll scrape her and shape her the best way I can.
So give us some coppers to bury the Wran.'

Enter the Wren, to whose clothes are sewn many turkey feathers. He speaks:

'The Wren, the Wren, the King of All Birds.
Saint Stephenses Day he was caught in the furze
She dipped her wing in a barrel of beer
And wishes you all a Happy New Year.
With porter the price that it is today
Its going to be hard to pay our way.
Add what you can to our little wealth.
Be it great or small, we'll drink your health
Whatever you give us goes into the pool
Now enter in my friend, Tom Fool.'

Enter Tom Fool, dressed as a jester with bells on his cap. He carries a stick to which a bladder is tied by a length of string; with this he strikes the other players as he speaks:

'Here I am, poor Tom the Fool
So I'm called, for I hated school
The very best days of your life, they said
I many a time wished that I were dead
See me now with bladder and staff
Doing my best to make you laugh.
If I had learned what came my way
I wouldn't be here like this today
They say its never too late to mend,
But a seasoned stick you cannot bend
So, ladies and gentlemen sitting round the fire
Give poor Tom his heart's desire
Lest he into despairing sink
Give poor Tom the price of a drink
If you give silver and no brass
We'll up with the music and have a bit of gas'.

Here Slick Slack strikes up a tune on his fiddle, joined by some of the others on other instruments. Some of the players dance and sing to entertain the audience, and Tom the Fool speaks a long verse composed for the occasion, with many topical and local allusions. The performance ends with the taking up of a collection by Little Divil.

Those who perform the play are variously known as Mummers, Christmas Rhymers or Hogmanay Men and, traditionally, their performances are given during the twelve days of Christmas, although more recently, groups have travelled about at any time between mid-December and the end of January. Most often the groups perform in the kitchens of living rooms of the houses they visit, but sometimes they appear in halls or barns lent for the occasion.

These mummers' plays are remembered in tradition or have been recently performed in parts of these Irish counties: Antrim, Armagh, Cavan, Derry, Donegal, Down, Dublin, Fermanagh, Kilkenny, Leitrim, Louth, Mayo, Tyrone and Wexford.

The characters vary from place to place. For instance, the fighting champions may be Saint Patrick and Saint George, Prince George and the Turkey Champion, or King James and King William. Other known characters are Bonaparte, O'Connell, the Tsar of Russia, Beelzebub, Jack Straw, Big Head, Devil Doubt, Johnny Funny, and, more recently, Hitler, Mussolini and other topical figures. There is much variation in the verses, of which several versions are given in Alan Gailey's *Irish Folk Drama*.

In a Wexford mummer's play, composed about the beginning of this century, all the characters are from Irish history, Colmcille, Brian Boru, Art MacMorrough, Owen Roe O'Neill, Sarsfield, Wolfe Tone, Lord Edward, Kelly of Killane, Michael Dwyer, Robert Emmet and Father John Murphy, all led by a captain who calls on each to speak his lines.

Wexford mumming differs from all the others in that the highlight of the performance is an intricate sword dance. There are always twelve players each with a wooden sword, and their dance is described by Patrick Kennedy in *The Banks of the Boro*, 231:

'Six men or boys stood in line, at reasonable distances apart, and six others stood opposite them, all armed as described. When the music began, feet, and arms, and sticks commenced to keep time. Each dancer, swaying his body to right and left, described an upright figure of eight with his fists, both of them following the same direction, the ends of the sticks forming the same figure, of course. In these movements no noise was made, but at certain bars the arms moved up and down, the upper and lower halves of the right hand stick striking the lower half of the left hand stick in the descent of the right arm, and the upper half of it in the ascent, and vice versa. At the proper point of the march each man commenced a kind of fencing with his vis-a-vis, and the clangs of cudgels coincided with the beats of the music and the movements of the feet. Then commenced the modulations, evolutions, interlacings, and unwindings, every one striking at the person with whom the movements brought him face to face, and the sounds of the sticks supplying the hooking in reels. It was a stirring but apparently confused, spectacle, which, when the music was good and the dancing combatants kept time, strongly interested and excited the lookers-on.'

Formerly, in County Wexford there also was a comical couple Darbey and Joan, the latter a young man disguised as an old woman. This pair took no part in the dance and had no set verses to say, but they kept the spectators amused by jokes and pranks during the performance.

In recent years there has been a revival of mumming in some areas, notably in south County Wexford, where competitions between groups are held annually. Wexford groups have performed in Dublin and elsewhere, as well as on television, and have travelled abroad to international folk festivals.

Some years ago a group of artillerymen from Kildare barracks were organised and trained in the Wexford-style mumming by a sergeant from that county; named 'Saint Barbara's Mummers' after the gunners' patron saint, they gave performances to raise money for charity. Similarly, busmen in Ballyclare, County Antrim raised money for charity in a like manner.

What the origins of mumming and the Mummers' Play may be, we do not know. It is clear that most of the verses and action of Irish traditional mumming are so closely related to that of England that the custom must be ascribed to English influence. How early this may have been is difficult to say. Hanmer's *Chronicle*, describing King Henry's celebration of Christmas in Dublin in 1172, tells of:

'. . . the pastime, the sport, and the mirth, and the continuall musicke, the masking, mumming and strange shewes, the gold, the silver, and plate, the precious ornaments, the dainty dishes . . .'

Christmas plays were popular in the medieval towns. For instance in Dublin in 1458 a different play was presented on each day of Christmas week, on a stage erected on Hoggen Green, before the Lord Deputy and the Lord Mayor and bailiffs. The carpenters' guild showed a nativity play; the shoemakers told the story of St Crispin their patron; the tailors portrayed Adam and Eve. Others presented more secular themes; the vintners showed Bacchus, the bakers, Ceres, and the blacksmiths Vulcan. In addition, and to restore the religious air proper to the season, the leaders of the clergy had the Passion of Our Lord and the Martyrdoms of the Apostles performed.

Holy Innocents

The festival of the Holy Innocents, 28 December, was generally regarded as an ill-omened day because of the commemorated event, the murder of the children by King Herod. It was known widely as *Lá Crosta na Bliana* 'the cross day of the year' and was a most unlucky day on which to begin any work or to plan or commence any new enterprise. Should some urgent matter present itself, ill luck could be avoided if the task was begun before midnight on the 27th: thus, for instance, if a grave must be dug on this day, one sod should be turned on the previous evening, thus beginning the work before the coming of the unlucky day.

In many places the ominous character of the day continued through the coming year. Thus, if 28 December fell upon Monday all Mondays were unlucky, and similarly for all the other days of the week.

Nurse Hedderman (*Glimpses of my Life in Aran*, 97–8), tells of 'a special day called the "Cross" (or unlucky) day . . . The particular day of the week in each year is the one on which we keep the feast of the "Holy Innocents". If this feast happens to fall to fall on a Monday, for instance, then every Monday throughout that year will be a "Cross Day". On these days no person in the south or Middle Island would transact business, commercial or otherwise, have a marriage solemnized, or open a grave; neither would they start the spring planting or the harvest gathering.'

This extension throughout the year of the ill-luck of Holy Innocents is noted by Dean Swift about 1731 (*Directions to Servants*, 39):

'. . . besides, Friday and Childermas-day are two cross days in the week, and it is impossible to have good luck in either of them.'

New Year

New Year's Eve and Day, 31 December–1 Jan. never seem to have been major festivals in Ireland. The first of January was not counted as New Year's Day until so designated by law in the new calendar of 1751, little over two centuries ago. Up to that time the legal year began in Ireland, as in England, on 25 March, while the country people still reckoned their working year as beginning on the first day of spring, 1 February. In Scotland, however, where Roman custom had long prevailed, 1 January traditionally began the year and thus was of much importance in popular celebration; a Scottish origin for some of the custom associated with the day in Ireland might thus be sought.

Divination of the future was common on New Year's Eve, especially, the forecasting of weather conditions for the whole of the coming year. Wind, sun, rain, snow, floods and all local weather signs were read and interpreted. Such omens often indicated much more than mere weather. In west County Kerry for instance, the direction of the wind indicated the trend of politics in the coming year; if it blew from the West the Irish cause would flourish, while an east wind foretold that the English interest would prevail.

Indeed, almost anything which happened on New Year's Eve and Day might be ominous of the future, and the nearer to the midnight hour when the year actually began, the more significant. A very popular belief held that the first person or creature to enter the house after midnight should be black or black-haired and also male to be lucky. To ensure their luck, many households sent out a suitably endowed member or friend before midnight to perform this office of lucky 'first footing' immediately after midnight. Others trusted to chance for their lucky first footing and were happy when their first visitor was a black cat or a dark haired boy. And since the latter was sure to be given a little present, small boys took advantage of the custom to get sweets or money at the neighbours' houses.

On New Year's Eve, girls put holly and ivy leaves, or a sprig of mistletoe under their pillows to bring dreams of their future husbands. One of the charms said was:

'Oh, ivy green and holly red,
Tell me, tell me whom I shall wed!

New Year's Eve was known as *Oiche na Coda Móire* (the night of the big portion) because of the belief that eating a very large supper on that night ensured food in plenty for the coming year. A further ceremony to banish hunger and ensure plenty was fairly widespread. Crofton Croker (*Researches in the South of Ireland*, 233) describes it thus, while casting doubt on its efficacy:

35   Breaking the New Year cake (*Ill. London News*, 1852)

'On the last night of the year, a cake is thrown against the outside door of each house by the head of the family, which ceremony is said to keep out hunger during the ensuing one; and the many thousand practical illustrations of the fallacy of this artifice have not yet succeeded in producing conviction of the same.'

Nicholas O'Kearney, some twenty years later, sees evidence of heathenish practice in it (*Trans. Kilkenny Archaeological Society*: 1849–51, 146–7):

'There is one custom which I found practised by a family moving in a very respectable sphere, and which I am informed was not long ago, probably still is, practised in the County of Kilkenny, and to which I wish to call your attention, because it appears to me to savour of Paganism of the rankest kind. On the eve of the Twelfth day a large loaf called the "Christmas Loaf" which is usually baked some days previously, is laid with great solemnity on the table; the doors and windows are closed and strongly bolted; and one of the family generally the housewife, then takes the loaf, and pounding it against the closed doors, etc. repeats three times, in Irish the following Rann:

260

Fógramuid an Ghorta,
Amach go tír na d-Turcach;
Ó nocht go bliadhain ó nocht,
Agus ó nocht féin amach.

(We warn famine to retire
To the country of the Turks;
From this night to this night twelvemonth,
And even this very night.)'

In County Kildare, 'Omurethi' is content to record the custom without comment (*Kildare Archaeological Journal*, v, 440–1):
'It was customary on New Year's Eve to bake a large barmbrack, which the man of the house, after taking three bites out of it dashed against the principal door of his dwelling, in the name of the Trinity, at the same time expressing the hope that starvation might be banished from Ireland and go to the King of the Turks. The fragments of the cake were then gathered up and eaten by all the members of the household.'
In west County Limerick the ceremony was similar; the cake was rapped upon the door with the words:

An donas amch
A's an sonas isteach
Ó' anocht go dtí bliain ó anocht
In ainm an Athar a's an Mhic, a's an Spirid Naoimh, Amen.

(Happiness in and misfortune out
from this night
Until a year from to-night.
In the name of the Father and of the Son and of the Holy Spirit,
Amen).

Many farmers repeated the ceremony at the door of the byre, to ensure plentiful fodder for the cows.
In some households the cake was tossed out through the doorway, to be caught by a person stationed outside. The invocation of the Trinity was usual in this as in so many other customs, which, incidentally, leads to speculation as to the degree of deafness of the smeller-out of heathenism quoted above.

261

People tried to ensure that no food was taken away from the house on New Year's Eve, and even shameless beggars hesitated to ask for a 'loan' of foodstuffs, and not entirely because of the fear of the householders' resentment.

From Rathlin Island, County Antrim comes word of a traditional ceremony which appears to be purely Scottish. A party of young men went about from house to house collecting oatmeal and money to help poor widows and other needy persons in the community. The leader wore a sheepskin tied about his neck and hanging down behind. On coming into the house he took a glowing turf sod from the fire and laid it in the middle of the floor, and he and his men marched around this, reciting an Irish verse while the second man in the line held up the end of the sheepskin and beat upon it with a stick. One man carried a bag to hold the gifts of meal, on receipt of which the leader cut a lock of wool from his sheepskin and having singed it over the red coal presented it to each member of the household to smell. The party then left for the next house, announcing their progress by blowing on horns. Another northern custom was the carrying about from door to door by children of a bundle of straw from which they presented wisps to the house-holders who were supposed to reciprocate with little gifts of money.

The welcoming of the New Year at midnight on 31 December by the ringing of church bells, band parades, fireworks, bonfires and general well-wishing has, over the past century or so, spread in Ireland from the larger to the smaller towns and villages, where it is usually now observed in this fashion.

When passing a graveyard on New Year's Eve or Day a prayer should be said for all those who died during the year.

Handsel Monday

Handsel Monday is the first Monday of the new year, on which day children approach or visit their neighbours, relatives and friends to solicit a 'handsel' – a small gift of money. In parts of Leinster, including Dublin City this bounty was known as a *suggit,* which may derive from Irish *so dhuit* – 'here's for you – here you are'. It was considered very unlucky to refuse a handsel to a child on this day; many thought it more lucky to anticipate the request and give the coin before the child's asking for it. In places the housewives baked special small sweet cakes to give, instead of coins, to the children who came to the door for a handsel; this may be why Amhlaoibh O Súilleabháin

262

calls the day *Luan na mBan maith* – Goodwives' Monday (6 Jan. 1834).

In parts of the west, and especially in west Kerry, the custom of asking for handsels was observed on New Year's day itself. Friends accosted each other with *Fograim iarsma ort!* (I cry a handsel, lit. a relic, remnant, on you) while children ran to the neighbours' houses with the same cry. According to some, the gift should go to the first claimer only; others, however, held that it should be given to everyone who asked.

Epiphany

Epiphany is commonly known in Ireland as 'Little Christmas' and is celebrated with a festive meal of somewhat milder proportions than that of Christmas Day. In Irish it was known widely as *Nollaig na mBan* ('Women's Christmas') which designation was usually explained by the assertion that Christmas Day was marked by beef, and whiskey, men's fare, while on Little Christmas Day the dainties preferred by women – cake, tea, wine, were more in evidence.

> Oiche na dTrí Rithe
> 'Sea deintear fíon den uisce

says the proverb, 'on the night of the three Kings the water turns to wine'. Some say that this miracle occurs in honour of the Magi, whose festival this is, others because this is the anniversary of the Wedding Feast of Cana. As in the case of the worshipping animals on Christmas Eve, it is most unlucky to spy upon this wonder, and, of the many tales told to emphasize this, one will suffice. Beside the blessed well of St Brendan in Cill a 'Ruith, near Ventry in County Kerry are still pointed out three boulders; these are the remains of three impious topers who sat up so as to drink their fill of wine, but who, at the moment of the miracle, were turned to stone. An old and formerly widespread custom still carried on in a few places is the lighting of candles on this night. It is mentioned by Sir Henry Piers in 1682 (*Description of the County of West-Meath*, 124):

'On Twelve-eve in Christmas they use to set up as high as they can a sieve of oats, and in it a dozen of candles set round, and in the centre one larger, all lighted; this in memory of our saviour and his apostles, lights of the world.'

263

A more specific version of this custom, of which the purpose was death divination, was known over a considerable area of north Leinster, east Connaught and south Ulster. The method was simple. A round cake of sufficient size was made of dough, or of ashes or clay, or even of dried cowdung, and in it were put standing a number of small candles, rushlights or bogdeal splinters, one for each member of the family, and each named for a particular individual. In the evening, when the whole household was assembled, these were lighted and then carefully observed, and the order in which they burned out or quenched was regarded as an indication of the order in which the persons represented by them would die. This was usually a solemn occasion, and no levity was permitted.

Indeed, this ceremony was almost always carried out during the family's evening devotions, when the saying of the rosary or other prayers was interrupted now and again by the announcement 'sé Tomás an chéad duine eile!' or 'Mary is the next to go!'

On 7 January, the day immediately following the Epiphany, the Christmas decorations were taken down. Those of a permanent nature were stored away for next Christmas but the holly and other now withered greenery were almost always burned, as it was thought wrong to throw them on the manure heap. According to a widespread custom, of which instances are known from all four Provinces, they were put aside for the time being and burned to heat the pancake griddle on Shrove Tuesday night.

Appendix – Church Feasts and Fasts

The feasts and fasts of the Catholic Church were much more numerous in the past than they are now. At the beginning of the eighteenth Century, after the institution by Pope Clement XI of the Feast of the Immaculate Conception of the Blessed Virgin in 1708, there were 35 days which carried for the faithful the dual obligation of attendance at mass and abstaining from servile or gainful work. These were, in Ireland:

1 Jan.	*The Circumcision
6 Jan.	*The Epiphany
2 Feb.	Candlemas
24 Feb.	St Matthias, Apostle
17 Mar.	*St Patrick
19 Mar.	St Joseph
25 Mar.	*The Annunciation
	Easter Monday
	Easter Tuesday
1 May	SS Philip and James, Apostles
3 May	The Finding of the Holy Cross
	*Ascension Thursday
	Whit Monday
	Whit Tuesday
	*Corpus Christi
24 June	St John Baptist
29 June	*SS Peter and Paul, Apostles
25 July	St James, Apostle
26 July	St Anne
10 Aug.	St Lawrence the Martyr
15 Aug.	*The Assumption

24	Aug.	St Bartholomew, Apostle
8	Sept.	Nativity of the Blessed Virgin
21	Sept.	St Matthew, Apostle
29	Sept.	St Michael Archangel
28	Oct.	SS Simon and Jude, Apostles
1	Nov.	*All Saints
30	Nov.	St Andrew, Apostle
8	Dec.	Immaculate Conception of the Blessed Virgin
21	Dec.	St Thomas, Apostle
25	Dec.	*The Nativity
26	Dec.	St Stephen
27	Dec.	St John, Apostle
28	Dec.	Holy Innocents
31	Dec.	St Sylvester

In 1778, Pope Pius VI abrogated 22 of these holidays, thus releasing the faithful from both obligations. Two further feasts, Easter Monday and Whit Monday, were abrogated by Pope Pius VIII in 1829, and one other, St John Baptist, 24 June, by Pope Gregory XVI in 1831, thus leaving ten to be fully observed by the faithful (those marked with an asterisk* above).

Further modification in the present century has left only eight with full obligation, which are The Epiphany, St Patrick's Day, Ascension Thursday, Corpus Christi, The Assumption, All Saints, The Immaculate Conception and Christmas Day. These later changes have scarcely affected folk tradition; as regards the earlier ones, however, their former observance may help to explain some of the usages which grew up around their dates.

Certain of the feasts abrogated in 1778, eight in all, carried the additional obligation of fasting on their vigils; these fast days were transferred to the Wednesdays and Fridays of Advent in Ireland (later changed for a period to the Fridays and Saturdays of Advent) on which days Lenten fast was ordered.

The obligation of fasting means that food must be restricted to one full meal in the day, while that of abstinence means that certain foods may not be eaten. Ordinary abstinence meant eating no meat; Lenten fast, however, prohibited the use of all animal products, including eggs and milk products as well as meat, in addition to fasting on one meal. Traditionally in Ireland, Lenten fast was observed on all days of Lent, including Sundays, as well as on the fast days of Advent. There were other days of ordinary fast and abstinence, as well as certain days of fast without abstinence, and abstinence without fast on certain other days. Moreover, the local ecclesiastical authority, that is to say the bishop in his own diocese, had power to modify the law in certain ways both as regards the holidays of obligation and the days of fasting or abstinence. Thus, in Ireland, observance was by no means the same all over the country, and here the local variations had some effect on local folk tradition.

The Advent fast was abolished in 1917, at which time also eggs and milk products were excluded from the law of abstinence. In certain parts of Ireland the faithful had already been released from either or both of these restrictions, while many older people continued to observe them voluntarily. The same tendency may be observed in the most recent change, the removal of the obligation of abstinence on ordinary Fridays, as many people continue to abstain voluntarily from meat as a private act of devotion.

Select Bibliography

Anon.: 'Ireland Sixty Years Ago', *Dublin University Magazine*, xxii, 1843, 655–76.
   'Skelligs Lists', *Journal of the Royal Historical and Archaeological Association of Ireland*, xix, 1889, 144–5.
   Annuary of the Kilkenny and South-East of Ireland Archaeological Society, 1855.
Andrews, Elizabeth; *Ulster Folklore*, London, 1913.
Armstrong, E. A.: *The Folklore of Birds*, London, 1958.
Arthurs, J. B.: 'A Tyrone Miscellany', *Ulster Folklife*, iii, 1957, 42–6.
Barrington, Sir Jonah: *Personal Sketches of his own Time*, London 1827.
Boate, Gerard: *The Natural History of Ireland*, Dublin, 1726.
Ní Bhrádaigh, Cáit: 'Folklore from County Longford', *Béaloideas*, vi, 1936, 257–69.
Buchanan, R. H.: 'Calendar Customs', *Ulster Folklife*, viii, 1962, 15–34; ix, 1963, 61–79.
Binchy, D. A.: 'The Fair of Tailtin and the Feast of Tara', *Ériu*, xviii, 1958, 113–38.
Camden, William: *Ireland and the Smaller Isles of the British Ocean*, London, 1610.
Carbery, Mary: *The Farm by Lough Gur*, London, 1937.
Chassanaeus, Bartholomaeus: *Catalogus Gloriae Mundi*, Cologne, 1617.
Cameron, Sir Charles: *Autobiography*, Dublin, 1920.
Caxton, William: *Mirrour of the World* (ed. Prior, Oliver H.) London, 1913.
Colgan, Nathaniel: 'The Shamrock in Literature, A Critical Chronology', *Journal of the Royal Society of Antiquaries of Ireland*, xxvi, 1896, 211–26 and 349–61.
Cooper Foster, Jeanne: *Ulster Folklore*, Belfast, 1951.
O Criomthain, Tomás: *Allagar na hInise*, Baile Átha Cliath, 1928.
   An tOileánach, Baile Atha Cliath, 1929 (translated by Robin Flower as: Ó Crohan, Tomás, *The Islandman*, Dublin and London, 1937.)
Croker, T. Crofton: *Researches in the South of Ireland*, London, 1824, reprinted Shannon, 1969.
   Fairy Legends and Traditions of the South of Ireland, London, 1825.
   Legends of the Lakes, London, 1829.
Davies, Oliver: 'Folklore in Maghera Parish', *Ulster Journal of Archaeology*, viii, 1945, 63–5.

Dinely, Thomas: *Observations in a Tour through the Kingdom of Ireland in 1681*, Dublin, 1858.

Donaldson, John: *An Account of the Barony of Upper Fews in the County of Armagh in 1838*, Dundalk, 1923.

Ní Dhonnchadha, Cáit: 'An Bhrighdeóg', *An Claidheamh Soluis*, 6 Aug. 1910, 3-4.

Dunton, John: *Letters*, in Mac Lysaght, Edward: *Irish Life in the Seventeenth Century*, Dublin and Cork, 1939.

Evans, E. E.: *Irish Folk Ways*, London, 1957.

    Mourne Country, Dundalk, 1951.

Farewell, James (attributed to): *The Irish Hudibras*, London, 1689.

'Fergus': 'Maypoles', *Ulster Journal of Archaeology*, iii, 1855, 164.

Fitzgerald, Rev. P. & M'Gregor, J. T.: *The History, Topography, and Antiquities of Limerick*, Dublin, 1826-7.

Four Masters, The: *Annals of the Kingdom of Ireland*, Ed. O'Donovan, John, Dublin, 1848-51.

Gailey, R. A.: *Irish Folk Drama*, Cork, 1969.

Gibbings, Robert: *Sweet Cork Of Thee*, London, 1951.

Gilbert, John T. (ed.): *Calendar of the Ancient Records of Dublin*, i, Dublin, 1889.

Giraldus Cambrensis: *Topography of Ireland*, (ed. O'Meara, John J.) Dundalk, 1951.

Gwynne, E. (ed.): *The Metrical Dinshenchas*, Dublin, 1913.

Hackett, W.: 'Porcine Legends', *Transactions of the Kilkenny Archaeological Society*, 1852-3, 308-10.

Haddon, A. C.: 'A Batch of Irish Folklore', *Folklore*, iv, 1893, 349-64.

Hall, Rev. James: *A Tour Through Ireland*, London, 1813.

Hall, Mr and Mrs S. C.: *Ireland, Its Scenery and Character*, London, 1841-3.

Hall, Spencer T.: *Life and Death in Ireland*, Manchester, 1850.

Hanmer, Meredith: *The Chronicle of Ireland*, Dublin, 1633.

Hardiman, James: *The History of Galway*, Dublin, 1820.

Hedderman, B. N.: *Glimpses of my Life in Aran*, Bristol, 1917.

Heron-Allen, E.: *Barnacles in Nature and in Myth*, Oxford, 1928.

Hilliard, Richard: 'Biddies and Strawboys', *Ulster Folklife*, viii, 1962, 100-02.

Hogan, John: *Kilkenny, The Ancient City of Ossory*, Kilkenny, 1884.

Hore, H. F.: 'An Account of the Barony of Forth', *Journal of the Kilkenny Archaeological Society*, iv, 1862-3, 53-84.

Hyde, Douglas: *Abhráin an Rachtúire*, Dublin, 1903.

J. L. L.: 'The Pattern of the Lough', *Dublin Penny Journal*, 7 Feb. 1835.

Jocelin: *The Life and Acts of St Patrick*, Dublin, 1809.

Jones, Walter (or Moffet W.?): *Hesperi-Neso-Graphia*, Dublin, 1735.

Joyce, Weston St. John: *The Neighbourhood of Dublin*, Dublin, 1913.

Keating, Geoffrey: *Forus Feasa ar Éirinn*, London, 1732.

Kennedy, Patrick: *The Banks of the Boro, A Wexford Chronicle*, Dublin and London, 1867.

    Evenings in the Duffrey, Dublin, 1869.

Kieran, Lily: 'Hunting the Herring', *Ireland's Own*, 26 Apr. 1916.

Leahy, David: *Abstract of Crime in Ireland,* London, 1839.

'Lageniensis': *Irish Folk Lore,* London, 1870.

O Laoghaire, An tAth. Peadar: *Séadna,* Baile Átha Cliath, 1904.

Mac Neill, Máire: *The Festival of Lughnasa,* Oxford, 1962.

'Mannanaan Mac Lir': 'The Folklore of the Months', *Journal of the Cork Historical and Archaeological Society,* i, 1895, 413–20, 553–7; ii, 1896, 157–60, 316–22, 365–7; iii, 1897, 22–5, 329–32.

Mason, Thomas H.: 'St Brigid's Crosses', *Journal of the Royal Society of Antiquaries of Ireland,* lxxv, 1945, 160–6.

Mason, W. Shaw: *Parochial Survey of Ireland,* Dublin, 1814–19.

Messenger, John C.: *Inis Beag, Isle of Ireland,* New York, 1969.

Merryman, Brian: *Cúirt an Mheadhon Oidhche,* Dublin, 1912.

M.F.D.: 'Letters from the Coast of Clare', *Dublin University Magazine,* 1841, 161–79.

Montbret, Coquebert de: 'Impressions of Galway City and County', *Journal of the Galway Archaeological and Historical Society,* xxv, 1952, 1–14 (ed. Síle Ní Chinnéide).

Moran, Rev. P. F.: *Spicelegium Ossoriense,* Dublin, 1874–84.

Morris, Henry: 'Marriage Customs', *Louth Archaeological Journal,* ii, 1908–11, 323–4.

'St Martin's Eve', *Béaloideas,* ix, 1939, 230–5.

O Muirgheasa, Énrí: 'An Scadan', *An Claidheamh Soluis,* 12 Apr. 1902.

'The Fern Seed', *Béaloideas,* iii, 1932, 331–2.

Müller, Friedrich Max: *The Science of Language,* ii, 1891.

Murphy, Michael J.: *At Slieve Gullion's Foot,* Dundalk, 1940.

Murray, Rev. L.: 'Omeath', *Louth Archaeological Journal,* iii, 1912–15, 213–31.

O'Kearney, Nicholas: 'Folk-Lore', *Transactions of the Kilkenny Archaeological Society,* i, 1849–51, 145–8.

'May Day and Midsummer', *id,* 373–82.

Omurethi: 'Customs Peculiar to Certain Days, formerly observed in County Kildare', *Journal of the Kildare Archaeological Society,* v, 1906–08, 439–55.

Paterson, T. G. F.: 'Harvest Customs in County Armagh', *Ulster Journal of Archaeology,* v, 1942, 2–7.

'Harvest Customs in County Armagh', *Louth Archaeological Journal,* x, 1944, 336–41.

'Harvest Customs in County Armagh', *Ulster Journal of Archaeology,* vii, 1944, 109–16.

'Brigid's Crosses in County Armagh', *Ulster Journal of Archaeology,* viii, 1945, 43–8.

Penn, William: *My Irish Journal, 1669–1670,* (edited Isabel Grubb), London, 1952.

Piers, Sir Henry: *A Chorographical Description of the County of West-Meath, A.D. 1682,* in Vallencey *Collectanea de Rebus Hibernicis,* Dublin 1770.

Pollock, A. J.: 'Hallowe'en Customs in Lecale, Co. Down', *Ulster Folklife,* vi, 1960, 62–4.

270

Prim, John G. A.: 'Olden Popular Pastimes in Kilkenny', *Transactions of the Kilkenny Archaeological Society*, 1852, 319–35.

Rinn Ó gCuanach: 'Sean-chainnt na nDéise', *An Claidheamh Soluis*, 15 Dec. 1906.

Roe, Helen M.: 'Tales, Customs and Beliefs from Laoighis', *Béaloideas*, ix, 1939, 21–35.

Shaw, Rose: *Carleton's Country*, Dublin, 1930.

Ó Súilleabháin, Amhlaoibh: *Cinnlae*, Irish Texts Society, xxx–xxxiii, 1936–7. Also de Bhaldraithe, Tomás: *Cín Lae Amhlaoibh*, Baile Átha Cliath, 1970.

Ó Súilleabháin, Seán: *Caitheamh Aimsire ar Thorraimh*, Baile Átha Cliath, 1961, translated by the author as *Irish Wake Amusements*, Cork, 1967.

A handbook of Irish Folklore, Dublin, 1942.

'The Feast of Saint Martin in Ireland', *Studies in Folklore*, Bloomington, 1957.

Notes to Mason: 'St Brigid's Crosses', *Journal of the Royal Society of Antiquaries of Ireland*, lxxv, 1945.

Stanihurst, Richard: *The Historie of Irelande*, London, 1577.

Stokes, Whitley: *The Tripartite Life of Patrick*, London, 1887.

'O'Davoren's Glossary', *Archiv für Celtische Lexicographie*, ii, 1904.

Story, George: *A True and Impartial History*, London, 1691.

Swan, H. S.: *Romantic Inishowen*, Dublin, 1947.

Swift, Jonathan: *Directions to Servants*, London, 1745.

The Journal to Stella, London, 1897,

Thackeray, W. M.: *The Irish Sketch Book*, London, 1879.

Threlkeld, Caleb: *Synopsis Stirpium Hibernicum*, Dublin, 1727.

Todd, Rev. James H.: *Cogadh Gaedhel re Gallaibh*, London, 1867.

Vallencey, Charles: *Enquiry into the First Inhabitants of Ireland*, Dublin, 1781.

Essay into the Antiquity of the Irish Language, Dublin, 1781.

'Of All Hallow Eve' and 'Of the Gule of August or Lammas Day', *Collectanea de Rebus Hibernicis*, xii, 443–511, Dublin, 1783.

Wakefield, Edward: *An Account of Ireland, Statistical and Political*, London, 1812.

Westropp, T. J.: 'The Beginnings of Historic Tradition', *Journal of the Galway Archaeological and Historical Society*, xi, 1920–5, 50–71.

Wilde, Sir William: *Irish Popular Superstitions*, Dublin, 1853.

Report on the Tables of Deaths, Census of Ireland 1851, Dublin, 1856.

Wilde, Lady: *Ancient Legends, Mystic Charms and Superstitions of Ireland*, London, 1888.

Ancient Cures, Charms and Usages of Ireland, London, 1890.

Wood Martin, W. G.: *Traces of the Elder Faiths of Ireland*, London, 1902.

Young, Arthur: *Tour in Ireland* (ed. Hutton, A. W.) London, 1892.

Calendar of the Justiciary Rolls of Ireland 1305–07, London, 1914.

Calendar of Papal Registers, Papal Letters, viii.

Calendar of State Papers, Ireland, 1574–1585, London, 1867.

The Ordnance Survey Letters, Typescript in National Library, Dublin.

Report of the Select Committee appointed to take into consideration the State of the Poorer Classes in Ireland, Parliamentary Papers, 1830, vii.

271

Reports of the Commissioners for inquiring into the Condition of the Poorer Classes in Ireland, Parliamentary Papers, xxx–xxxiv, 1836.

The Anglo-Celt, Cavan.

The Annual Register, London.

Béaloideas, Dublin.

Belfast Mercury, Belfast.

Finn's Leinster Journal, Kilkenny.

Freeman's Journal, Dublin.

Folklore, London.

The Graphic, London.

The Irish Times, Dublin.

Irisleabhar na Gaedhilge, Dublin.

The Longford Leader, Longford.

The Morning Post, London.

The Sunday Press, Dublin.

Ulster Folklife, Belfast.

Index

274